MIND OVER MONEY

MIND OVER MONEY

MATCH YOUR PERSONALITY
TO
A WINNING FINANCIAL STRATEGY

JOHN W. SCHOTT, M.D.

with

Jean S. Arbeiter

Little, Brown and Company

Boston   New York   Toronto   London

First Edition

Library of Congress Cataloging-in-Publication Data

Schott, John W.
    Mind over money : match your personality to a winning financial
strategy / by John W. Schott, with Jean S. Arbeiter.
        p.   cm.
    ISBN 0-316-77378-6 (hc)
    1. Investments — Psychological aspects.   I. Arbeiter, Jean S.
II. Title.
HG4521.S3563   1998
332.6 — dc21   97-27781

10 9 8 7 6 5 4 3 2 1

Text design by Bruce Hamilton

MV-NY

Published simultaneously in Canada by Little, Brown & Company (Canada)
Limited

Printed in the United States of America

FOR

Sally

Contents

Important Note to the Reader   IX

Acknowledgments   XI

1:   What a Psychiatrist Can Teach You about Investing   3

PART ONE: THE BASICS

2:   The Psychology of Getting Started   21

3:   The Psychology of Building a Stock Portfolio   39

4:   The Psychology of Selling   59

5:   Psyching Out Greed in a Bull Market   77

6:   Reality Testing: Fear in a Bear Market   94

PART TWO: THE PROFILES

7:   The "I Can't Stop Worrying" Investor   109

8:   The Power Investor   129

9:   The Inheritor   151

10:   The Impulsive Investor   179

11:   The Gambler   196

12:   The "Make Me Safe" Investor   213

13:   The Confident Investor   228

Appendix A:

    Why I Picked My Core Portfolio Stocks   230

Appendix B:

    Net Present Value: A Calculation for Confident

    Buying   233

Resources Section   239

Index   249

Important Note to the Reader

Although several of the chapters in this book contain sample portfolios, and certain stocks are used as examples in the text, we offer no specific investment recommendations. Indeed, no book can reliably recommend individual securities, because companies and conditions change. Before you make any investment, you should investigate it for yourself, *at the time of purchase,* a point I will make several times in this book.

I personally own shares in the following stocks and funds mentioned in the text: AFLAC, Berkshire Hathaway, BHC Communications, Capital Southwest Corp., Chris-Craft, Exxon, Leucadia National, Markel, Merck, Mid Ocean Ltd., New Plan Realty, PepsiCo, Philip Morris, PICO, Royal Dutch Petroleum, St. Joe Companies, ServiceMaster, Texaco, Thermo Electron, Third Avenue Value Fund, Tweedy-Browne Global Value Fund, United Asset Management. But again, I recommend none of them for purchase (or sale) by anyone.

The stock called "Acme National," used several times as an example, is a fictitious company and no resemblance is intended to any real company.

All of the names of the clients and patients I discuss in this book, and personal facts about them, have been changed to protect their privacy. Needless to say, it would be inappropriate for me to give specific investment advice to my patients, and I never do.

Acknowledgments

I had long hoped to write a book about investing but would not have done so without the encouragement and guidance of our agents, Herb and Nancy Katz. Their assistance and friendship saw us through the process. I thank them very much.

Jean and I also thank our editor, Jim Silberman, whose insight, skill, and diligence are evident on every single page of this book.

My knowledge of investment psychology might not have grown beyond the rudimentary without the encouragement of my longtime friend Jack Templeton, and the subtle, intellectual guidance of his father, Sir John Templeton.

I am also grateful to the readers of my monthly newsletter, who support me in both material and spiritual ways. Thanks go to a special group of readers, the physicians who participated in my psychological study of investors.

The following people also contributed to my development in the field in ways they will not recognize: Dr. Larry Lifson, Dr. Richard Geist, Marianne Held, Leota Miller, Ray Brolley, and Dr. Mary Weeg.

We would be remiss if we didn't thank Jean Arbeiter's husband, Solomon, for his patience and support.

Finally, but certainly most important, my thanks and love to my wife, Sally, and to our daughters Anne, Hannah, and Lilly. They cheerfully endured my absences and being surrounded by the stacks of books and papers that are part of writing a book.

MIND OVER MONEY

CHAPTER 1

What a Psychiatrist
Can Teach You about Investing

The advice investors most often get goes something like this: "Investing is a simple matter — buy good stocks, hold on to them, and time will make you rich. Control your fear in tough times and your greed when the market is high, and everything will be just fine."

I happen to agree with the first part. Investing *is* basically a simple matter. What complicates it is the unrecognized power and diversity of the emotions that investors bring to it. The psychology of investing is considerably more complex than its two most familiar components — fear and greed.

Every drive associated with money gets played out in investing — the longing for security, the guilt engendered by feelings of greed, the quest for power and esteem, the fear of being abandoned, the search for love, the dream of omnipotence. Emotions are not peripheral to the investing process — a matter of "keeping one's head" when the bull tops out or the bear roars in. *Emotions are central; they are the entire ball game. If we want to make money, we need to know the rules.*

A basic investing rule is that our emotional patterns are so often hidden from us that they can pull our strings without our ever realizing it. They become our "invisible advisers," and they don't always act in our best interests.

When emotions gain the upper hand, we can find ourselves losing money, or not making as much money as we had hoped — all the while feeling insecure, anxious, or overwhelmingly disappointed. Some investors accept worry as a given, but this need not be.

Investing is meant to be a rewarding experience, and by that, I mean rewarding psychologically as well as financially, because investing symbolizes your taking care of yourself. It's a grown-up matter, and grown-ups should feel good about the work they're doing for themselves.

Therefore, if you're not achieving both wealth *and* a healthy amount of esteem from your investing, you're not getting all the success you deserve. My goal in writing this book is to tell you how to correct that situation.

Success begins with accepting the *centrality* of emotions in investing. We need to understand that behind the basic mechanics — getting started, selecting stocks, selling stocks, taking appropriate action at the height of a bull market or the depth of a bear market — there are always emotional factors.

Whenever we buy a stock, a psychological process of identification begins that affects everything that happens next, especially whether we sell too soon or hold on too long. When we inherit a stock, psychological forces come into play that affect our ability to judge the stock on its own merits instead of our own past history. For psychological reasons, some stocks look "good" to us and some look "bad," even though a bad stock may be in better position to do well than a good one.

Once you identify your own psychological patterns, you can utilize your strengths and curtail your weaknesses in the interests of financial success. You can follow your own blueprint — the investing strategies that are *best* for you because they are based on your own emotional prototype. This book will help you do that.

With this book, you can also learn, in detail, how to analyze, employ, and alter your investing emotions. You'll be given basic investing advice — in fact, an entire investing program, which covers both the basics and your own psychological profile. Your behavior may contain elements of several of the prototypes you will learn about. As you read, you will decide which behaviors apply to you, and you will arrive at solutions that fit you.

My recognition of the need for such guidance grew out of research — by myself and other pioneers — into the psychology of investing, a field that is currently recognized by psychologists and economists alike as "the missing link" in our understanding of the stock market. With two colleagues, Dick Geist and Larry Lifson, I cochair an annual Congress on the Psychology of Investing, which brings together hundreds of therapists and professional money managers for two days of sessions. I teach a popular extension course, "The Psychology of Investing," sponsored by the Harvard University Medical School. And I've been interviewed widely by the media about the insights of this new field.

For centuries we've known that emotions influence the market — indeed, today they seem to be dominating the market entirely — but, until now, we haven't known how to put our insights to practical use for the individual investor. Now the knowledge is available, and I believe it is vital that it be shared with the people who stand to benefit most — the investing public.

THE IMPERATIVE TO DO WELL

There are reasons why sharing this knowledge is vital now.

Currently, more people have invested in the market than at any other period in history, due, in part, to changes in retirement laws that have made individuals increasingly responsible for their own financial futures. "Guaranteed" retirement plans, funded by corporations, have been rapidly replaced by such do-it-yourself programs as 401(k) plans, self-directed SEPs (self-employment plans), and other arrangements.

We have entered the age of financial autonomy, an exciting period, but one fraught with anxiety as well as promise.

The growing insecurity of the workplace contributes to anxiety. No longer do firms offer the unspoken promise of "lifetime employment" in return for loyalty and diligent effort: witness the continual waves of corporate "downsizings" and "restructurings" that often mean "you're out."

"No one knows where the ax will fall next," one client, a systems engineer, told me. He is still employed by one of the high-tech firms located along Route 128 outside Boston, but he no longer has the limitless optimism about his lifetime prospects that he had when I first met him in the early 1980s.

My client, like millions of others, understands that the profitability of his investments will be the major determinant of his future security. He cannot depend on his firm or on Social Security as a "safety net" for retirement.

As a result, the record numbers of investors include many people who never imagined they would be in the market. That group includes baby boomers who once thought investing was something their parents did but now find it high among their priorities and concerns.

Recently, a thirty-three-year-old sales executive, the daughter of a friend, told me that although she has been investing through her 401(k) plan for several years, she never feels satisfied that she has picked the right securities. "I lie awake at night thinking about it," she said, "because my whole future is riding on this. As a kid, I could never save a dime, and my dad always said that money went through my fingers like sand. Since I've been working, I've been doing okay, but I still think of myself as a financial screw-up. Being in the market just ratchets up the emotional ante for me. I want to do well, but can I? It all seems so complicated, and scary, too."

Investors know that they *must* do well, yet they are frightened of making mistakes that can undermine and conceivably even destroy the very security they seek. When they look around for help, they find that they are inundated by an overload of information, contradictory advice, and persistent theorizing about the stock market that only serves to increase anxiety because it cannot be reconciled into a coherent whole.

At a time when investors are confused, and when the market has become more driven by psychology than ever, they must be self-aware as well as self-directed. Over the long term, independent thinking is the surest path to wealth and to a feeling of ease.

In this book, I intend to show you how to meet the unique challenges of our time and how to emerge as a winner by making money in the way that is psychologically most appropriate for you.

Now let me explain how this book came about, and how it relates to my personal investing philosophy, which is central to what I will be telling you and where I intend to lead you.

HOW I BECAME "THE MONEY DOCTOR"

My life's work has been dedicated to two specialties that aren't usually combined in one individual: money management and psychiatry. True, there are plenty of money managers who think they should be licensed as psychiatrists, but I doubt that many of them are. As for therapists, I don't know of many who are also money managers and, therefore, the relative uniqueness of my position sometimes causes people to look at me skeptically.

"A shrink *and* a market guru," they wonder, "how did *that* come about?"

Well, as with many things psychological, the answers lie in the past, and in my case, investing goes back a long, long way.

I bought my first stock when I was eight years old (fifty shares of Virginia Carolina Chemical), and I come from a long line of investors. My great-grandfather, an immigrant from Germany who started out pouring molten lead in a zinc plant and wound up as a leader in the industry, was an investor. My grandfather, a successful businessman and real estate investor in the midwestern town where I grew up, was an ardent investor. I accepted investing as a wonderful thing to do, and wealth as a wonderful thing to have. I always studied a great deal about investing, but I never gave much thought to its emotional aspects until I was in Harvard Medical School and planning on psychiatry as a specialty.

I had the good fortune of having as a housemate Jack Templeton, the son of the famed mutual fund investor Sir John Templeton. Jack became a close friend, and to this day we turn to one another in times of personal crisis.

I got to know Sir John during occasional visits to the family's summer place on Fishers Island, New York. I always wanted to talk with him about investing, but I felt timid, and I may have been put off by his natural air of reserve and the fact that he is much my senior.

But one night, after dinner, I got up the courage to ask him what one quality above all made him a great investor. At that time, I thought there had to be *some* marvelous secret to success, at least on a scale such as his.

He replied that what made all the difference was having studied with Benjamin Graham. Further, he added, virtually every great investor since World War II was a Graham disciple.

I knew that Graham was a money manager who taught economics at Columbia University and that he had written, with David L. Dodd, *Security Analysis*, the classic work on the subject. But until I got John Templeton's advice, I had never read any of his writings. After I returned home, I read everything of Graham's I could find, including his popular book on value investing, *The Intelligent Investor*.

Since I read from the point of view of a psychology student as well as an investor, I saw immediately that Graham's essentially mathematical approach to finding undervalued stocks was actually the product of a psychological process that recognizes the market's mood swings between mania and depression. (I'll have more to say about these swings and how they can actually benefit you later on in this book.)

Still, I was puzzled by Templeton's revelation and by my own insight. I thought to myself: If John Templeton was doing what Graham said, and Warren Buffett was doing what Graham said, not to mention all of the other famous disciples, why wasn't everyone else?

On reflection, I concluded that the answer was also psychologically based. To follow Graham's principles required the ability to think independently. One of the best-known facts about the stock market is that the "crowd" is particularly susceptible to manias. Less recognized is the fact that marvelous businesses can sell at absolute bargain prices simply because they are out of favor.

But to be able to buy such stocks, you need a great deal of self-confidence and innate self-esteem, because you can't count on others for verification. And to hold on to those stocks until their value comes to be recognized by the market requires the ability to delay gratification.

Thus, to follow Graham's economic advice meant truly understanding your own emotions, perhaps better than most people were prepared to do.

Until then I hadn't thought much about the role of emotions in investing, but now I began to ponder it and, like any good psychiatrist-to-be, I started by analyzing my own feelings and memories.

I thought about the Wednesday afternoons when our entire extended family — my grandfather, grandmother, parents, aunts, and uncles — would gather in the living room of my grandparents' Victorian mansion to discuss investments.

We were joined each week by our broker, Fred Rubel, from Chicago, a "circuit-riding stockbroker," who systematically visited the small towns of north-central Illinois.

As we went over the family portfolio, I had happy feelings of belonging. I identified strongly with my grandfather, who had been so successful in life, and I wanted to prove how wise and capable I was by understanding something that clearly was important to him.

So for me, early on, investing was associated with feeling good about myself and with striving for achievement. Most important, for me, was that investing was a normal activity, because everyone in my family did it, so I never experienced the common anxiety about "getting started," a subject I will deal with in the next chapter.

Nonetheless, there was a certain amount of anxiety, because despite his expertise, my great-grandfather had lost a million dollars in the 1920s in a utilities scheme manipulated by financier Samuel Insull, which became a national scandal. In our family, the words *remember Insull* were a warning for everything, but especially in regard to investing, and so I developed a cautious, investigatory attitude toward buying stocks, and I steer clear of investments that could be considered speculative or easily manipulated.

Thus I brought to the market several crucial emotions — a basic sense of confidence based on familiarity with the process, a drive to succeed based on my identification with my grandfather, and an attitude of conservatism (which has actually served me well in investing) that was based on the Insull incident.

I realized that this constellation of emotions defined me in the market and that other investors undoubtedly had their constellations.

I also realized that I could continue to pursue both my serious interests, psychiatry and investing, which I had once thought would be mutually exclusive. Now I saw that they would inform one another in beneficial ways.

While I was a medical resident, I got my broker's license, and worked part time as a stockbroker. When I went into private practice, in the 1970s, I gave up my brokerage work, but because I wrote and lectured about money issues so frequently, I achieved a reputation in the Boston area as "that psychiatrist who knows all about investing," and soon I was known as "the money doctor."

During the 1980s, a period of strong growth for the stock market, first colleagues and then other people started coming to me with questions about their investments. In 1985, I became a professional investment adviser with a noted Boston firm and started a market newsletter about the psychology of the market — *The Schott Letter* — that is today one of the top-performing market letters in the United States, with a twelve-year record of 21.1 percent annual compound growth. I also became involved in the work I mentioned earlier that helped to develop the prestigious Congress on the Psychology of Investing. (Needless to say, I never mix psychiatry with investing. I keep treatment of patients and financial counseling of clients totally distinct.)

THE IMPORTANCE OF FINDING THE "INNER INVESTOR"

Currently, I manage millions of dollars of other people's money. I work with hundreds of clients. I respond to queries from the subscribers who read my newsletter. I know that most investors have hopes, fears, and fantasies that I need to understand as well as I understand their concrete investing goals, because if I don't — and they don't — these feelings can take over the money management.

When I talk with clients, I always listen very carefully for the "inner investor," realizing that each investor is different, and every feeling expressed is intensely human and valid. Here are some of the statements I typically hear, and the ways they might be interpreted:

- "I came to see you because I'm having trouble getting started. It's all so complicated. You need to know so much to do well." (I'm afraid that the market is a place where I am going to be tested and found wanting.)

- "I'm feeling a bit anxious. After all, my family wasn't well off and I'm the first person to try investing." (I am trespassing in an area where I don't belong. Maybe I'll be punished for it.)

- "I hope it's not unrealistic to expect that I can double my money in six months or so." (I'm very much attracted by immediate gratification. If I don't see quick results, I may feel disappointed and drop out of investing.)

- "Can't you tell me the right time to get into the market?" (I'm looking for certainty so that I can avoid the emotional pain of loss.)

- "Yes, the stock sounds pretty solid, but as soon as I buy, it will probably go down." (I'm worried that I can make bad things happen. Perhaps I'm going to be a loser.)

- "I know you want me to sell the stock because you think it's a loser. But my gut tells me it's about to make a big comeback." (If I can control the market, I will be seen as powerful. It's important to me not to lose the self-esteem I've been getting from the stock.)

- "I spotted this wonderful new product in a store, and I don't see how the company can miss. I think buying the stock is a brilliant move." (I'm guided by my feelings, and I enjoy expressing them. Most likely, my investing will be on the impulsive side.)

- "I was talking with my cousin, and her broker does about 20 percent for her. I hope we can do better than that." (Competing is very important to me. I may take extreme risks because sibling rivalry, or something like it, is playing a role in investing.)

- "I can't sell that stock. My father left it to me." (I'm still grieving for my father. Perhaps by holding on to the stock, I can keep him with me.)

- "I only want to invest my inheritance in a way that's socially responsible." (I feel guilty about having money that I didn't work for. If I can invest it with "virtuous" firms, the money will seem more palatable to me.)

- "I noticed that in the newsletter you advised selling off a bit, but I've been doing so great. The market isn't really that overpriced yet, is it?'' (This bull market is making me feel terrific about myself, so I don't want to give it up. I'm trying to rationalize away the need for caution.)

- "I know I've been making a lot of trades, and maybe I've lost some money, but all I need to make it all up is that one great trade." (I'm investing for the thrills, rather than long-term profits. By thinking magically, I hope to make things come out my way.)

You may recognize some of these emotions as your own. If not, I can assure you that later in this book you will find feelings and behaviors that are familiar to you.

Of course, my objective is not only to have you recognize aspects of yourself, but also to help you utilize your feelings in the interest of investment success. Throughout the book, I am going to combine specific investment principles — growing out of my own investment philosophy — with the psychological reasons why I think they are valid, in order to provide a sense of direction both financially and emotionally.

The material is divided into two sections.

The first section deals with the basic mechanics of investing and the psychological issues associated with them, particularly the key issues of overcoming anxiety, building a portfolio, making selling decisions, and handling greed in a bull market and fear in a bear market. *This section is an investing program, designed to help you become and stay centered in the market.* These are the basics from the point of view of a conservative, traditional investor — myself — who is very much committed to the principles of value investing, even though I don't insist, of course, that everyone follow this approach.

The second section deals with the investing styles of individual personality types, which I call "the profiles." Each of these styles is based on feelings that are common to all of us, even if not expressed by all of us to the same degree.

These feelings, human though they are, often produce investing losses, or at best mediocre results, and can result in frustration and disappointment. When people are disappointed, they may drop out of investing altogether, or get caught in a revolving door — going in and out of the market, but usually exiting and reentering at just the wrong times, a situation that is virtually guaranteed to produce loss.

The worst result is that people wind up soured on investing, believing that the market is a "gamble" or a "circus" or convinced that investors get manipulated in one way or another by Wall Street, when the truth is that investing, if done in a psychologically sound manner, is a straightforward process and the best opportunity we have of achieving wealth over the long term.

As I noted earlier, I come from a background of wealth, I've gained substantial wealth through my own efforts, I understand the advantages of wealth in terms of achieving individual goals and opening options; in sum, I think wealth is a wonderful thing that should happen to everyone. And it can.

THE "MIND OVER MONEY" PROGRAM

Let me tell you what you will learn about in this book.

THE BASICS

• *The Psychology of Getting Started.* The trick to getting started, if you are anxious about it and fearful of being tested, as most new investors are, is simply to normalize the process. In this chapter, I show you how to take the first steps, in psychological comfort, and explain why you *must* limit the amount of information you try to master and, indeed, the amount to which you let yourself be exposed.

• *The Psychology of Building a Stock Portfolio.* Your portfolio should be your emotional home in the market, a long-term base that you tend and care for, while it protects you. You need to feel psychologically comfortable with the companies you buy, and that means you have to know how to evaluate them and establish reasons for trusting them. The more focused your investigating and the more secure the standards you have in place, the less emotions will intrude into the building process.

• *The Psychology of Selling.* Selling is such a difficult decision that investors are rarely given rational advice about it. That's too bad because indiscriminate selling — in response to such emotional triggers as fear of making a mistake, fear of losing self-esteem, fear of not being perfect, or even the desire to punish yourself — is the *primary reason* for long-term loss in investing. I explain how you can establish and adhere to disciplines for selling. I also tell you how to relieve anxiety and deal with the triggers *before* they cause financial pain.

• *Psyching Out Greed in a Bull Market.* At the height of a bull market, greed gets the upper hand, but often we don't realize it, because no emotion gets rationalized away as completely as greed does. In this chapter, I show how to recognize what's happening inside yourself when things are going ahead full steam; how to discern when the end of the bull market may be near; and how to take effective steps to prevent your portfolio and your psyche from getting hurt in the downturn. Also, you'll learn what investors are not often told — why greed is, surprisingly, just about the most important ally you can have.

• *Reality Testing: Fear in a Bear Market.* In a bear market, the absolutely universal fantasy among investors is that the end of the world has come. Obviously, this is a distortion, yet it's so powerful that people almost inevitably give in to it. You don't have to, and you won't, if you recognize that what you have to deal with is not fear alone, but the entire range of negative emotions that compose the bear market depressive syndrome (BMDS). Only when you overcome the syndrome — and I'll provide guidance for doing that — can you be prepared to take advantage of the real opportunities that occur during a bear market. I'll also tell you how to know when to start buying again.

THE PROFILES

• *The "I Can't Stop Worrying" Investor.* Some investors constantly rethink their investing decisions, wondering if they made the right moves, comparing themselves to everyone else, and never getting a good night's sleep. If you're constantly torturing yourself, your anxiety can actually produce the outcome you fear most — poor investing results. I'll explain why you may be putting yourself through the ringer and how you can use your considerable intelligence and love of figuring things out to control your obsessiveness, so that you can make investing decisions once, and only once — and then let them go.

• *The Power Investor.* When we invest to impress, we seek out stocks we consider powerful, generally "concept stocks" in hot areas; we become excited about them, and we pour not only our money but our self-esteem into them. We get a big charge out of investing, and that's wonderful, but we *overidentify* with our stocks in a way that can cause us to get hurt because we don't want to look too closely at their foibles. If you've ever felt that "This stock is me," if you've ever hung on to a fading investment because you were certain things just *had* to get better, if you've ever crashed emotionally as the losses piled up — you can benefit from the strategies I offer for restraining your enthusiasm and selecting stocks with greater objectivity.

• *The Inheritor.* Inheriting money has the same emotional impact as winning the lottery — in fantasy, it's great; in reality, it can also be great, but fraught with psychological and practical problems. Inheritors often suffer from grief and from unexpected feelings of guilt that make it difficult to invest the money or, if they've inherited an entire portfolio, make necessary changes. What's crucial here, for both widows and adult children who inherit, is to examine the reasons for the inhibitions and then move on to develop a portfolio that suits their new needs. I demonstrate how to do this, and I also advise how to find a money manager who meets the special emotional requirements of an inheritor.

• *The Impulsive Investor.* If you usually lead with your feelings in other areas of your life, you are going to do it in the market. Impulsive investors tend to buy a stock because something about it — "an intuition" is the way they sometimes describe it — resonates with them emotionally. These people often do have a wonderful sense of what's going to do well, but the danger of a "love at first sight" approach to stock picking is that one can fall out of love just as quickly, and sell in a way that is certain to lose money. If you have a pattern of frequent buying and selling, and it's tripping you up (as it inevitably does), I'll give practical strategies for curbing your impulsiveness in ways that don't curb your enjoyment.

• *The Gambler.* Gamblers are extreme enthusiasts who relish the thrills of "playing the market." They see themselves as traders, even successful traders, but usually they are less successful than they believe, and their obsessive connection to the market may be worrying family members — and themselves as well. If you've seen more trades go sour than you care to admit, if you believe that you need only that one good trade to turn things around, or if you've ever found yourself hiding losses from loved ones, you need to learn how to steer a more emotionally balanced and profitable course in the market. I'll discuss how to do this, in an emphatic way, because the market is *not* for gambling.

• *The "Make Me Safe" Investor.* Some people find the market a very scary place; they search for certainty (which doesn't exist), they are extremely risk averse, and they feel forever locked into that stance. Yet they know that over time investing is the best way to make money. Their conflict is: Should I be at the party or pass it up? If you do want to be in, but feel hesitant, I'll show you how to exchange your extreme risk aversion for prudent risk aversion of the kind that can increase your returns and build your self-esteem.

• *The Confident Investor.* Many investors are naturally confident; they trust their ability to weather the ups and downs of the market, and they know how to manage their emotions. But whether or not you have such confidence at present, you can attain it, if you follow the principles I set down in this book.

I hope you'll read all of the profile chapters, not only the ones you think may be relevant to you, because they are *all* relevant — and there are important points to be learned from each in terms of investing strategy.

Every emotion discussed in the profiles is an emotion that's common to all of us. There is something of the gambling instinct in every investor, because we all hope to control fate. There is something of the "Make me safe" fearfulness in every investor, because we all long for certainty and none of us wants to lose. *We are all human. That's a theme I'll repeat a number of times in this book, because frequently investors think being human isn't good enough, and this idea inhibits success.*

Many investment books and articles divide investors into two categories — the market sophisticates, like the author (and, by inference, his or her readers), and the less knowledgeable folks "out there," who are vulnerable to crowd psychology, fear, greed, and so forth. A dichotomy gets set up between "them" (the human) and "us" (the superhuman).

But the fact is that we are all "them"; we are all influenced by human emotions, and this includes, in particular, the very top money managers — the people who run the mutual funds and investment firms and who on some level are even more driven by emotions than the ordinary investor.

We need to understand that being human is fine, but recognize that certain feelings can cause us trouble. Fortunately, there is a whole host of things we can learn to distance ourselves from these feelings, while accepting them and ourselves. When we know we are able to control our own self-defeating behaviors, we approach the market with a sense of comfort — and we increase our success.

We also need to make ourselves comfortable with the vast amount of theorizing about investing that is currently in vogue. We read a great deal in financial publications about a "new paradigm," a substantial shift in the underlying nature of the market caused by the vast amounts of institutional money pouring in and the fact that individual investors have been persuaded that they have nowhere else to go but the market to make their futures secure. Some theorists have even proclaimed a "new era," in which these vast sums of money will create such a demand that the stock market can only go up.

This new money may be good for the capital growth that business expansion requires, but I'd be amazed if it has eliminated business and market cycles. These will continue, as will investor psychology, which has existed since the very beginning of markets.

There certainly are new things happening today, but most notable is the fact that the market has become more psychologically driven than ever, and therefore the psychological knowledge of ourselves as investors is more important than ever.

We need to remember that in the long history of the stock market, paradigms have come and gone. *Yet the task of the individual investor remains the same: not to master theories, but to master oneself.*

I believe that no matter what happens in the market, and we can be sure to expect the unexpected, the investor's individual behavior is the key to winning or losing. Learn how to manage your emotions, and success will follow. In this book, I will show you how to do that, beginning with the basics of getting started.

PART ONE

THE BASICS

CHAPTER 2

The Psychology of Getting Started

Getting started can sometimes be so difficult that people never get started at all. This is unfortunate, because investing in equities is simply the best way, over time, of building wealth, of becoming more financially secure than you ever imagined possible — in short, of turning your dreams into reality.

In order to claim the rewards that are waiting for you, rewards that I assure you are possible, you need to make yourself feel secure about taking those first steps.

Powerful inhibitions block people from getting started, and among the strongest are feelings of guilt, which may have to do with trying to surpass one's parents or siblings, with having risen in social class, or with having accumulated wealth when so many in the world live in poverty. Or, if the money is inherited, guilt can come from thinking it is wrong to have money not earned, or because the inheritance came from relatives who were secretly disliked or even hated.

Fear is another important obstacle — the fear of making mistakes and errors and, especially, the fear of "losing everything."

But the most common reason for not getting started is simple. Most people don't know very much about investing, and this makes them feel frightened and often angry, because they were never told they would need this knowledge one day. The result can be a pattern of procrastination that can be difficult to get over.

One of my clients is an attorney who finally came to see me after repeatedly breaking appointments for several months. That was ten years ago, and today, after listening to my advice, this man is about ten

21

times wealthier, having earned an annualized return of 24 percent on his money.

Returns like this astonish people who are unfamiliar with the wonders that can arise from investing. There is a marvelous principle called the Rule of 72, which approximates the time it will take for a given amount of money to double at a given rate of compound interest. If you divide 72 by an annualized compound return, you will get the number of years required to double your money. In my client's case, that was three years, since 72 divided by 24 equals 3. Taxes do lower returns somewhat, but over the long term, if the increase is primarily from capital gains as opposed to dividends, taxes can be less.

Recently my client said to me, "When we first met, I bet you thought I was a jerk for being so nervous about getting started." What he didn't realize is that his fears and inhibitions were entirely normal.

I told him, as I tell many prospective investors, that feelings of anxiety are perfectly natural, since money has highly charged symbolic value. In addition to its being essential as a medium of exchange, money carries with it a host of subconscious references to love, power, self-esteem, shame, and security. Though these references are different for each of us, they are always intense.

The emotions generated by money obscure a truth that surprises many potential investors — *Getting started in investing is no different from getting started in any other new endeavor.* The novice investor feels "I have to know a lot because there's money involved." But in investing, as in anything else new — learning to swim, for example — you don't have to be a gold medal champion, at the beginning. *The rule is to approach it slowly and simply and without distorting its ordinariness. Normalize investing.*

If you are a hesitant investor, you may feel the need to learn everything at once. Learning is, in fact, a helpful defense against your lack of self-confidence, but not too much learning. If you try to read every bit of available advice and reconcile it into a coherent whole, you are going to sink, and you will make yourself miserable, too.

I advise clients to begin with a small portfolio of conservative investments, acquired in planned stages. Because of what I tell them and the amount of reading I suggest they do, they know they are not at high risk at this point in their investing and they can become knowledgeable gradually. Step by step, they learn to give up the paralyzing thought that they have to be expert before they begin.

This psychological approach reduces anxiety, builds gratification, and fosters motivation. These are the same principles I am going to teach you in the next pages. I also ask you, as I ask my clients, to make a commitment to staying in the market at least three years — the average length of time of one market cycle. Hopefully, you'll stay a good deal longer than that.

In investing, there are few friends as useful as experience and few advisers as wise and omnipotent as time. Time is the great key to becoming rich, a point that has been made over and over again, but what most people don't realize is that time is also the key to becoming psychologically secure. Just as time evens out the market's fluctuations and makes you a financial winner, it evens out any rough edges you may have emotionally and makes them less hazardous to your success.

The first steps, as I have designed them, should be easy to take since they were formulated with your sense of security as the foremost consideration.

THE "GETTING STARTED" PROGRAM

When I meet with clients for the first time, I do what all good investment counselors do. I work with people to develop a financial plan that analyzes current and future resources and determines long-term goals. I make sure that, before investing, they have enough money set aside to cover expenses for three to six months in the event of an emergency. I ask whether they have sufficient life insurance. And I also make certain that they are already regularly investing in whatever tax-advantaged resources they have available to them, a 401(k) plan at work, an optional investment program in company stock, an IRA (individual retirement account), or, if they are self-employed, a SEP (self-employed individual account). I consider their likely Social Security benefits and any probable inheritances.

As we talk about these basics, I look for signs of uneasiness, and I try to put the people at ease psychologically because, as a psychiatrist, I know that at the beginning, reassurance is important and that often, as we talk about first investment choices, vestiges of procrastination — a "pull back" mentality — can linger.

If you feel yourself hanging back, remember that this basic program for hesitant investors is designed to help you get over procrastination by making things *very simple and very sound, yet giving you choices.* Here are some of the approaches you can take.

First, decide whether you want to begin with mutual funds or stocks, bearing in mind that there are psychological benefits to each. As you probably know, a mutual fund buys securities and you own a percentage of everything the fund owns. With mutual funds, you get the emotional security of professional management, instant diversification, and ease of record keeping. With stocks, you take control, and you have the possibility of doing better — or worse — than you would with a fund. You also get a greater amount of satisfaction from identifying with your investments since stocks are more "personal" than funds. Therefore, you have to decide what makes you more comfortable — being in someone else's experienced hands or testing your own talents.

I find that the majority of my clients feel more comfortable with mutual funds since funds are less anxiety provoking as a first investment. This chapter will focus on funds, particularly stock funds, and I will discuss developing an individual stock portfolio in the next chapter.

Psychologically, rules help, so here are some for building a mutual fund portfolio:

IF YOU HAVE UNDER $10,000 TO INVEST

The rule: Buy a single fund first. Gradually buy shares in one mutual fund, and preferably *only one fund,* until you have accumulated between $10,000 to $25,000. If you're earning between $30,000 and $50,000, it will take you about three years — making investments monthly or every few months — to reach your goal.

The idea of restricting yourself to one fund up to a certain amount is based on an important psychological principle. It is more gratifying to be able to watch money grow in one place, and at a certain point — usually around the $10,000 to $15,000 mark — you begin to feel really terrific about what you have accomplished.

A technician at the hospital where I work has been putting a fixed amount each month into a mutual fund for four years. He was quite hesitant to start, telling me that investing was something that "just isn't done in my family." With my encouragement, he got going and by January of the fourth year, he had about $10,000 in his mutual fund. By year's end — a banner year for the market — the fund had gone up by 39 percent, and the technician saw his assets jump to over $14,000. For him, this was the "emotional payoff" point, and he went around beaming for several weeks, murmuring "wonderful" to me each time we passed in the hall.

Probably, my coworker could have accumulated $14,000 by investing in three strong-performing funds, but the emotional impact would not have been the same because, psychologically, *a single sum of money seems to add up to more than the same sum divided.*

For several years, I've been doing a study of the investing habits of doctors. One of the physicians told me that when he had all of his money in one fund (the Magellan Fund) he "felt" that he was doing better than when he became diversified among several funds, even though he's been making money that way, too.

Particularly for a beginner, it's important to get the greatest amount of gratification possible, since gratification will encourage you to continue, and that often comes from watching your money increase steadily in one place to the "emotional payoff" point and beyond.

The "emotional payoff" point is important because that's when most investors begin to *think ahead* in a positive way — "If the fund's at $14,000 now, I'll probably have $20,000 in another year or two" — and since time is the key to successful investing, the sooner you link yourself emotionally to a time horizon, the better off you are.

After you have contributed regularly to one fund to a set maximum, $25,000 let's say, start a second fund and contribute to the same maximum, and then a third. After you have $25,000 in each fund, alternate contributions among the three funds.

A word about diversification: Building up a single fund to an amount that will *gratify* you is more important, to my mind, than having several funds to begin with in the interests of diversification. The principle of diversification, though an important one, has become overdone. Even if you have only one mutual fund, remember that the fund itself is diversified.

> "Put all your eggs in the one basket and — watch that basket."
> — Mark Twain, advice frequently quoted
> by Bernard Baruch

IF YOU HAVE $50,000 TO INVEST

The rule: Invest half right now and the rest next year. Put $25,000 in a mutual fund and $25,000 in one-year U.S. Treasury bonds. Next year, cash in the bonds, and put $25,000 into a second mutual fund.

IF YOU HAVE $100,000 TO INVEST

The rule: Invest half right now and the rest over the next two years. Divide $50,000 between two mutual funds. Put $25,000 in one-year Treasury bonds and $25,000 in two-year Treasury bonds. Next year, cash in the one-year bonds, and put $25,000 in a third mutual fund. The following year, cash in the two-year bonds and divide the money among the three funds or put it into a fourth mutual fund.

Feed your money into equities incrementally — over several years, if you have a large amount to invest.

The psychological reason is that you don't want to risk consigning everything you have to a falling market. Nothing discourages a new investor more than suffering a substantial loss at the very beginning of an investment program. Anxieties and fears can become overwhelming, leading to abandonment of the program.

There is a psychological principle behind this: The money you make — while marvelous — never seems as valuable as the money you lose. The emotional arithmetic is that money lost is twice as important as money gained.

Warren Buffett, one of the greatest investors of our time, says there are two rules to successful investing. The first rule is "Never lose" and the second rule is "Never forget the first rule."

I assume Buffett was referring to *significant* losses of a size that damage capital creation, because rebuilding from a smaller base is so difficult.

Let me show you what I mean. If I asked you whether you'd rather put $100 in a savings account at 5 percent compound annual interest for three years or a mutual fund that goes up 50 percent the first year, down 50 percent the second year, and up 50 percent the third year, you might well choose the mutual fund. In fact, the savings account is the better choice because it would be worth $115.76 at the end of three years, while the mutual fund, having undergone significant losses in that second year, would be worth $112.50.

If you can protect against *significant* losses by investing prudently, you are virtually assured of building significant wealth — and in succeeding chapters, I will show you how to do that. In the meantime, you have to act on the *most important rule* of investing, which is: *Begin.*

CHOOSING THE FUND FOR YOU

Start with a fund that emphasizes value as opposed to growth. My second choice would be a fund that combines both value and growth. (I'll have more to stay about investing styles in the next chapter.)

These recommendations are based on my personal opinion — that the value approach to investing, inspired by the teaching of Ben

Graham, is the most successful. The records of great value investors, such as Warren Buffett, Charley Munger, John Templeton, and Walter Schloss, attest to the virtues of value, and I find that value fits my psychological profile best because I am the sort of person who gets excited at the thought of buying a dollar for twenty-five cents, and I'm willing to wait two or three years to reap my reward.

Since you'll be working with a single fund for a while, you need the security of selecting one that has a record of success. Here are several factors to consider:

• *Past record.* Look for a top rating by *Morningstar Mutual Funds* or *Forbes* magazine or a place on the *Forbes* Honor Role of funds with great long-term records, which appears in the magazine's end-of-summer issue. I prefer the *Forbes* ratings because I think they are better at taking bear market performance into account, but acquaint yourself with both valuable sources and see which you prefer. (*Morningstar* is a newsletter, published every other week, that evaluates funds in detail and rates them. Five stars is the highest rating, one star, the lowest. See Resources Section.)

Ideally, you want a fund that has a *Forbes* A rating in a down market and at least a B rating in an up market. Why not an A rating for both markets? There aren't many funds that meet that criterion, but the main reason is that in an up market, there isn't much difference between A, B, or even C — your real need is for the best protection you can get in a bear market. That's when an A rating really counts.

Look at the fund's record over five years and ten years, comparing its variations to the Standard & Poor's 500 (S&P 500), or whatever index is appropriate for the fund. Let's say that in a fund's best year, 1986, it went up 34 percent — above the average in a very good year — and in its worst year, 1987, it went down 14 percent — less than the average in a poor year. Then such a fund is a pretty good choice.

Always judge a fund by its long-term record, not a sensational six months or past year. Much has been written questioning the validity of long-term records, but no other measure has been developed that offers greater *emotional security,* particularly when you are just starting out.

• *Continuity of management.* Make sure that the manager who created the good record is still managing the fund.

• *Volatility.* Suppose you find a fund with a great record that nevertheless took a dive of 39 percent at one point, but hasn't gone down recently. It may be due for a correction just when you decide to invest, and as I said earlier, you want to avoid an initial dip for emotional as well as financial reasons.

• *Assets.* The larger the fund, the slower the growth, and the more difficult it is for the manager to outperform other funds. Look for a fund with less than a billion dollars in assets.

• *Tax considerations.* If you don't need dividend income to live on, you'll do better, tax-wise, buying a fund that mainly gives you capital gains. Check to see what percentage of a fund's reported total return comes from dividends rather than capital gains. Check the fund's average holding period for a stock. A low turnover rate means lower costs and lower taxes.

• *Leverage.* No more than 10 percent of the fund's assets should be in funds borrowed from banks and financial institutions. If they are, the fund is too speculative for you.

• *No-load — usually.* All things being equal, a fund with no sales charge is preferable. But remember: In investing, all things are rarely equal, and some load funds are worth the additional cost because of their superior returns. If you plan to be in the market at least three years, a load may not be as big a drawback as it first seems. (You'll find in the Profiles section of this book that load funds have positive psychological value for some investors.)

If you're investing a large amount of money — $25,000 at once, or $75,000 over a three-year period — you can negotiate the load, and this can give you a great lesson in investor assertiveness.

GOOD FUNDS TO GET YOU STARTED

The following funds are excellent first choices for beginning investors or, for that matter, for any investors. Although not all of them meet each of the criteria above, and not all are value funds, I recommend them because their performance is above average, they are extremely well managed, and I have found them to be highly trustworthy. From a psychological point of view, trustworthiness is extremely important for a new investor, and indeed, any investor.

1. *Vanguard Index 500 Trust.* (No-load. Minimum initial investment required: $3,000. *Forbes* rating [August 25, 1997]: B for up markets, C for down markets. Five-year annualized total return: 19.62 percent; ten-year: 13.65 percent. *Morningstar* rating: 4 stars.)

This passively "managed" fund is the flagship of the Pennsylvania-based Vanguard Group, which is known for its low costs. Vanguard Index 500 Trust invests in the 500 large- and medium-size companies that compose the S&P index. Its results mirror the index, less costs of 0.2 percent, which are small. The annual turnover rate of stocks is 4 percent, which means that you delay most capital gains taxes until you sell the fund.

A beginning investor may ask, "Why an index fund? I want to do better than average." *What's difficult to accept, psychologically, is that doing "average" is actually doing very well.* In any year, the average of the Index 500 Trust beats 80 percent of stock funds and balanced (stock and bond) funds. And those 20 percent of funds that top the averages are not the same ones from year to year. The result is that, over time, only a small number of funds actually surpass the Vanguard Index 500 Trust.

2. *Third Avenue Value Fund.* (No-load. Minimum initial investment required: $1,000. Not yet ranked by *Forbes*. Five-year annualized total return as of August 31, 1997: 22.45 percent. *Morningstar* rating: 5 stars.)

Third Avenue Value is managed by Martin J. Whitman, who came to investment management after a brilliant record as a bankruptcy and stockholder litigation specialist. He is focused on stockholder interests and operates the fund according to the principles of Ben Graham and Warren Buffett. Third Avenue buys good companies selling at bargain prices because their industries are depressed, companies that foster asset growth rather than earnings momentum, and special bankruptcy situations. If I ran a mutual fund, I would hope to run it as competently as Marty Whitman runs this one.

3. *Lexington Corporate Leaders Trust.* (No-load. Minimum initial investment required: $1,000. *Forbes* rating [August 25, 1997]: C for up markets, B for down markets. Five-year annualized total return: 19.38 percent; ten-year: 13.22 percent. *Morningstar* rating: 4 stars.)

This is a fascinating fund, founded in 1936 with the idea of buying and holding companies the managers subjectively identified as being the leading thirty U.S. companies. Mergers, acquisitions, and one bankruptcy have reduced this number to twenty-four, which includes General Motors, Ford, Union Carbide, Dupont, Praxair, International Paper, and Alcoa. Lexington's results have been excellent, slightly better than the S&P 500. Key to the fund's success is low costs, low turnover, and an odd quirk — the trust has to invest in an equal number of shares of each company rather than an equal dollar amount of each company (as most funds do). This favors higher-priced companies, whose prices reflect their success; if such a company splits its stock, shares must be sold off to equalize the number of shares. This rule has led to a successful contrarian approach, because the trust must sell shares in the most popular companies and reinvest in companies that are currently out of favor, taking advantage of value opportunities.

4. *Guardian Park Avenue Fund.* (Load: 4.50 percent. Minimum initial investment required: $1,000. *Forbes* rating [August 25, 1997]: B for up markets, C for down markets. Five-year annualized total return: 24.02 percent; ten-year: 15.37 percent. *Morningstar* rating: 5 stars.)

While Guardian Park Avenue is a load fund, its long-term record merits consideration. Using a quantitative modeling system to discover high-quality stocks, the fund practices both value and growth investing strategies. The management team is thorough and has a great sense of value; Guardian is a blend of value and growth at a reasonable price.

AGE NEEDS, PSYCHOLOGY, AND FUND CHOICES

Your "asset allocation," the percentage mix of stocks, bonds, and cash in your portfolio, depends on your goals, your age, and the way that age makes you feel. What follows applies to portfolios that consist of individual stocks and bonds as well as funds. Let's focus on funds for the moment.

In your twenties and thirties, you're saving for a home, the kids' educations, and other expenses, so look for a top-rated equity fund. The one you choose should reflect your own aggressiveness and risk tolerance. At your age, there are several psychological factors that can cushion the risks of being more aggressive. Time, the great partner in investing, is on your side, so if you have a bad year, you know you will make up for it eventually, and your income is probably growing, since you're at the age when people move up the career ladder most rapidly. A loss can be weathered more easily than if you were older and on a fixed income.

From your middle forties through your fifties, your psychology naturally shifts toward caution. You want to make your retirement secure, you have a shorter timeline, and you realize that there may not be many more promotions on your career horizon. Growth with safety may be your theme, so look at balanced funds, a mixture of stocks and bonds.

In your retirement years, allocation depends on how much money you've accumulated and how secure you feel. If you have enough money to maintain your standard of living (a million dollars, if you need yearly income of $40,000, or two and a half million, if you need $100,000) and you want to grow capital to pass on to your estate, look to equity funds, remembering that if need be, you can afford to dip into capital. A wealthier retiree can afford to feel more expansive psychologically. If you need investment income to live on, you must behave defensively, and you may well be feeling defensive emotionally. You can increase your sense of security by looking to a balanced fund or a bond fund.

In making allocation decisions, most retired people will be psychologically affected by the longevity of their parents and grandparents. Long-lived families are usually more conservative because they expect to need the money for a longer time, but that's not such a sad state of affairs, after all.

THE "NO ANXIETY" WAY TO LEARN

Whether you start out buying mutual funds or stocks or both, you'll undoubtedly feel you want to do some serious reading first, but piling up information often creates anxiety rather than relieves it.

Beginners sometimes feel they have to "catch up" with what they don't know, but when they try to do this, they quickly get overloaded. The danger of overload, like an initial loss in the market, is that it can turn you off. So I advise my clients to relax and follow a system of "sifting and skimming."

What you have to do is to *sift* through books on investing, and pick out several that seem valuable to you; then *skim* the ones you have selected, and gradually read more deeply — as you feel like it, making sure that you keep the pressure off yourself.

Avoid any book that tries to lure you with promises of extraordinary results or quick wealth. For me, Ben Graham's *The Intelligent Investor* is the best first book, and no one should invest without having read it. I've found it so valuable that I reread it annually.

The "next most valuable" investment book is Philip Fisher's *Common Stocks and Uncommon Profits*. The Graham and Fisher books are short and clear, and mastering them leads to an understanding of the investment process.

Other useful books are Louis Engel's *How to Buy Stocks,* Peter Lynch's *One Up on Wall Street,* Jane Bryant Quinn's *Making the Most of Your Money,* and Martin Zweig's *Winning on Wall Street.* (You'll find a complete list of recommendations in the Resources Section.)

Further preparation for becoming an investor is to skim through the *Wall Street Journal (WSJ)* or the *Investor's Business Daily* (one or the other, not both) every day, looking for items that interest you, the way you would in any other newspaper. Almost everyone finds the human interest stories on page one of *WSJ* captivating. Try reading "Heard on the Street," which appears in Section C (where you will also find tables of daily stock, bond, and mutual fund quotes). This column will introduce you to Wall Street's way of thinking, and can help you to become an investor mentally, even as you work toward becoming one in practice.

Eventually you may find yourself reading more and more of whichever paper you have chosen, but if you don't, that's all right, too. Becoming a regular financial reader, even if you're just a skimmer, can do wonders for your investing self-esteem.

A publication that's fun to skim (and you want to have fun investing) is the wonderfully down-to-earth advice that Warren Buffett gives in the annual reports of Berkshire Hathaway, the fantastically successful holding company he founded. In fact, there is probably no better investment "book" than this compilation of Buffett's remarks in the Berkshire Hathaway annual report, which you can obtain by writing to Berkshire Hathaway at 1440 Kiewit Plaza, Omaha, NE 68131.

An adult extension course can be informative and psychologically valuable if you can utilize the support of your classmates — people who are also new to investing — to encourage yourself to get started. But courses can be inhibiting if you compare yourself to others, decide they know more than you do, and use them as an excuse to keep on procrastinating.

A warning: If you decide to take a course, check out the credentials of the instructor before you sign up. A person who is associated with a brokerage firm or a financial company may be more interested in obtaining clients than in providing objective instruction.

PUTTING HESITATION TO REST

If you find that you are hesitant about getting started, there can be several concerns that are serving as roadblocks.

All of these concerns are understandable, and they've been "common wisdom" for quite some time, but they are distortions, so work at readjusting them — at letting in a bit of light.

Let's start with the idea that you think you have to wait for "the right time" to begin. These three little words can cause more trouble for beginning investors than any others.

Often a new client will ask, "John, can't you tell me exactly *when* I ought to get in?" When I hear that question, I know that it has two meanings. On a financial level, the person is asking me to predict a market low, in order to start investing at the most advantageous time. But on a psychological level, the person is asking, "Can't you protect me from getting hurt?" and expressing all of the angst that investors feel.

Waiting for "the right time" is an attempt to avoid the issues of fear, risk, and loss that are a natural part of the investing process. There is no way of avoiding these issues, but they can be eased with the certain knowledge that over time, and with patience, you will emerge from investing a financial winner. *This knowledge is the powerful antidote to the down times you may experience.*

Realistically there is no "right time" to begin, because it is not possible to time the market. Absolutely no one knows when the low has been reached. If you wait, you are more likely to miss an opportunity to make money by not being in the market than you are to lose by being in.

In July 1995, I thought we might be near the top of a bull market but, of course, I could not be sure, since no one can predict the market. If I had advised new clients not to come into the market at that point, they would have been deprived of gains averaging more than 20 percent over the next year. If you wait, you may never make your move, and the great likelihood is that you will always be shadowed by regret.

Another reason people may fail to get started is that they think they are at a big disadvantage compared to "the professionals." What many investors don't realize is that in certain ways, the advantage belongs to the individual investor.

Consider this: Professionals — the people who run mutual funds and institutional investments — are under intense pressure to perform over the *short term* or lose their jobs.

When rumors spread on Wall Street, as they do every day, big-time managers feel compelled to go along with what the crowd is doing; they can't take the risk of standing apart. (This is one reason I try to pick independent-minded managers in the funds I recommend and recommend you stay with the fund over the long haul.) If you're selecting your own stocks, you don't need to produce short-term results, so you need not follow the herd.

The *only* advantage professional managers have over you is that they are working at investing full-time, and even that is not completely true because much of their time is spent on other parts of the money management business, such as meeting with clients, marketing, and record keeping. On occasion, professionals do have better sources of information, but even this advantage is much less important today, with the electronic dissemination of news.

Many investors hesitate because the market seems so unpredictable. While the market is by no means a certain place, it is actually *more predictable* than you might think because of two important *psychological* laws, which can even out the playing field. Remember them, and you have an important leg up.

THE LAW OF UNEXPECTED RESULTS

This law was discovered by noted money manager and *Forbes* columnist David Dreman. I call it the "Law of Unexpected Results," a principle that my unpublished research suggests is applicable to many sets of expectations besides investing.

Psychologically, the market expects *more* of the stocks it favors, the stocks that are currently popular, as indicated by their high price-to-earnings ratios (P/E), and it expects *less* of stocks it does not favor, those that are currently not popular, as indicated by their low price-to-earnings ratios.

When the earnings of a high P/E stock come in modestly higher than forecast, the stock hardly goes up at all, because the market's psychological expectation was that the earnings would be much better than forecast. If the earnings are only as high as forecast or below, the stock drops, because the market is extremely disappointed.

On the other hand, when the earnings of a low P/E stock come in as high or higher than forecast, the stock goes up more than the market in general, since the psychological expectation was that the earnings would not be as good. If earnings are lower than forecast, the stock hardly drops at all, because the psychological expectation was that the earnings would be poor.

This law gives you a great advantage, for it helps you predict how the market is likely to behave when earnings reports are released. It also should encourage you to buy out-of-favor (low P/E) stocks when you start to invest, since you are likely to do a lot better when they do well and lose less when they do poorly.

The "Law of Unexpected Returns" is an argument in favor of value investing because it leads you to where the gains are high and the risk low. But even if you don't adopt a value style, the "law" will give you a reliable insight into market behavior.

THE LAW OF EXTREME NEWS

The market will react vigorously to extreme news events, going up when the news is good and down when it is bad, and it will react more vigorously to bad news than to good news. Victor Niederhoffer, a financial analyst, studied newspaper headlines from 1950 to 1966 and discovered that the more extreme the news, the greater the market fluctuations. He also discovered that in the days that followed, there was a rebound if the news had been bad and a decline if it had been good. So this law helps you *know* what to expect, and often you can look upon bad news — especially political or economic news — as a buying opportunity.

Finally, if the stock market is a gamble, it's a good one, because the odds are in your favor. *Historically, the market has gone up twice as often as it has gone down, and the rewards have been impressive.* Since the beginning of the century, the Standard & Poor's 500 — the index of 500 major stocks listed on the New York Stock Exchange — has averaged an annual return of 9.5 percent, compared with 7.0 percent for corporate bonds and 3.3 percent for Treasury bills, *making stocks the best wealth builder available* (excluding real estate, which did very well from 1933 to 1986).

For all the seeming volatility of the market, investing is just about as far from gambling as anything could be. Unlike gambling, it requires work, judgment, patience, and a commitment to the long term, and best of all, it produces results.

If you're committed to your financial future, if you want to do the very best for yourself and those you love, you have already achieved the emotional positioning that underlies successful investing and are more than halfway there. It's only a matter of setting out on that slow, sure path that, over time, can bring you the riches you deserve.

CHAPTER 3

The Psychology of Building
a Stock Portfolio

Most people are comfortable starting out in mutual funds, but eventually large numbers of investors want to choose their own individual stocks. For them, this choice is what "being in the market" means.

The appeal of buying stocks, as I told you in the last chapter, is that you take control, you challenge yourself, and you can do better than you can with funds. Psychologically, you are more likely to identify with stocks than with funds. So when you choose wisely, and your stocks do well, you get a boost to your self-esteem that you can't get with funds, and this stock/self-esteem connection is a positive one, provided you don't fall into the trap of identifying too closely with your stocks. You can also nurture the pleasing fantasy of finding an unknown company that turns out to be the next Johnson & Johnson or Coca-Cola, though, to be truthful, this fantasy rarely comes true.

THE EMOTIONALLY SECURE PATH TO WEALTH

You become *financially secure* through building a diversified, limited-size portfolio that you change infrequently, buying and selling only for specific reasons. You become *emotionally secure* by following the same approach, so there is a happy confluence of economic and psychological principles at work that comes down to the word *stability*.

What you want from your portfolio is maximum stability, combined with maximum growth over time, which will give you an "emotional home" that reflects your own perspective and makes you feel good about investing. *The rule is: Build your portfolio and your portfolio builds you up.*

You need an emotional home to withstand the extreme anxiety investors experience today — greater than at any other time I have seen.

There is an irony in this. With the current information explosion — the proliferation of financial newsletters, magazines, and, particularly, access to computer sites — so-called insider knowledge is no longer restricted to market "insiders." This ought to make the individual investor feel less anxious, because the playing field has been leveled, but rather than being reassuring, the information overload is anxiety provoking and results in constant portfolio turnover — nervous buying and selling in order to respond to all the "opportunities." Rather than assuaging anxiety, continued turnover serves only to increase it. *Successful investing consists of doing less — not more. It consists of picking a few good stocks and hanging on to them for as long as possible.*

Every good money manager realizes that clients today are under psychological bombardment from too many stimuli. Our job is to show them how to slow down and relax. The *really new idea* is to get back to basics, because that's the road to sanity. One of my colleagues, Ted Rorer of Rorer Management in Philadelphia, says it best, I think: *"Buy one good company at a time and ignore the noise."*

THE CORE PORTFOLIO

I recommend to my clients that they build up to a maximum of ten quality *core* stocks, diversified among leading industries, and perhaps a smaller *satellite* portfolio, which I will discuss later on. Ten is the highest number most individuals can follow in *sufficient detail*. (I'll talk more about what sufficient detail means in the next chapter.)

Building my own portfolio, I look for core companies that have the following characteristics:

- Profitability. A return on equity (ROE) of at least 15 percent and preferably 20 percent. ROE is net income after taxes, divided by stockholders' investment.

- Predictability of earnings, based on the company's past record, and my conviction that the nature of the business is not likely to change.
- Products with low risk of being made obsolete by technological changes.
- A low need for capital reinvestment, because the company doesn't have to invest in new buildings or plants, pay off a lot of debt, or spend much money on research and development.
- Shareholder friendliness — a company that buys back its shares instead of, or in addition to, paying dividends, so that the value of the shares increases. (While dividends are often recommended as a criteria for selecting a company, they can have substantial tax consequences, so unless you need the income, you are generally better off with a company that reinvests in itself.)
- Honesty and integrity — two qualities that are of great psychological importance. I will have more to say about them later in this chapter.

It's most important to me that the company be unique in some way so that its products, distribution system, or management style is difficult or impossible to copy. *A unique company has an economic "moat around it," to use Warren Buffett's phrase, but that also forms a psychological moat that increases an investor's inner security.*

A good example of what I mean by unique is Thermo Electron, one of the companies in which I own shares and that I have recommended in my newsletter. Thermo Electron makes hundreds of complex products, including instrumentation for technological processes, bomb and smoke detectors, lasers for hair removal, and even the first FDA-approved artificial heart. But what makes the company unique is a corporate culture that rewards entrepreneurship by spinning out new companies and giving shareholders a stake in them. This culture, which has made Thermo Electron enormously successful, is not easily reproducible, since most companies are not structured to operate in such a flexible and imaginative manner, and since many managers cannot bear to share power in the way that John Hatsopoulos, Thermo Electron's CEO, does.

Banks and insurance companies are unique in another way: They

are unlikely to become technologically obsolete and, if managed prop-
erly, they can go on forever. That's why they rank among my favorite
investments.

Different qualities make a company unique, but my point is that
this criterion has a place in your selection process. (In Appendix A, as
an example of both financial and psychological reasoning, you'll find
a list of the companies in my portfolio and why I selected them.)

RULES FOR BUILDING YOUR PORTFOLIO

As I recommended with mutual funds, you should follow a system-
atic approach related to the amount of money you have.

*If you have less than $3,000 to invest: Save up $3,000 in a money
market account and invest it in one stock.* Then save another $3,000,
invest it in another stock, and so on until you have your ten-stock portfolio. This program may take you three to five years, depending on your
income and how much you can save. It's advisable to buy stocks in
100-lot shares — for reasons of convenience, record keeping, and commission costs — so $3,000 is about the minimum you need to make a
purchase. Many companies allow you to buy additional shares under
DRIPs (Dividend Reinvestment Plans), but about fifty companies also
allow you to buy your initial shares directly from them, thus saving
commission costs. Sometimes the automatic reinvestment of dividends
is not only commission free, but even at less than market cost. (You
will find a list of these initial investment companies in the Resources
Section, and a further discussion of DRIPs in chapter 12.)

Once you have built your portfolio up to ten stocks, keep on purchasing additional shares in each company in rotation.

A technique for saving: If you find saving difficult, put 10 percent
of your net pay into a money market fund as soon as you get your
check. David Chilton, in his book, *The Wealthy Barber,* suggests this
approach. He has found that people who cut their salary by 10 percent
never miss it. But even if you do miss it, and you find making cut-
backs difficult, remind yourself that there is a tremendous tradeoff:

Gaining your own personal ticket to independence can be enormously motivating.

While you save, investigate stocks you might want to buy (I'll show you how to do that later in this chapter), so that mentally you turn yourself into an investor. The sooner you see yourself as an investor, the easier it becomes to put money aside for stock purchases.

If you have $10,000 to $25,000 to invest: Buy one company right now and two at intervals over the course of the year. Divide the money equally among the companies you buy. There is great psychological value in making purchases incrementally. You temper the emotional trauma of initial loss, should you run into a market downturn with your first investments, and time — even a few months — gives you a fresh perspective as you select subsequent stocks. Finally, by making yourself delay, you reinforce the principle that *a buy decision need never be rushed.* The only exception to this rule is if there is a merger or some unusual activity on the drawing board that you believe is a compelling reason to buy right now.

If you have $50,000 to invest: Put $25,000 into a one-year U.S. Treasury bond or CD. With the other $25,000, buy three good stocks over the course of the year. The next year, cash in the bond, and gradually buy the rest of your portfolio.

If you have $75,000 to invest: Put $25,000 in a one-year Treasury bond or CD and $25,000 in a two-year Treasury bond or CD. With the remaining $25,000, buy three good stocks over the course of the year. The next year, cash in the one-year bond and, at intervals, buy another three stocks. The following year, cash in the two-year bond and gradually buy the rest of your portfolio. The reason for investing slowly over a three-year period is that you do not want to risk putting large sums of money into a declining market.

While your goal is to keep the portfolio balanced, with 10 percent of the money in each of your ten stocks, you'll find eventually that some of your investments are more successful than others (that's the reason for being diversified) and the portfolio has gotten out of balance. There are several ways to deal with this.

Some mutual fund managers sell off shares of a stock if it gets above a certain percentage, but my approach is more flexible. If a stock gets up to 20 percent of my portfolio's dollar value, I may sell some of it, or I stop buying it in rotation and focus on my other stocks.

Another approach is to sell off some shares in your more successful stocks, put the money aside, and after taking time to think about your next move, buy an eleventh stock, eventually a twelfth stock, and more. These stocks can be the basis of a smaller, satellite portfolio that is more speculative than the core portfolio.

THE SATELLITE PORTFOLIO

A satellite stock is an undervalued stock that has good short-term prospects, but hasn't yet achieved stability in terms of profits and predictability of earnings to make it a long-term hold. A satellite may not even have a solid business as yet. It may be a biotech company awaiting FDA approval on a new drug, or it may represent a sector of the market that is currently undervalued — a utility company when interest rates are high at a point when the rates may be about to go down. A satellite is a good bet, but a bet nonetheless.

A good example is Sepracor, an emerging pharmaceutical company in Massachusetts, that I purchased in June 1996 at 15$^3/_8$. Sepracor has the uniqueness that I seek. It is the world's leader in "chiral chemistry" — the study, isolation, and purification of drugs existing in optical isomer forms. An optical isomer is a compound with the same chemical composition as other compounds but with a different spatial relationship of its atoms, which are commonly mirror images of each other. Sepracor has a number of products, in various stages of FDA approval, that would be improved and cheaper versions of current drugs. Sepracor could become a real star — maybe even fulfill my fantasy of discovering the next Johnson & Johnson — but I know it is risky, since the company has no profits yet and invests a lot of capital in research and development, as do all early biotech companies.

Remember that you should not invest more than 10 to 20 percent of your money in satellites. The percentage depends on your age, financial circumstances, and risk tolerance. Satellite stocks tend to take over, especially in a bull market, but they can never provide the stability you need to feel emotionally secure. For that, you need to concentrate on the care and feeding of your core portfolio.

GETTING FOCUSED

In portfolio building, nothing is more important than having a sense of focus, a feeling of being centered. To center yourself, you need to adopt an investment style and follow it, not rigidly, but confident that you are on the right track most of the time. Even if you don't pick your own stocks, you can't feel confident unless you understand the reasons for the choices your broker or adviser makes.

As you undoubtedly know, the two most widely followed styles in investing are value and growth.

Value investors look for soundly managed companies that are selling at prices below the basic value of the business because they are out of favor. David Dreman's research shows that value investing produces higher returns over time because when a value stock gains favor with the market, it benefits both from the rise in stock price and from earnings growth. Value stocks tend to be less risky because there is less market reaction to earnings disappointments than is the case with growth stocks.

Growth investors look for soundly managed companies that seem to be poised for an extraordinary rate of earnings growth and that currently have a growth rate of at least 15 percent.

A good rule-of-thumb is to buy companies whose P/E multiples are less than their compound earnings growth rates. (P/E multiples are listed in the stock charts in every financial newspaper. The compound earnings growth rate is reported every day in *Investor's Business Daily.*) From 1990 to 1997, Intel's average P/E ratio was in the 10 to 14 range while its earnings compounded at better than 40 percent annually.

Momentum investing is a variation of growth investing that has become popular only in the past four or so years. For momentum investors, a stock becomes desirable because unexpected accelerations in earnings have caused the price to rise more than the prices of other stocks. Once this trend becomes established, the stock tends to keep on rising ahead of the pack. Momentum investors buy a company simply because it is going up in price. Value investors seek to buy low and sell high; momentum investors seek to buy high and sell even higher. (I suspect that momentum will turn out to be yet another variation on the "Greater Fool Theory": that there will always be someone else who will buy a popular investment regardless of price.)

My major reservation about momentum is that when the market turns around, what has gone up can come down even faster and, if you don't get out more quickly than most people can, you may incur punishing losses that will take years to make up. In the market correction of June 1995, a major mutual fund based on momentum lost 35 percent of its value in just a few days.

As for charting or technical analysis — to which momentum is closely related — my opinion is that charting is reasoning after the fact. The charts can give you past data, such as where stocks have met points of resistance to rising further, but they can't predict what will happen in the future, and that is what you want to know. John Train, a noted financial analyst, has a standing offer: He'll give $10,000 to the technician who, having seen half of an existing chart, can make an accurate prediction of what the other half shows. So far, nobody has been able to collect.

In short, momentum and technical analysis are not, to my mind, the best approaches to selecting stocks.

A PSYCHOLOGICAL LODESTAR

Momentum investing and other faddish styles that preceded it — go-go stocks in the 1960s, one-decision stocks in the 1970s, and "relative strength" stocks in the 1980s — run on the market's own psychology. This psychology generates excitement for the latest trend, then abruptly changes its mind and goes on to seek excitement elsewhere, leaving investors high and dry.

I am not the first person to observe that the market's enthusiasms and mood swings are neurotic. In fact, the market might clinically be described as manic-depressive, and as a psychiatrist, I've been tempted to put it on the couch.

But as an investor, I know I have to understand the market's churning emotions, but separate from them as much as possible. Investors also need to understand where their own emotions intersect with the market's in a financially dangerous way, a subject I will deal with in the Profiles section of this book.

One of the reasons I am so committed to value investing is that it provides the major psychological mechanism you can use to put distance between yourself and the mind-set of the market.

This mechanism, which is to think like the owner of a business rather than someone who is simply seeking to make money in stocks, has been my inner compass in investing. I credit it with my substantial financial success and I believe it can make you wealthy, too, whether or not you choose value investing.

Decades ago, Ben Graham, the father of value investing, said that when you invest, you are buying a share of a business, so the purchase should be looked upon as a business partnership, rather than an alliance with the stock market.

If you know the fair market value of the business (the price a competitor would pay for it, which I will show you how to figure later), if the basic fundamentals are sound, if the potential for growth is strong — if, in short, it's a good business — it doesn't much matter how the price fluctuates because, eventually, you are going to come out ahead.

The psychological power of this principle is that it can help liberate you from the market's emotions, since price fluctuations are related more to emotional responses than economics. And when you are liberated, the market's strange behavior can work to your advantage.

Graham gave this example: Imagine that you have a business with a fair market value of $10,000,000 and your partner is a manic-depressive character named Mr. Market. Some days, Mr. Market is placid. Some days — and you have learned that you cannot predict when they will occur — Mr. Market becomes wildly enthusiastic and offers you the full $10,000,000 for just your half of the business. Other days, equally unpredictably, he becomes totally morose and offers to sell you his half of the business for just $1,000,000.

Either way, you would win. And you will win in any investment if you learn to judge it by its fair market value, and not by Mr. Market's gyrations.

Whenever I have to make an investing decision, I ask myself: Am I thinking in a business way or in Mr. Market's way? The business way is psychologically the best way, because my feet are planted firmly on the ground.

I've worked with a great many clients, and those people who have a "business partner" psychology about their investments — whether they are value investors or growth investors or a combination of the two — are more likely to be successful than those who listen to Mr. Market.

FIRST STEPS TOWARD BUSINESS PARTNERSHIP

The first objective is to find "leads" — companies that look like good prospects, which you will want to investigate further to see if you should become a partner. Before I suggest how you might do this yourself, let me talk about my own approach.

Like many investors, I begin with the weekly publication *Value Line Investment Survey,* known as the investor's "bible." Peter Lynch has called it "the next best thing to having your own private securities analyst."

If you've done any investing, you are probably acquainted with *Value Line.* Its combination of comprehensiveness and historical depth cannot be equaled. *VL* reports on more than 1,700 companies, updating each company four times a year; the data covers a fifteen-year period, and is presented in an easy-to-read format that includes stock history, earnings, growth rate, dividends, cash flow, capital spending, book value, and shares outstanding. There is a commentary and the latest information on insider selling and institutional holdings. *Value Line* also has an expanded edition which covers an additional 1,800 smaller companies.

The *Value Line* ranking system for stocks — one is the highest, five the lowest — was for many decades not very predictive of success, but since the system was updated several years ago, it has proven to be very accurate and it can be used effectively by any investor.

For historical data alone, *Standard & Poor's Reports*, published annually, is the best reference. *Standard & Poor's* also comes out in a weekly edition that is similar to *Value Line* but is not as detailed.

The *Wall Street Journal* is, in my opinion, the best daily source of financial information. (As I mentioned in the previous chapter, it has only one daily competitor, the *Investor's Business Daily*.) In addition to its comprehensive stock tables, *WSJ* publishes news articles and features that can give you leads to good companies, even if you only skim the *Journal*, as I recommended.

I've gotten on the trail of some of my best investments simply by noticing items in the *Journal* and then following up. A few years ago, I read an item about Chris-Craft, the one-time boat manufacturer, which had sold a sugar company that it owned for $40,000,000. I called up the president, Herbert Siegel, and asked what he planned to do with the money. His answers were so interesting — he was going to expand into the media area — and he sounded so well informed and reliable, that I eventually bought both Chris-Craft and its sister media company, DHA Communications; both stocks that have done quite well for me.

I have also found valuable leads in *Barron's Weekly*. In addition to stock tables, each issue of *Barron's* publishes at least three to five feature articles and a number of interesting regular departments. I also get *Forbes*, *Business Week*, and many other business and financial publications.

Online, I subscribe to the *Dow Jones News Retrieval Service*, which downloads everything that has appeared in print or on one of the wire services about a particular company, set of companies, industry, or sector for the past three months. *Dow Jones* tracks up to thirty stocks for its basic fee and more can be added at a modest additional charge.

I regularly use two business services, *First Call* and *IBES*, available both online and in hard copy, which track the stock analysts' earnings projections and which could be called the Associated Press or Reuters of the financial world.

If, in my research, I find a company that interests me, I send for the annual report and 10K form, which I'll say more about shortly.

After looking over these documents, the next step in my investigation is to talk to management. In almost any company, you can speak with the person in charge of investor relations — whose information can be useful but somewhat limited — but what most investors don't realize is that it's often possible to talk directly with the chief financial officer (CFO), the president, or the chief executive officer (CEO).

Admittedly, it's easier to get these officials on the phone if you are a professional money manager or newsletter publisher, but you would be amazed at how frequently top management will respond to an individual investor.

When I speak with management, my first objective is to get the earnings picture for the next quarter. If I'm talking with the CFO, for example, I ask whether he or she is comfortable with analysts' forecasts. If earnings are going to be lower, the answer may not be forthright, or at best equivocal, but if I hear something like "Well, we're actually doing a little better," that's a good sign.

If the company has been developing a new product, I ask whether they've shipped it yet and how sales are going — information that gives me a *business partner's* feel for what's happening inside.

Another question I often ask is "Do you have any assets off the books?" When a company — particularly a high-tech company — develops a new product, it frequently creates a venture company for this purpose, taking the costs off the books of the parent company. If things go well, and the product is successful, the assets get shifted back to the parent company, causing the stock price to rise, so assets off the books can be an indicator of potential income growth.

I like to talk directly with management so I can "feel them out" psychologically. If I get a lot of evasive answers, I begin to wonder about trustworthiness; if management seems poorly informed, that's certainly a negative sign. On the other hand, if I encounter an open attitude like Mr. Siegel's, one that is welcoming even on the telephone, I begin to make an emotional connection to the company, and I'm certainly encouraged to think of myself as a potential partner and to find out more.

SETTING LIMITS ON THE WORK YOU DO

Some people in public administration are called "policy wonks" because they love poking around in governmental issues. I am a "business wonk." I get enthusiastic about researching a company — everything from the history of the founder and his family to changes in management and new products under development — and I get a great many psychological clues that way, too.

What I do gives me a real high, but it is not essential for the average investor. You can do very well without reading every business publication, subscribing to news or business services, or calling up management — unless you want to — and most important, it is not helpful to worry about not having the time or the inclination to do these things.

What's important is to make a commitment to doing some basic work, but limit the number of publications you look at regularly. You can do well by simply relying on *Value Line*, as the trust departments of many small banks do in making selections for clients' portfolios.

Whenever you can, use what has been researched and predigested for you — by reliable people. Here is one of the ways that I narrow down the selection of smaller companies I may want to purchase. In September, *Forbes* magazine publishes a list of 200 of "the world's best small companies." In May, *Business Week* puts out a similar list, which overlaps *Forbes* by about 100 names. If you put the two lists together, you have a universe of between 300 and 400 companies to work with.

These lists have already been screened for growth and return on equity, so if you are following the growth approach, you have the basic information in front of you.

If you are following the value approach, you want to select from the combined list those companies with the lowest 10 percent of P/E (price-to-earnings ratio) and PSR (price-to-sales ratio). This information is also noted in the lists.

A P/E of 10 or less would be considered low at any time, but since P/E fluctuates with market conditions, what constitutes a low P/E can be a relative matter. You are looking for a P/E that is low *relative* to the current average for stocks in the same category, as measured by the appropriate index — the Dow Jones index for large capitalization stocks, the S&P 500 for medium-to-large-cap stocks, and the Russell 2000 for small cap stocks. A relatively low P/E is one that is 70 percent of the average for the index or less. If the S&P 500 has an average P/E of 18, you seek a company with a P/E of 13 or less; if the Russell 2000 has an average P/E of 22, you seek a company with a P/E of 16 or less, and so forth.

PSR is the ratio of price (market capitalization) to sales (revenues). A company's market capitalization is its share price multiplied by all of its shares. If a company had one million shares outstanding at $10 per share, its market capitalization would be $10,000,000. If its sales were $5,000,000, the ratio of price to sales would be 2. What constitutes a low PSR varies by industry group. (This information can be found in *Value Line* or *Standard & Poor's*.) Grocery store chains run on a low profit margin, so a 1.5 PSR would not be a bargain for a supermarket chain, but would be low for a software or manufacturing company.

Once you have narrowed down the companies you want to consider, you can look them up in *Value Line* or *Standard & Poor's*, or simply rely on the *Forbes/Business Week* information, remembering that you may want to take both value and growth factors into consideration in making your decisions.

Let's say that you are looking at a company with a P/E of 20, which is relatively high, and a PSR of 0.5, which is relatively low. If the company is profitable, and its growth rate — which is in the *Forbes/Business Week* lists and also in *Value Line* — is above 20 percent, it may well be a good buy. But if it is not much of a grower, and its earnings are increasing at a rate that's lower than inflation, you would definitely want to stay away.

Or, you might find a company that has a growth rate of 20 percent a year, a PSR of 5, and a P/E of 30. Such numbers indicate an overpriced growth stock, because despite the good growth rate, the PSR and P/E are too high. Seasoned growth investors would point out that a generation ago, IBM and Polaroid seemed to be overpriced, and in more recent years, Microsoft and Cisco Systems, but they all turned out to be excellent investments, even at high prices. These companies are exceptions to the rule because of their long-term success. The danger with most overpriced stocks is that when they have earnings disappointments, their prices tumble precipitously.

CALCULATIONS THAT CAN BENEFIT YOU

P/E and PSR are commonly used measures that give you an approximate idea of a stock's fair market value, but there is a more exact way of evaluating whether the company is worth the price being asked for it, and this is to do calculations for net present value (NPV). The NPV is the current value of a company based on the predicted future cash flow of that business for a given time period (usually ten years), discounted at prevailing interest rates.

It takes some work to do this calculation (also known as "the two-stage dividend discount method"), but the psychological benefits are tremendous, because when you understand what you're buying is really worth, the market's opinion — so greatly influenced by emotion — becomes far less important.

If you have a clear idea of a company's net present value, you can avoid being influenced by Mr. Market's manic-depressive behavior, manage your own emotions, and do well for yourself. In 1993, when the Clintons' health plan was being debated, the prices of drug companies fell precipitously. By performing the NPV calculations, I discovered that two of the greatest drug companies in the world, Johnson & Johnson and Merck, were at one-half of their NPV. That told me that these companies were great buys, no matter what the market's *psychological* opinion of them was at the time.

In Appendix B, you will find a discussion of how to figure net present value, along with an example of a worksheet I used to do these calculations.

THE ANNUAL REPORT AND THE PSYCHOLOGY OF TRUST

Before buying a stock, you need to get a sense of the company's trustworthiness, because you want to invest in companies that have integrity as well as expertise.

Some companies have a good level of management competence, but are dishonest. *This is one of the worst situations a shareholder can face psychologically, because it pulls the rug out from under you.*

You can't know for certain about the integrity of a company, but you can form a pretty good opinion by looking at the annual report and the 10K form, required by the Securities and Exchange Commission. The company's investor relations department will be happy to send these documents to you.

The reason you want both documents is that certain accounting information, particularly cash flow, can be left out of the annual report but is mandatory on the 10K. In its annual report, a company wants to demonstrate a smooth flow of earnings growth. You can accelerate or slow the way you record items on the books so as to demonstrate favorable growth, but cash flow — monies paid to the company and monies paid out by the company — cannot be manipulated, and therefore the 10K can be a more accurate barometer of how a company is doing.

You can get a good sense of what the company does by reading the narrative in the annual report. It should be straightforward and free of hyperbole, because hyperbole, which is quite common in such reports, can be a way of hiding difficulties. If a company frankly discusses its problems as well as its successes, in language a lay person can easily understand, that is a good sign.

Look at the earnings trend for the last seven years. Have earnings accelerated in the past two or three years? Is there profitability of at least 15 percent based on return on equity (ROE)? ROE, as I said earlier, is net income after taxes divided by stockholders' investment. I consider it the most important financial ratio because it is the best indicator of how well management is running the business. A rise means that costs are being controlled.

Check capital expenditures. If a company regularly requires huge capital outlays, it will need to borrow, thereby eating away shareholders' profits.

Compare the trend of earnings on the balance sheet in the annual report with the item on the 10K form called EBIDTA (earnings-before-interest-depreciation-taxes-and-amortization). EBIDTA is more reliable than annual earnings because it is a true reflection of cash flow. Earnings can be legally manipulated by accepted accounting principles. When Coca-Cola spun off Coca-Cola Enterprises, it charged the bottlers for goodwill, and although the amount was paid in full, it continues to be amortized on the balance sheet. The recurring noncash charge makes CCE earnings look less than they actually are.

Be on the lookout for red flags, such as the cost of sales going up faster than earnings or an inventory that is growing significantly faster than sales. Both indicate a potential for lowered profitability. Let's say that a company has a million dollars in sales, a profitability of $100,000, and two salesmen, each earning $50,000. If the company hires more salesmen, and the cost of sales goes up, but earnings don't go up proportionately, the company will be less profitable. If inventory goes up faster than sales, the company is not selling what it makes, and will be less profitable.

A change in accounting firms — which has to be publicly reported — is a large red flag, particularly if the switch is from a leading accounting firm to a smaller, less-known firm. A change can signal an attempt to keep red ink off the balance sheet, the setting up of a subsidiary where the profits go to insiders rather than investors, or, more seriously, even fraudulent reporting. You can't tell the exact meaning of the change, but you can know that a change from a large accounting firm to a smaller one is always a danger sign. Many times it has preceded the bankruptcy of a fraudulent firm. Be wary.

Another issue you need to consider: Is this company shareholder oriented? Are the interests of management aligned with your own?

Take a look at salaries. If management is paid modestly, compared with the rest of the industry, and receives stock bonuses based on performance, you know the managers are committed to having the company grow, just as you are. Other evidence of commitment includes: plowing profits back into the company to fund research, new products, plant modernization, and all moves directed at future growth. A company that buys back its shares increases the value of the remaining shares because they represent a higher percentage of ownership. In essence, the company gives shareholders a tax-free dividend.

Look carefully at the footnotes below the balance sheet. Here, tucked away, you may find the opposite of a shareholder orientation, private deals spelled out between the company and its officers, for example, or sweetheart real estate deals. You might read that the CEO bought a parcel of land for $1,000,000 and sold it back to the company for $2,000,000, making a profit at shareholder expense. You want no part of a company that would do such things, not only because it is dishonest, but because it demonstrates that management puts its interests ahead of stockholder interests. Sometimes positive items can be gleaned in the footnotes, assets being carried on the books at a fraction of their real value, for example.

A company that seems to have integrity, combined with sound fundamentals and good management, gives you the sense of security that to my mind, you *always* need to feel before you make your purchase.

Several years ago, on the recommendation of a shrewd investor, I learned that a sleepy little medical malpractice insurer, Physicians Insurance Company of Ohio (PICO), was being transformed into a financial holding company. The company had brought in new management, Ronald Langley, whose portfolio had gone up a hundredfold over the decade he was an analyst for Industrial Equity, and John Hart, another investment manager with an outstanding history. Their records gave me the confidence to buy the stock and recommend it in my newsletter. (PICO went up 120 percent in one year's time, but more significantly, its book value, the value at which assets are carried on a balance sheet, rose 400 percent.)

Even after you've developed a feeling of confidence about a company, remember that you rarely have to make a buy decision hurriedly. Try to avoid an inner sense of urgency or a broker who tries to force a sale by telling you that "I need an answer today, and I wouldn't let this go if I were you." A statement like that tells you more about the integrity of the broker than about the need to act quickly.

Always contemplate a buy decision — and a sell decision, too — in a quiet, neutral place where phones aren't ringing and no one is bothering you about other matters.

CONNECTING TO YOUR STOCKS

When you buy a stock, you can expect to feel even more positively about it *after* the purchase than you did *before*. This emotion has to do with another principle of behavioral psychology — *we tend to validate and justify purchasing decisions once they have been made.* (Investors who are intense worriers or extremely anxious may not validate in this way, and I'll talk about that problem in the Profiles section of the book.) It's normal to think well of our choice, to feel pride of ownership, and to derive self-esteem from bonding with the stock.

An experiment done at Princeton University demonstrates how this process works. One half of a class, called the "owners" group, was given Princeton coffee mugs, which they were encouraged to look at and handle. The other half of the class, dubbed the "observers" group, received no mugs.

At the end of the experiment, the owners were asked to estimate the cost of their mugs, which they were told was somewhere between

$1 and $10. Their average estimate was $8. When asked whether they wanted to keep the mug or sell it for the actual value, the overwhelming majority of owners elected to keep their mugs.

The observers, however, valued the mug at only $1.75. And, when given the option of getting a mug from a box outside the room or taking the cash value, only 30 percent elected to get a mug.

Since the mugs were identical, the researchers concluded that being placed in an "outside" group and made envious led the "observers" to devalue the mug, while being called an "owner" and handling the mug created "psychological value."

This psychological value extends to the stocks we buy; it plays a major role in the process of identifying with our stocks, and it becomes particularly important when we have to think about selling decisions, which is the subject I will discuss next.

CHAPTER 4

The Psychology of Selling

Deciding when to sell is the most difficult decision faced by the investor, and the most important.

The best answer to the question "When should I sell?" is "Never." If you buy stock in a well-run business at the right price, it may be possible to own the stock all your life. In that happy circumstance, your investment compounds free of capital gains taxes, and when it enters your estate, a new cost basis is established for your heirs, so that the stock is valued at the market price at your death, rather than the price you paid originally.

In the last fifteen years, I have seldom had to drop a stock from my core portfolio. But no matter how well you choose your investments, there *are* times when you have to think about selling. The rule is to limit your selling to the *absolute minimum,* for both economic and psychological reasons. Economically, the best way to make money is to buy good companies and stick with them, not only because they are likely to do well, but because you avoid the substantial tax consequences and the transaction costs associated with frequent selling. Psychologically, being committed to a stock enhances your own self-worth. Keep your portfolio intact — perhaps tinkering with it occasionally, but not in any extreme way.

If you can think of selling as a lifetime ticket on which you have very few punches (to paraphrase Warren Buffett's metaphor for investing) you can avoid one of the biggest causes of losing money *over time:* frequent, haphazard selling. The irony is that it is fear of some *imminent* loss that triggers much selling.

It's not unusual for the same person to sell one stock because it's going down ("I've got to get out before I lose more"), another stock because it's finally back up to the price where he or she bought it ("Thank goodness I didn't really lose; I better get out before it goes down again"), another stock because it's correcting a bit after going up ("If I get out now, I can save at least part of what I made"), and yet another because it seems to have gone up too much ("This can't go on forever; I'm sure to start losing pretty soon").

Responding indiscriminately to these "triggers" assuages anxiety, but at the price of investment success.

A 1996 *Wall Street Journal* story on the investment portfolio of former congressman Jack Kemp demonstrates what a pattern of frequent selling can do. According to the article, Mr. Kemp bought Mercury Finance in May and sold in July, picked up Telefonos de Mexico on January 31 and dropped it a week or ten days later, bought Aetna Life & Casualty on February 9 and sold on February 14. His trades, totaling $2 million, resulted in a short-term net loss of $12,000 and a long-term net loss of $65,000 — in a year when the average investor was doing well. Had Mr. Kemp paid more attention to the stocks' underlying businesses and less to trying to play the market, he could have profited handsomely.

It's obvious that if you sell in an unfocused fashion, you are going to lose money, or best case, make very little — yet people behave this way time and time again, and wonder why they're not doing well. Sometimes, when they reach a certain point of frustration, they quit investing altogether.

One of the physicians in my ongoing survey of doctor investors bought Intel in 1991 at $46 and unloaded it a few months later when the stock corrected to $42, breathing a sigh of relief at not having lost much. When Intel resumed its upward climb, he started kicking himself, particularly since colleagues, who had also purchased the stock at $46, constantly gloated about how well it was doing. At $55, he bought again, and sold some months later at $82, feeling that he had made "enough money" on Intel. He went on to buy a stock his colleagues didn't yet know about that he had read was certain to be "the next Intel." When it turned out not to be, he sold at a loss, and told me that he was giving up on investing because "everything is so confusing and you can't trust what you read."

This doctor had confused himself because he had no set expectations for stock performance, he had no consistent standards for selling, and he allowed himself to be driven by competitive feelings.

I empathize with his distress because generally investors are not given much guidance about selling, though they get plenty about buying. It's hard to pick up a personal-finance magazine that doesn't have an article on "Ten Hot Stocks to Buy Right Now" and the reasons for picking them, but on the subject of selling, far less is said.

Brokers are often loath to suggest selling because clients are unforgiving when they get talked into selling and a stock goes up, but they can be very forgiving when a stock they were advised to buy goes down. Years ago, when I was a psychiatric resident doubling as a stockbroker, a stock I recommended to a customer fell precipitously. When I called him apologetically, he not only forgave me, but was actually comforting. "Don't fret," he said, "everyone makes mistakes." If I had advised him to sell a stock that went up, he would not have been as compassionate.

Despite the general silence, an understanding of the psychology of selling is urgently needed, because *if you want to win, if you want to grow wealthy, you need to achieve discipline about selling.* The single major advantage professional investors have is that they maintain this discipline. They have specific expectations for their stocks and specific standards for selling.

A few years ago at a meeting of money managers, a colleague told me, "I'm going to bail out of my Philip Morris because it's at nineteen times earnings and the dividend is down to 3.2 percent and in Philip Morris's history, when these things happen, there's almost always a correction." I didn't agree that it was time to sell, but I admired her market-oriented standard. Professionals rely on such reasoning all the time.

The psychological benefit of having standards — even though they are by no means foolproof — is to reduce your dependency on emotions, to alleviate the fear and anxiety associated with selling. *Having standards in place is more important than having them be 100 percent accurate.* "I may be right and I may be wrong," a noted money manager once told me about his standards, "but at least I don't lose any sleep over selling."

This is a great achievement, so let's talk about how you can obtain such peace of mind, while keeping yourself on the path to long-term financial success.

SELLING BEGINS WITH BUYING

As soon as you buy a stock, you need to establish your expectations for its performance — expectations that, if not met, would lead you to sell. Some investors are reluctant to set standards, and the reason lies in the psychology of buying.

When we buy a stock, we don't usually make a snap decision. We watch for a while, tracking the price and news about the company, and when we feel confident, we buy. The result is that by the time we make the purchase, we're optimistic about the stock, and beginning to identify with it. *We've started a relationship, but the relationship is not with the real company. It is our psychic picture of the company, which is both conscious and unconscious.*

To think about selling during this honeymoon can seem like a betrayal, and is often the farthest thing from our minds. But this is the best time to plan ahead. If we wait until we're disappointed in the stock, we'll be in a defeated frame of mind — not the best time for decision making.

Write down or enter into your computer the date you bought the stock, the price, and the reasons you bought it, something similar to my chart in Appendix A, which explains why I purchased the stocks in my core portfolio. Then note your expectations for the stock's performance, for the next year if it's an established company, and three years if it's a venture company in your speculative satellite portfolio.

With my core stocks, I look for them to continue to be strong as businesses and to perform well in the market relative to other companies of the same size and in the same industrial sector. I write down the following expectations:

- Performance that puts the stock in the top 5 percent of its industry group.
- Performance that beats a given index by a set amount. My own general standard is to beat the S&P 500 Index by 3 percent annually.
- Profits that put the company in the top 20 percent of all companies in the sector.
- A growth rate higher than most Standard & Poor's businesses.
- Return on equity (ROE) of greater than 15 percent a year.
- Sales and earnings that are growing faster than the Dow Jones Industrial Average or the S&P 500.
- Management that will continue to be competent, shareholder friendly, and ethical in its behavior.
- A unique niche in its industry that the company will continue to occupy.
- No significant "sea change" in the nature of the business due to technological changes or changes in societal attitudes.

In addition, I may set a specific price expectation for a stock, based on analysts' forecasts of earnings or my own discussions with the company. For example, "Bought Acme National at $10. Expect earnings to grow from 15 percent a year to 25 percent. Price expectation: $15 within two years."

For the venture companies in my satellite portfolio, my expectations are different, since most are in the early stages of a long-term development cycle, and may not yet have a product on the market. Here is what I wrote down for Sepracor, the biotech firm with a drug awaiting FDA approval when I bought it for $15:

- FDA approval within one year.
- Product on market within two years.
- "Burn expenses" of capital for research and development not to exhaust the company's capital within two years.
- Technology that continues to be unique.
- No serious competition from other "start-ups" or major drug companies.

I postulated that the company's earnings by the year 2000 would be $5 a share and that the price would be $75 to $100, if all of my expectations were met.

Venture companies are risky, so I usually place trailing stop/losses (orders to sell if the price drops below a certain level) on these stocks. I determine the stop/loss point either as the amount I'm willing to lose (usually 20 to 25 percent) or at a point on a company's chart (the history of the company's price movements), where it has resisted further decline in the past.

"Stops" have both pluses and minuses. They relieve anxiety because they limit decision making and protect against too much loss. But they are a commitment to selling, and that runs counter to my general principle of buying and holding. I do not use stops when I judge a business to be excellent and its price to be a relative bargain, but rather when there are a great many imponderables, as is true of all venture companies. It may be true of some established firms as well. I regard Philip Morris as less secure than I once did because public opinion, long tacitly supportive of tobacco companies, seems to have turned permanently hostile to them.

Though I rarely employ stop/losses, using them frequently can be an extremely valuable psychological tool for an investor who is anxious about losing money or who tends to rethink decisions obsessively. (I'll have more to say about this in chapter 7 on the "I can't stop worrying" investor.)

EXPECTATIONS FOR FUND PERFORMANCE

Expectations for mutual funds are easier to establish than for individual stocks, where you need to evaluate the entire business. With a mutual fund, all you need to do is evaluate it according to the standards of the areas in which the managers invest.

You should expect a blue chip fund to outperform the Dow Jones Industrial Average by 2 percent a year, a growth fund to outperform the S&P 500 by 3 percent a year, and a small cap fund to outperform the Russell 2000 Index by 2 percent a year. A bond fund should outperform the Lehman Bond Index by 1 percent a year.

These results sound easily achievable, but do not be deceived. As I said in chapter 2, in any single year, only about 20 percent of equity funds do better than the S&P 500. Over a three-year period, that percentage declines to about 10 percent, because the same funds aren't the "winners" year after year, and beyond three years, the percentage goes down further still.

Because of the fees (2 percent annually for the average fund), the huge size of many funds, requirements for diversification, and the limited number of stocks available, many funds come to approximate the market, and very few top the averages. Meanwhile, their competition, the various Vanguard index funds, have extremely low costs that enable them to keep performance close to the actual indexes. So for many investors, index funds are the most intelligent choice, though they are by no means infallible.

Whatever type of fund you purchase, give yourself at least three years to judge its performance unless results are way out of line with the averages. (A recent study by Mark Hulbert, editor of the *Hulbert Financial Digest*, indicates that as long as twelve years may be necessary.) One year is too short a period to evaluate a fund because either luck or the momentary popularity of an investment style can skew results.

Your mutual fund expectations should be recorded. Writing them down is an important psychological mechanism, because it can give you the impetus to follow through with selling if your expectations aren't met. I'll explain later why following through can sometimes be difficult.

I also ask clients to write down any emotional reasons that may have played a role in their buying a stock or mutual fund.

One of my clients, who was competitive with his brother, hoped his stock would outperform a similar stock his brother owned. Another client was excited about a popular biotech stock because an executive she admired talked about it at a company cocktail party. A third client bought a fund because he enjoyed being associated with the glamorous "guru" who managed it.

The more you expect a stock to fulfill you emotionally — to compete for you, make you feel important, or bring a sense of excitement into your life — the more quickly you are going to become disappointed and think irrationally about selling. That's why you need to be aware of any such motivations from the very beginning.

THE BEST WAY TO TRACK YOUR STOCKS

At quarterly intervals, evaluate how a stock is meeting expectations by looking in the *Wall Street Journal, Barron's, Value Line,* or any other comprehensive market report.

You should *not* check prices every day, though many people seem to feel compelled to. Checking every day is a sure way to make yourself nervous and trigger premature selling. Once a week is often enough.

Although I don't, of course, ignore price, I devote my serious attention to news articles about the companies I own, since news is the true indicator of whether one's expectations are likely to be met. Psychologically, reading the news reminds me that I have bought a business and not just a stock listing. *Every time I read a news item, the image of myself as a business partner gets behaviorally reinforced.* I do not hesitate to call management to learn more about company news that has caught my attention.

I look for information that could impact sales, earnings, and profits — delays in shipping, the purchase of a new plant or the sale of an old one, large inventories, accounting problems, a potential merger, a change in management, are examples.

But in particular, I look for news of technological or societal changes that could *permanently* alter the future of a company or a sector. These occurrences are *primary reasons* for thinking about selling.

An example of a societal change is the impact of antismoking sentiment on the tobacco industry; an example of a technological shift was the replacement of mainframes by networked personal computers in the early 1990s.

In the 1980s, American Software experienced wonderful growth because it produced the best banking and insurance software for mainframe computers. The replacement of mainframes constituted a sea change in American's business. Although the company now produces software for PCs, it must compete with Oracle, Microsoft, and other companies that dominate the market, and although sound, it's simply not the same business it was a decade ago. Yet American bears watching because it has high-caliber management and is trying to respond to a changing market with new products, both for mainframes and for networked PCs.

News can alert you to a sea change, often before price does. I began to read negative news about the mainframe market about eighteen months before American Software started to fall. It can be crucial to know what's new.

A good way to follow the news of your companies, as I said in the last chapter, is to subscribe to the *Dow Jones News Retrieval Service,* which will track up to thirty stocks for you for a set fee, and more for an additional fee, sending you every day, online or by fax, items from the *Wall Street Journal,* the *New York Times,* the *Boston Globe,* the *Washington Post,* the *Chicago Tribune,* the *Los Angeles Times,* and Reuters. (See the Resources Section.) You can get almost as much information by reading the *Wall Street Journal* or *Investor's Business Daily.* In addition, many companies will fax you their news releases, if you call the company representative in charge of investor relations.

As you read the information you acquire, always have your expectations for the companies in mind.

In terms of expectations, there are three things an investment can do — fail to meet them, meet them, or exceed them — and each of these outcomes requires you to evaluate what to do.

IF THE STOCK FAILS TO MEASURE UP

If expectations aren't met, you have to think about the possible reasons why.

Generally, I am more interested in a company's business performance than price performance, although I do expect good business performance to be accompanied by a price rise at some point.

If a business is doing well, and the market has not yet reacted, the stock may be in a sector that is out of favor for psychological, rather than economic, reasons — banks from 1989 to 1990, for example. (The psychology of the market always favors some sectors over others. That is simply its nature. Inevitably, favor shifts, which is why you always want to keep your stock portfolio balanced among sectors.)

If the business is not performing up to expectations, I ask myself whether this is due to some short-term factor that may well be corrected next year, such as an unavoidable delay in shipping, or cost-cutting measures that have temporarily decreased sales but are actually a sign of good management because they are likely to increase sales in the future.

I give my companies the benefit of the doubt, because I chose them carefully and I know that in most cases, a strong company is recognized by the market within a reasonable time. My portfolio, based largely on value investing, had an annualized return of 19.3 percent for the period from 1982 to 1995. Remember, it's no good owning the greatest company in the world if the market never responds to it. If a company with good business performance fails to achieve a price rise within three years, I usually sell.

If a stock fails to meet business expectations *and* price performance expectations, and there are no good reasons that you can determine, you should sell, and promptly, because your money can be growing more elsewhere. (If you are a momentum investor, interested only in price, you *must* sell the minute the stock drops out of the top 5 percent of performers for its index or industry group.)

If you fail to sell a disappointing stock, you negate the entire psychological advantage of writing down expectations and establishing a schedule. These acts are intended to direct you away from uncertainty and toward action, even if you're not always 100 percent right.

It can be painful to sell a stock that has not met expectations, particularly if you have lost money. Feel some regret; acknowledge having made a mistake ("I'll do better next time"); and move on. Accept the fact that you can't win them all.

But for some people, admitting a mistake is emotionally devastating. It torments them, and they hang on to the stock in the hope that it will at least go back up to the price where they bought it and perhaps even higher. Emotionally, they feel that by waiting they can somehow force the stock to go up and, thereby, reverse their error.

A doctor I know absolutely refused for over a year to sell a declining stock until he "finally got it back up" to the price where he bought it. When it did, he experienced great feelings of relief, because it proved that he hadn't actually "been a loser," as he feared. Extremely proud of his reputation as a physician, yet not as self-confident as he appeared, in investing, as in so many other areas of his life, he was struggling to prove himself. His wife's grandfather had been a successful investor, and although she encouraged her husband's fledgling efforts, he feared disappointing her and, at some level, perhaps even losing her love.

Losing money always brings up fears of more losses or memories of previous losses. Indeed, when a stock goes down, a whole flood of forgotten feelings about earlier losses can come rushing back.

Most important, losing money constitutes a blow to our narcissism — the natural sense of self-love we all have — since we identify with our stocks. If they go down, we're wounded, and we seek to repair the psychic injury by insisting that they go back up.

I've done this myself. Early in my investing career, I bought a real estate investment trust for $20 that I figured had a fair market value of $70. Within a year, the trust was bought out by a mortgage management company and went to $100. But then it fell to $50. I thought, "Well, I won't worry, it's really worth $70," but the descent continued to $40 and then to $30. I talked to people who knew real estate, and I found out that the trust was overextended — some of its projects had gone bankrupt. My great investment was a lemon, but still I had trouble selling, because I couldn't accept that I had made such an error in judgment. I finally sold at $15, but it was a wrench — because I still had hopes of a turnaround.

Even if a turnaround does occur when we hang on to a stock, it rarely happens quickly enough to make up for our failing to put our money to work more productively someplace else. *So we achieve our emotional goal at financial cost — an outcome we constantly have to guard against.*

If you find it difficult to accept an investing mistake, you're probably hard on yourself about other mistakes, too, on the job or in relationships. You need to kick yourself less and ask, "What's so terrible about a mistake?"

The answer is — nothing, especially if you learn from each one. Although the first rule of investing is "Don't lose," realistically a certain number of losses are to be expected. After all, we're human and therefore not perfect. We need to deal with our losses in a businesslike way and limit the damage to our portfolio and our feelings.

If you have trouble selling at a loss, consider what may be holding you back — perfectionism, fear of facing up to an error, perhaps even getting a certain amount of gratification out of castigating yourself. Quite often, simply realizing that your hesitation to sell may be emotionally based can give you the impetus you need to act.

Another reason why investors fail to sell is simply blind devotion. People who subconsciously look upon investing as a means of expressing power can identify so closely with their stocks that they persist in making excuses for them. People who have inherited stocks can be devoted to them out of loyalty to the deceased loved one. Both of these situations can lead to major financial losses, and I'll talk about solutions in the chapters on the power investor and the inheritor.

IF THE STOCK MEASURES UP — AND THEN SOME

When a stock meets or exceeds expectations, let yourself feel good about your success, since positive feelings are important for keeping yourself committed to investing.

If your reading of *Value Line,* the annual report, and the 10K form indicate that the stock is likely to continue to meet expectations, hold on to it, and write down the same or a new set of expectations for the coming year. My experience is that if I buy a good company and it meets expectations, it is likely to keep on doing so.

If the stock more than meets your expectations, you are in a happy situation, but you also face one of the most difficult investing decisions — whether to sell all or part of a winning stock. You may want to unload some shares to keep your portfolio in balance, but the most important reason is that you fear a correction because the stock has become overvalued or overpriced.

There are two ways to respond to this. You can decide not to sell and to ride out any correction — a philosophy that may be appropriate if you have an investment horizon of ten or more years. Or in your satellite portfolio you can sell all or a percentage of your overpriced speculative stocks, the approach I favor myself.

There are several standards professionals use for upside selling decisions. Here are some commonly used criteria:

- Sell as soon as a stock reaches the fair market value you assigned to it. Let's say I purchased Acme National at $20, after projecting a fair market value of $36 based on expected earnings of 20 percent. As soon as the stock reaches $36, I would sell.
- Sell as soon as the stock reaches a certain percentage of the fair market value you assigned to it, such as 80 percent of fair value. Under such a system, I would sell Acme National at $29.
- Sell as soon as the stock reaches a price/earnings ratio (P/E) that is average for stocks in the same index, the Dow Jones index for large capitalization stocks, the S&P 500 for medium-to-large-cap stocks, and the Russell 2000 for small cap stocks, and so forth.
- Sell as soon as the stock reaches a P/E that is 25 percent higher than for other stocks in the same index.
- Sell when dividends are in the bottom 25 percent of their historical range. (You can find dividend histories in *Value Line*.)
  Some criteria based on price are:
- If the stock doubles in price, sell.
- If the stock doubles in price, sell half.
- If the stock goes up 50 percent, sell.
- If the stock goes up 50 percent, sell half.

(If you decide to keep half of the stock, you can protect against a correction by putting in trailing stop/losses that are always 10 percent below the current price.)

My own general standard is to sell when a stock exceeds 125 percent of the net present value (NPV) I calculated using the system described in Appendix B — when, in other words, it becomes 25 percent overpriced. Sometimes, instead of selling, I enter a stop/loss order. Just because a stock is overpriced doesn't mean it won't become *very* overpriced, and I'd like to go along for the ride if possible.

Tax planning is an additional consideration in deciding when to sell. My wife owns Exxon stock she received as a child. I project long-term growth (dividends and capital gains combined) of 12 percent per annum for Exxon. I believe certain investments will outperform Exxon, but given the taxes we would pay on selling, those investments would have to compound at 18 percent per annum for seven years for us to catch up.

No set of selling standards is foolproof, and that is why several standards exist. But the psychological value of having standards *is* foolproof, because if you don't develop some kind of consistency, you are likely to resist selling altogether. *Selling on the upside is much more difficult than selling on the downside, and you must prepare yourself for this.*

When you identify with a stock, and it does well, wonderful things happen to your self-esteem. You feel terrific, powerful, and brilliant. You want to tell everyone about the stock's performance — and perhaps you do — so the mere thought of selling becomes anathema. You ask yourself, "Why do I have to get rid of something that's making me feel so good?"

Then you attempt to rationalize your way out of selling. You may convince yourself that the stock isn't as overpriced as it seems, that the danger of a correction is probably exaggerated, that the stock undoubtedly has plenty of room to go even higher. You work to reinforce your attachment, and subconsciously you decide to do nothing, a decision you may well regret.

Standards give you enough objectivity to cut through strong feelings of attachment. But standards alone aren't enough. You also have to *use* them, telling yourself that you are making the *best move possible* under the circumstances.

You need confidence to avoid torturing yourself if the stock continues to go up after you sell. This form of torture is common and you can control it by convincing yourself that you are making the right decision, even if the stock fails to correct after you sell it.

One of my colleagues, a top money manager, sells when a stock has doubled. He says, "I don't care if it goes higher after that. I made money, I'm happy, and I'm grateful."

Investors who berate themselves because they think they could have made more should remember that money lost becomes twice as important as money gained and that *money you might have gained is counted as money lost.* Due to the odd accounting our psyches perform, it is natural to feel you've lost, even when you have won.

One of my clients, a marketing consultant, sold Amgen, the biotech company, in 1990 after the stock had gone up 50 percent, the discipline he had adopted. He felt confident that it was "time to sell," since the stock had had a meteoric rise, was overpriced, and, he was sure, was due for a correction.

But when the rise continued, my client became depressed. He had advised his older sister, with whom he frequently compared portfolios, to sell her shares, but she had not. Every time they had one of their frequent phone conversations, she managed to mention the stock's new price, making my client's blood boil, particularly since he believed his sister wasn't half so well informed an investor as he was. Subconsciously, he felt he should have been "rewarded" for his discipline by a decline in price and his sister should have been punished for being both undisciplined and cocky, as she had frequently been when they were children. He started calculating, on a daily basis, exactly how much he had lost by selling "too soon" and when we had our regularly scheduled consultation, he showed me "the bill."

I told him to throw it away, since it had nothing to do with reality, and was only making him suffer. Rather than losing, as he imagined, he had protected against *future losses* by being disciplined, even if he was wrong about Amgen.

Wealth accrues from a pattern of generally right behavior, not from trying to extract the maximum profit out of each and every situation, since one never knows what the maximum might be. If you ignore a selling standard, and the stock continues to go up, you're being rewarded for the wrong behavior, but you may not be so lucky next time — and in the long run, which is what counts, you definitely will not be. My own experience has been that in 80 percent of the cases when I thought I should sell and I didn't, I was wrong.

WHEN YOU SHOULD NOT SELL

There is one situation when you should *not* sell, even though you may feel a strong emotional pull to do so, and that is when you buy a stock and it *immediately* goes down, within a matter of days or weeks. A common investor fantasy is "As soon as I buy a stock, it's sure to sink," so when this actually occurs, panic rises — "Oh, my God, it's happening, I better get out fast."

Many investors don't know that running into an "air pocket" initially is common, because of the timing of the buying decision.

We wait to buy until we're feeling optimistic, after watching the stock go up for a while. But when we buy at the moment of greatest optimism, we are buying when the stock is most likely due for a correction. If the stock has had a big run-up, the correction can be as high as 20 percent.

What undoes most investors is not the correction itself, but being mentally unprepared for it.

If you *are* prepared, you can tell yourself that the dip is normal — even with a very good investment — that you have not made the stock go down, that it will most likely go up soon, and that you need to give the stock *all of the time* you had allotted to it to meet your expectations.

Although it's disappointing when it happens, you can look at an air pocket as a positive experience. If you ride it out, you become used to the natural rhythm of the market, to having a long-term horizon, and to being disciplined, rather than fear-driven, about selling.

The ideal time to buy is at the point of greatest pessimism. Then you can avoid an initial air pocket, and increase your chances of making money. But achieving the control to buy in this way takes time and experience. If you're not there yet, remember that at some point, you will be, and in the meantime, running into an initial dip is not a disaster, but simply a fact of investing life.

You also need to resist an urge to sell when there is bad news about a company that causes the price to go down. I'm not talking about bad news that bodes a permanent sea change in a company's fortunes — which, as I've said, is one of my major criteria *for* selling — but a set-back — a delay in getting FDA approval on a new drug for technical reasons, not research problems with the drug itself, or a production problem that's easily corrected, or a delay in plant construction. The price of Intel took a beating when investors learned of a problem with the Pentium chip, which caused it to make errors in rare higher math calculations, but didn't affect the chip's usefulness to most consumers. There was no long-term effect on the company and Intel's price soon turned around.

It can take fortitude and experience to buy on bad news, as most of the great investing "gurus" do. But even if you find such news too anxiety producing to act on it, remember that it should never make you so anxious that you sell.

By contrast, it can be astute to sell on good news — when, for example, the FDA approves a new drug for a small biotech company — especially if you have profited from a price run-up in expectation of such news.

THE PSYCHOLOGY OF THE "FORCED" SELL

Sometimes you are forced to sell because you need the money to cover financial reverses, to pay for medical expenses, or some other emergency. Or, you may sell for happier reasons, because you've finally accumulated enough money to buy the vacation house you wanted or the perfect home that just came on the market. In short, you've achieved one of the goals that motivated you to start investing in the first place.

Although this kind of selling sounds as if it should be emotionally cut and dried, it's not. You may feel a loss of control, because in an emergency the timing of the decision isn't in your hands. Even if the money is going to be put to a happy use, you can have feelings of sadness, too, because accumulating wealth is itself a source of pleasure. "The joy can be more in the journey than the destination," as an old expression goes.

The sadness comes from surrendering investments that have provided you with a great deal of gratification over a period of years. When you've been in the market long enough to accumulate $200,000 for a house, you've nurtured and created wealth. You have a relationship with your portfolio that's not merely a matter of money. And you have a strong subconscious desire to see what you've built keep on growing. A client of mine, who was delighted to have made enough money to finance a comfortable retirement, was, nevertheless, disappointed that from now on she'd be living off her investments rather than increasing them at the rate she had previously.

If you find yourself feeling angry or sad or depressed over a "forced" sell, you can balance these feelings by reminding yourself that you have the money to solve a crisis or that you have achieved your happy goal, and can anticipate yourself enjoying it, being in your new vacation house on a midsummer weekend. You can make selling after years of hard work what it should be — a cause for satisfaction and an affirmation of your skill as an investor.

CHAPTER 5

Psyching Out Greed in a Bull Market

Greed and fear are the most dangerous stock market emotions. In fact, the "psychology of investing" used to consist primarily of this advice: Resist greed in a bull market and fear in a bear market. If you get swept away by "crowd psychology," which encourages greed and fear, you'll lose a bundle of money, and you'll look pretty foolish in the bargain.

Until recently, money managers had little practical advice for handling greed and fear because not much was known about the psychology of investing. When it came to resisting these powerful emotions, the standard answer was "Just say no."

Today, as a result of research by people like David Dreman, Josef Lakonishok, Richard Thaler, and myself, we understand a good deal more about how people can be motivated to protect their portfolios against the disastrous financial losses that can result from our *natural* vulnerability to greed and fear.

In this chapter, I'll talk about how you can recognize and control greed in a bull market. In the next chapter, I'll talk about fear and a bear market, but remember that if you know how to rein in greed, you'll have less to be frightened of in a bear market, since you will have protected your portfolio.

WHO'S BEING GREEDY?

In a bull market, greedy behavior tends to become normal, which is why it can be difficult to recognize and control. Although we invest as individuals, the market is a crowd, and when we are in a crowd, the natural response is to act like everyone else.

There appears to be safety and security in herd behavior, as sociologist Gustave LeBon first pointed out in 1895. Although as investors we're often warned against yielding to "group psychology," practical experience in other areas of our lives — working in a corporation, for example — has taught us that indeed there is, as Freud suggested, security in adopting group values. So we easily transfer this knowledge to investing, and we don't need to berate ourselves for doing so. It takes a rather uncommon person to behave differently from the crowd, whether it is being greedy or fearful.

But in the market, uncommon behavior is the key to building wealth long-term; thus you must adopt the goal of becoming an uncommon investor in this respect.

To achieve this status, particularly when it comes to greed, you need to know that our subconscious works to conceal greed-oriented behavior from ourselves, and this, rather than crowd psychology, is what makes greed so powerful. (It is also what makes the simple advice "Don't be greedy" so difficult to follow.)

From childhood, we all understand that greed is not an admirable trait — we may remember being told we were greedy for wanting our sister's toys or all of the Halloween candy — so *we defend against greed by rationalizing it.* We may tell ourselves that we're buying speculative investments not to get rich quickly, but because we have become more "sophisticated" investors. We may argue that it's only "sensible" to keep on buying more of a good thing, no matter how overpriced the "good thing" has become because the nature of the market has changed. Most dangerous, we convince ourselves that we should take substantial risk because we're emotionally prepared to cope with losses, when the reality is that most people are not at all prepared.

When we rationalize, it's almost as if a change in brain chemistry takes place, a change that can make something like trading our houses for tulip bulbs seem sensible, as investors did during the famous tulip "mania" that swept Holland in the seventeenth century.

Because rationalizations can be so powerful, our future wealth depends on our ability to reverse the chemistry — by bringing the greed to light. You can't fight greed unless you can see it. That's why you *must* make yourself see it.

Be alert for changes in your *usual ways* of feeling and acting about investing. In a strong bull market, such changes are often signs of greed. Here are nine of the most common signs:

• *You experience wonderful feelings of control.* Although you usually recognize that there are many uncertainties in the market, they seem to vanish, and you feel that little can go wrong with the investments you choose. If your stocks are making substantial gains, you believe that *you* are somehow responsible.

• *You find you want more, more quickly.* Perhaps your investment plan calls for a return of 12 percent, annualized over a three-year period. Suddenly, in a strong bull market, this goal doesn't seem very ambitious. With mutual funds, the Dow Jones Industrial Average, and the S&P 500 surpassing 12 percent, you feel you should be able to double your money in a year, or maybe even six months. You forget that historically, equities have averaged 9.5 percent (dividends and capital gains combined) compounded annually, so a goal of 12 percent actually is aggressive and not easily attainable, even for professionals in their own portfolios.

• *Speculative investments don't seem so speculative.* It appears only sensible to "just look into" such things as commodities trading that you have always judged to be risky. In 1985, an acquaintance, Hank Russell, prevailed on me to help him make "just one" commodities trade. Although he had never traded, two of his colleagues were doing so well that he wanted to "test the waters." After warning Hank that commodities are just about the riskiest of all investments — even a small price change in the wrong direction can wipe an investor out totally — I traded $10,000 in lumber and made a profit of $75,000 for him in a few months. Unfortunately, this confirmed Hank's opinion that commodities were, despite my warnings, pretty much of a sure thing. Against my better judgment, I agreed to "just one more trade." I bought several contracts totaling $120,000 against the yen and pyramided them, a technique by which commodities speculators use the increased value of existing contracts as margin to add more contracts to their position. By the time the contracts came due nine months later, they were worth $1,400,000.

Hank was euphoric, but I pulled out, because success in commodities is *always* the result of a good bet, nothing more. Hank took over the trades himself and created an inverted pyramid, one in which the position becomes top-heavy with recent contracts, the contracts at greatest risk. Then, a short-term drop in the yen's value created losses in the many contracts he had added, and within a short time, he had lost more than his gains. It wasn't that I was smarter than Hank, but that the good bets had run out, and by creating an inverted pyramid, he had turned the odds against himself. Greed distorted his good bets, so that success appeared to be inevitable, when it definitely was not.

• *You increasingly favor overpriced stocks.* Your usual criteria for buying stocks may be that price/earnings (P/E) ratios are low or at least average relative to the current average for stocks in the same sector measured by the appropriate index. Now you buy stocks with high P/Es — the stocks a bull market favors. Although you know rationally that these companies are overpriced, they get so much favorable attention from the media that you're certain prices will go even higher.

• *You can't stand the idea of being left out.* Usually you follow your own plan. Now, you're more worried about missing out on what other people are doing than reaching your personal goals. A client of mine wanted to buy 200 shares of Boston Chicken, a stock that I thought was already overpriced. I advised against it, told her my reasons why, and she agreed. A few weeks later, after the stock had risen another 15 percent, my client called, very angry indeed. "I don't know a living soul who isn't making money on that stock," she said. "You cost me two thousand dollars." Notice that my client expressed her concern about being left out before she got around to berating me for not making her money.

• *You're more impressed with "tips" than you used to be.* You never listened to tips, but now you seem to run into them everywhere, and they make more sense than they used to. Remember, the more glamorous the setting, the more vulnerable you are likely to be. A few years ago, I heard this story: A midlevel executive, who normally paid no attention to tips, was thrilled to be invited to a cocktail party attended by several top executives, including a man who was the founder and president of a company with $400 million in sales. The entrepreneur's wife, after chatting with the midlevel executive, said casually, "I shouldn't be telling you this, but right now might be a good time to buy some stock in Tom's company."

The excitement of being privy to "insider" knowledge flattered the man, even though he knew she should not have discussed the matter. Without investigating the company, he bought some stock, and a short time later, heard rumors of a merger. The next time he met the entrepreneur's wife, at a community theater performance, she confirmed the rumors, and quietly advised him to buy more stock. A few weeks later, the merger was called off, the stock tumbled, and the man lost 50 percent of his investment. Fortunately, the story has a happy ending. He held on to the stock and the merger was ultimately consummated, but he suffered so much angst in the meantime that he permanently reinstated his "no tip" rule.

• *Your competitive juices accelerate.* It's suddenly important for you to do better than friends and relatives, particularly people with whom you may have a competitive relationship. I know a man who doesn't usually have much to do with his wife's brother, a powerful figure in the family and a truly terrible investor. When my friend's stocks are soaring, he delights in inviting his brother-in-law to dinner and steering the conversation around to their market results. Though he knows that it's easy to beat his brother-in-law, he has to make absolutely certain that he is coming out ahead.

• *You develop "diversification resistance."* Usually, you have divided your investments among several companies or funds to balance the market sectors that are doing well against those that are not. Now you start to imagine that you are losing out if all of your investments aren't doing as well as the best ones. You experience a strong temptation to rearrange your portfolio so that all your eggs are in the "winning" basket. I have one client whose portfolio is about 30 percent in Microsoft. In 1995, Microsoft had another banner year and my client remarked,

"It's up a lot and I'm really happy. Why don't we put all my money into Microsoft?"

• *You know for certain that "it's different this time."* No matter how much you have read about tulip mania in Holland and other "bubbles" and manias of the past, no matter how often you have watched up and down cycles of the market, you become convinced that this bull market is going to last forever because of some entirely new circumstance.

Two decades ago we were told that Japanese stocks could only continue to rise because the government was the market's partner in Japan, and that was why "it's different over there." But in the early 1990s, the Japanese stock market declined by 75 percent.

The new reason "it's different" is that 401(k) plans have brought immense amounts of money into the market. Since these investors, particularly the baby boomers, are counting on the market to fund their retirements, they are committed to staying in, and, in any case, they can't use the money for any other purpose unless they leave the company, and they are more sophisticated than investors were in the past. Their needs and their psychology, the "new paradigm" goes, have fostered a bull market that may well be permanent.

I do not believe that one should swallow whole the idea of the new paradigm. It is true that we are experiencing a "sea change" in the expanded and democratized market — a market that is far more inclusive than at any time in history. In that sense, it *is* different this time, but that has not changed the fundamental behavior of the market.

I believe that market cycles will continue and that the next bear market could be particularly severe. Because vast amounts of money are concentrated in the hands of a small number of managers, I believe there is great potential for panic. If interest rates should go up to 8 or 9 percent, and the market sags, money could flow quickly from stocks to bonds, perhaps causing a stampede.

The words "it's different this time" are still ominous — perhaps even more ominous than when John Templeton first called them "the four most dangerous words in the English language."

When you hear these words all the time, you have to believe that greed has gotten out of control and that the bull market may be topping out. If you don't believe it, if you continue to find yourself deep into the greed-oriented behaviors I have described, you need to perform a reality check, looking to see if the market is displaying what have traditionally been its own danger signs.

MARKET SIGNALS TO WATCH

In the past, certain signs have predicted the topping out of a bull market. They are not foolproof, of course. If they were, it would be possible to forecast market cycles accurately, and it definitely is not.

Nevertheless, there is great *psychological value* in reviewing these factors to focus yourself on controlling greed. If you can recognize what have traditionally been the market's trouble signals, it may be easier to control your own responses. As Samuel Johnson once commented, the prospect of being executed in two weeks' time can improve a person's concentration immeasurably.

Here are the signs that a hangman's noose may be tightening:

- A sharp increase in the number of initial public offerings (IPOs) — a company's first sale of its stock to the public. In this regard, it may be instructive to point out that in 1996, there were 875 IPOs compared with ten in 1993. In the first four months of 1997, there were 158.

- Ratios of prices to companies' earnings, sales, and book values are at record heights. (You can find this information weekly in *Value Line* and in *Barron's* in the "Market Laboratory" section.)

- Dividend yields are at record lows. In early 1997, they were the third lowest in history, just behind 1929 and 1995. But note that low dividend yield is less significant than it used to be since many companies buy back stock with excess cash rather than increasing dividends.

- Volume is weak on days when the market goes up, strong on days when the market goes down, a sign that professional investors are selling, while individual investors are buying.

- The advance-decline line — the ratio of the number of stocks that have advanced to the number that have declined — points down over a period of weeks. (You can find the graph of the line in the *Wall Street Journal* every day in the "Stock Market Data Bank" in Section C.) Be wary, though, that computerized trading has made the market and, therefore, the advance-decline line more volatile; you need to consider the data over a period of time.

• There is market divergence. The Dow Jones Averages — industrials, transportation, and utilities — no longer go up together, as they do in a solid bull market. Toward the end of the cycle, the industrials tend to continue rising after the transportation and utility stocks have topped out.

• *Time* or some other news or financial magazine has a cover story about the strength of the current bull market. Martin Zweig, the newsletter author and money manager, first described this phenomenon in *Barron's*. He discovered a pattern of market declines within thirty days of a *Time* or *Life* story on bull markets, and dubbed it the "Time-Life Indicator." Significantly, the reverse is also true. In a bear market, a pessimistic cover story may signal an impending market rise.

• When 60 percent or more of market newsletters are bullish, it's a contrarian sign of the beginning of a bear market. As a group, the "experts" who write newsletters, including myself, tend to be wrong.

When there is widespread consensus that a bull market will continue indefinitely, that market may have about run its course. My favorite sign is what I call "the lunch table indicator." If all the people I'm lunching with agree that the market can only continue to go up, I know it's time to worry.

The reason contrarian signals can be so accurate is not that people are dumb, but because of a psychological principle that has been set forth by Josef Lakonishok, professor of finance at the University of Illinois. The human psyche resists change, and this seems to be particularly true in the market, so we tend to remain emotionally committed to one economic cycle, although another has already begun. The deeper our own attachment — and for this, you must examine your own feelings — the greater the likelihood that the market is headed elsewhere.

Use this rule as a guide: The more secure you feel about the market's continuing to go up, the more important it is to take steps to protect your portfolio.

A "PORTFOLIO PROTECTION PLAN"

Post these words someplace where you can always see them: "Never confuse a bull market with genius." This ancient Wall Street maxim is absolutely invaluable, because it helps to counter the false sense of control that greed confers. Being in control ("genius" is just another word for it) is the aspect of greed that really thrills us. I have a "Post-it" slip with the maxim on my bathroom mirror, so I can see it every morning.

A bull market has the psychological components of mania — an excitement and ebullient optimism that are infectious. The happy consequence is big profits, usually spread around the entire market, but with huge gains going to the more speculative sectors. The less happy consequence is that the asset allocation in individual portfolios gets dangerously out of balance because of the increase in speculative commitments. When this happens, it is the most pragmatic evidence that greed is at work.

Let's consider the case of Jodie and Jeffrey Dexter, a professional couple in their late forties with twin children who have just graduated from college. Jodie, a city planner, and Jeffrey, an engineer, earn a joint income of $175,000. They have a net worth of $1,350,000 and a $600,000 portfolio.

The Dexters' primary goal is to accumulate enough capital to retire without compromising their standard of living, and they would like to leave a substantial estate to their children, and to grandchildren as yet unborn.

Before the boom market of the 1990s, the Dexters' portfolio was

60 percent equities and 40 percent bonds. The equities portion was allocated this way:

- 50 percent value stocks selected for quality
- 30 percent growth stocks (all with P/Es 50 percent lower than the average P/E of the S&P 500)
- 20 percent speculative small stocks

By September 1996, when the Dexters became my clients, their portfolio had shifted to 82 percent equities and 18 percent bonds. The equities portion was allocated this way:

- 35 percent value stocks
- 35 percent growth stocks
- 30 percent speculative small stocks

This shift reflects the success, and also the excess, of the great bull market of the mid-1990s. The market had excited the Dexters' greed, luring them like a siren's song away from their safe, conservative course.

Since his investments were doing so well, Jeffrey had added to his goals an expensive new car and two overseas vacations yearly, another sign of greed at work. Jodie talked about the "new paradigm" and how it had changed the entire nature of investing so that stocks could only continue to go up — a greed rationalization.

When I suggested to the Dexters that they rebalance their portfolio by selling off a portion of their more speculative stocks, and holding some of the cash for a possible market correction, I met with the resistance I expected.

Then I explained that the fact that they didn't *want* to rebalance, or think they *needed* to rebalance, meant that they *had* to rebalance. *This external action was the best protection they could have against inner forces that were hidden from them, because greed conceals itself so well.* Without making some shifts, they were open to real danger in a bear market.

When you rebalance by selling off speculative stocks, trimming down the number of stocks if you've accumulated too many, perhaps adding more bonds, and also holding some of the cash for the correction you anticipate, you are making an educated guess about what will happen in the market. You may not be right, but *errors are acceptable because your goal is to control greed and prepare for any eventuality.*

Sometimes a client will ask, "Well, let's say I'm *very* sure a bear market is coming. Why bother with this rebalancing business, why shouldn't I just put *everything* in cash?" This is a corollary to the question asked in chapter 2 on getting started: "Can't you tell me exactly *when* I ought to get into the market?" The emotional question that's really being asked is "Isn't there some way I can protect myself totally from the pain of loss?"

The answer is you cannot, because you cannot time the market, and if you try, and the market goes up instead of down, you will lose in a very big way. You've probably read those figures from a University of Michigan study showing that if an investor missed the market's twelve best months between 1926 and 1993, a $1 investment would be worth only $65, instead of growing to $637.30. That's a big penalty for getting out of the market.

So rather than doing anything extreme, stick to a moderate course that will offer you substantial protection against a downturn, yet still enable you to make gains should the bull market continue for longer than you expected.

Here is what you need to do:

• *Reinstitute your criteria for selling.* Look over the expectations you wrote down for your portfolio and your standards for selling, particularly on the upside. (See chapter 4.) If greed is on the rise, you may have been letting these standards lapse, as the Dexters did. If your satellite portfolio — the speculative portion — has grown to more than 20 percent, you need to lighten up. This is the time to remind yourself that speculative stocks, without a product or without earnings, are likely to take the biggest hits in a bear market.

If you find yourself loath to sell, try this technique: Imagine that a favorite stock has fallen 50 percent in one day and allow yourself to experience the pit-in-the-stomach feeling you would get if that really happened. Really feel it. This type of "aversion therapy" can actually make you feel less fond of the stock and help move you toward selling.

• *Dump losers and trim down winners.* If you can, sell off equal amounts of a losing stock and a winning stock to eliminate the potential capital gains tax. Psychologically, you gain from your loss and you don't lose from your gain. This combination can make selling easier.

• *Clear up the mess.* When greed makes you hungry, you tend to fill up on more stocks than you need because everything looks appetizing. The result is that your portfolio gets messy, and messy is, by nature, out of balance. Go back to your core portfolio of around ten stocks, diversified among seven to ten industry groups. If you've accumulated too many stocks, sell off the weakest stocks in each industry group over a period of months. Remember, a messy portfolio can have a subconscious meaning, serving as a means of obscuring your greed from yourself.

• *Increase your holdings of defensive stocks.* You do want to create one slight imbalance toward defensive stocks — companies that tend to do better in a bear market because they produce such products as food or household products, which are always in demand, including utilities companies and broad-based consumer stocks, like Kellogg, Procter & Gamble, and Hershey.

• *Look to preferred stocks for increased safety.* Preferred stock — stock that receives a fixed dividend and tends to trade like a bond — can be useful to the investor seeking both higher-than-average yields and a temporary haven in the event of a bear market. A high-quality preferred stock with a near-term maturity date provides a yield superior to government bonds and often better liquidity than corporate bonds. When you own preferred stock, you have a claim on the company's assets in bankruptcy prior to the claim of common shareholders, but subordinate to bond holders.

• *Select appropriate bonds.* Although stocks and bonds have moved in tandem for several decades, bonds offer safety in a bear market because they provide guaranteed income, even though until maturity rising interest rates can affect the value of principal. I advise individual investors to buy only U.S. Treasury issues. While corporate bonds offer higher yields, they are less liquid and they have higher brokerage costs.

• *Make sure you hold on to a portion of the cash you accumulate from rebalancing.* If the bull market continues for longer than you expected, you may be tempted to use your cash to buy more at inflated prices because you are afraid of being out of the market for too long. Avoid this temptation by reminding yourself that you set the cash aside to buy after a correction, even if the correction doesn't fit your mental schedule. If you don't hold on to cash, you will defeat an important benefit of rebalancing your portfolio.

SHOULD YOU HEDGE A BIT?

If an investor is pretty sure that the market is overpriced, that the bull is topping out, and that prices will soon go down, a classic hedging technique is to sell short.

To sell short, you borrow stock through a broker, sell that stock (receiving the sale proceeds), and assume the obligation to replace the stock at a future date. Your hope is that the stock falls, enabling you to buy it back at a lower price. The difference between what you received when you "sold short" and what you paid to replace the stock is your profit or loss. (Of course, commissions and taxes must be subtracted to determine your real return.)

Because there is great risk in selling short, I don't recommend it. As Warren Buffet has sagely commented, "Just because something is ridiculously overpriced doesn't mean it won't get bid to even more ridiculous levels." The maximum possible gain in a short sale is 100 percent (if the stock drops to zero in bankruptcy). *However, the maximum possible loss is infinite because the stock can keep going up and up.* Many a stock has been driven up in price because short sellers were forced to buy more to cover their positions when the stock's owners called their brokers, who loan out the shares, and demanded them back. On Wall Street, this scenario is known as the "short squeeze," and is definitely not something you want to get caught in.

A second reason for not shorting is that it is difficult to get good "sell" information from conventional brokerage houses, who don't want to criticize companies for whom they are investment bankers.

Buying puts is an alternative to selling short. A put is an option that allows you to sell a security at a predetermined price for a specified time period. Suppose I buy a six-week put on Kellogg stock at a "strike price" of $65. If during the six weeks, Kellogg never closes below $65, I would lose what I paid for the put. If Kellogg went below $63, I would collect the $2 difference between $65 and $63, and the further Kellogg went below $65, the more money I would make.

Puts have a distinct advantage over short selling because the risk is limited, and psychologically, it is important to know that you can limit loss. The two disadvantages of puts are that they expire in a relatively short time period and become worthless if the stock price either goes up or remains unchanged.

Rather than buying puts, or selling short, if you think your greed, and the greed of the market, may signal an approaching bear, it's best to take the portfolio protection measures I outlined above. Hedging is inherently complicated and, therefore, creates more emotional stress than it relieves, particularly if you are inexperienced at it.

The best way to "hedge" against a bear market is to recognize your own internal greed so you can readjust your portfolio in a reasonable way — not drastic, not infallible — but, simply, common sense.

WHAT ABOUT THOSE "RISK-FREE" INVESTMENTS?

Some brokerage firms exploit the fear of an approaching bear market by selling so-called risk-free investments that are supposed to protect you against loss by guaranteeing that you will at least get your original investment back. A buyer invests $10,000, let's say, in a fund, but must hold the fund until a specific date. The fund purchases zero coupon bonds that mature on that date, so the original investment is, indeed, guaranteed — and the fund also purchases stock. ("Zeros" pay no current interest and are sold at a deep discount to their face value. The difference between the purchase price and what the buyer gets back at maturity is the interest.) Investors are given the impression that they are purchasing "risk-free" equities, when in fact, they are making two separate investments — zero coupon bonds and stocks. This you can do by yourself at far lower cost, and without the psychological hazard of believing in such a thing as a "risk-free" investment.

THE ENORMOUS VALUE OF GREED

While you work at protecting your portfolio both against yourself and possible shifts in the market, you can discover new ways of looking at greed. One factor that drives greed underground — and keeps investors from recognizing it or doing something about it — is that greed evokes feelings of guilt.

You need to understand that greed is normal; it is universal; it is one of the most basic human drives, evident from day one of infancy.

A baby has an all-consuming need for food. It cries to be fed, sucks vigorously when its cries are answered, and experiences relief from tension until the process begins all over again. A baby seems to be "greedy" by nature, and comes to associate the satisfaction of its need for food with love.

If the parents are able to satisfy the baby emotionally in a consistent, caring manner, it is easier for the adult offspring to make the transition to a mature love, where his or her needs don't always have to come first. Without giving parents, strong feelings of greed can persist into adulthood and express themselves through money, a substitute for parental love. Since the stock market is *about* money, greed plays a significant role.

But greed, when controlled, is the most valuable emotion an investor can have.

Greed is valuable because it motivates us to participate in the market. We want, we need, we are hungry for profit, so we will take the reasonable risks necessary to get it, and we will take the time to investigate investments that we think may be profitable. Greed piques our interest, it makes us work at investing, and it holds our attention. If we weren't hungry, we wouldn't be in the game.

Controlled greed — greed we can recognize and direct to our own advantage — is the hallmark of all great investors from J. P. Morgan to Warren Buffett.

The danger of greed is that it's a basic appetite, difficult to control, no matter how good our intentions.

People who have strong feelings of deprivation are particularly at risk, since they expect their investments to compensate for what they feel they have missed.

Trudy Connors, a thirty-eight-year-old recently divorced saleswoman, decided to invest half of her divorce settlement in stocks. Since Trudy had two small children and could not afford too much risk, I recommended several solid blue chip companies — Merck, Philip Morris, and Microsoft. When I said our goal was for her to earn about 12 percent compounded annually, Trudy shook her head. "I need something that will double in six months," she said emphatically.

Trudy's financial situation was certainly not desperate enough for her to set such an unrealistic goal, but as we talked, I learned that Trudy felt the divorce settlement had been unfair. "He just about got it all," she said. "I don't know what that judge was thinking of."

Unconsciously, Trudy wanted the market to make it up to her for the wounds to her self-esteem. Trudy didn't realize she was being greedy; she was simply driven by that bottomless "I need it now" feeling that greed generates, particularly when we are unhappy.

Remember: You don't have to *be* very deprived by most objective standards to feel that you *are* deprived.

As I wrote in an earlier chapter, in my research into the psychology of investing, I have for more than a decade been studying a sample of twenty-five physician investors. When I first surveyed these doctors, some had recently completed their residencies and had been in private practice for only a short time. I found that several were greed-oriented, buying and selling impulsively in order to make a quick profit, but, of course, failing for that very reason.

I was surprised to find that the physicians' "need it now" attitude was, like Trudy's, based on a feeling of deprivation. As interns and residents, they had earned very little, while their friends who were not physicians were making good money. Now their financial prospects for the future were excellent and even enviable by the standards of most people, but the doctors still saw themselves as poor relatives who had been left out. This sense of deprivation, firmly embedded in their self-image, fueled greed-oriented investment practices.

Sibling rivalry also can awaken greed. In childhood, we want all our parents' love, but if we have siblings, their presence makes it impossible to satisfy this need. Through investing, we try to ensure that at last we get all the love by surpassing our siblings, relatives, and friends.

The feeling that we *must* satisfy this competitive drive accounts for the enormous competitive tension that permeates the late stages of a bull market.

This tension is psychological, so you must apply the most rigorous "antigreed" measures not to your portfolio, but to your mind. You must recognize that greed cannot be satisfied, no matter what rate of return you achieve on your investments. *Greed is absolutely bottomless. Don't struggle to meet its demands; they cannot be met.*

You can experience enormous relief through understanding this truth because it will dispel the endless strain greed creates. Released from your prisoner's chains, you will feel lighter and free to choose your own course.

Encourage the positive side of greed, its ability to keep you involved in the investing process, while negating its bad aspects, its competitiveness and the dangerous rationalizing you now have the power to eliminate forever.

CHAPTER 6

Reality Testing:
Fear in a Bear Market

A bear market usually begins slowly, when a steady pattern of erosion develops in the most speculative and popular stocks. At this point — the first phase of the bear — you can still protect your portfolio by rebalancing. Or, if you are an investor who maintains the same portfolio balance through "thick and thin," in my opinion a perfectly reasonable thing to do, you need to recognize that "thin" may be approaching.

Those who do rebalance should sell off 10 to 20 percent of their portfolios at the beginning of the bear, hold on as the bear makes its descent, and buy when they think the bear is starting to bottom out. The psychological difficulty is that the instinct is to do just the opposite — hold on at the beginning and sell as the descent becomes frightening.

At the top of the bull market, we feel confident, convinced that prices will keep going up, maybe forever, so when the first signs of a bear market appear, we can't integrate them with our mental picture and we simply deny them. Investors say, "This can't be happening"; "It's just a slight correction"; "We'll get back on track soon" — and similar evidence of full-blown denial.

If you hear yourself making such remarks, and feeling *intense relief* when they put the world back into order, you need to realize that you are at risk. It's not too late yet, if you can be clear-minded, to take steps. This may well be your last chance before the train starts down the mountain, so you can't afford to let denial rob you of the opportunity.

By the time a full-scale bear market is under way — after a series of ups and downs, including perhaps record highs, a steady downward course gets established — you're not in denial anymore because the trend is obvious. This is when you are going to *want* to sell. But you have to prevent yourself from selling, even though it seems that you *must*, particularly if the market takes a sudden nosedive. The following story illustrates how hard it can be to control that impulse to sell, and why clients sometimes need help in holding back.

On October 20, 1987, the day after the stock market had suddenly dropped 508 points (an astonishing 22.6 percent), money manager Ted Rorer got a visit from an agitated client.

The client told Rorer that he wanted to sell everything. He was sure the market was going to collapse. Rorer tried to dissuade him, but the client was adamant.

Rorer pulled out the client's portfolio and said, "Okay, let's start with Bristol-Myers. Until yesterday, you had a big profit. You still have a nice profit. It's a great company at an undervalued price. Are you telling me to sell Bristol-Myers?"

"Yes," the man answered. "Sell the whole portfolio, while I'm still ahead."

Ted tried to reason with his client, explaining that the worst thing to do in the middle of a panic is to sell. The client looked unconvinced as he sat slumped in his chair. "Sell," he murmured gloomily.

There was silence for a moment. Then Ted said, "Joe, if you really want to do this, walk over to me, grab me by the collar, and shout, 'I'm *telling* you to sell.'"

The client couldn't quite make that move, so he decided to go out and walk around for a few hours to think it over. While he was gone, Bristol-Myers went up 8 points, the rest of the market started to recover, and it looked as if this particular "bear market" might be on its way out.

When Joe returned, Rorer gave him the good news. The client beamed. "Thank God, we stuck to our guns and didn't sell," he said.

This story graphically demonstrates just how irrational fear can take hold in a downturn, how quickly it can dissipate when the downturn appears to be over, and how easily an investor, in order to restore shaken self-esteem, can forget that he ever panicked.

Fortunately, this "bear market" turned out to be short lived, and some people assume that such brief bears will continue to be the pattern, because investors have become too "sophisticated" to panic when the market drops sharply. Instead, the theory goes, they will "buy on the dips," and keep the bull market going.

Many of those who believe this scenario have not been investors for long enough to experience an extended bear market — I define a bear market as a decline of 15 percent or more — and the mental torture that goes with it. Eighty-seven percent of the money ever invested in U.S. stock funds has come into the market since late 1990, which marked the start of the longest bull market in history. From October 1990 to October 1996, the Dow Jones Industrial Average soared 3,644.90 points, or 154 percent.

Despite this extended bull market, I don't believe that a law has been passed repealing traditional bear markets — the kind where fear can hang around for a long while and force you to sell irrationally at the very time you know you should hang on. Investors must be prepared to cope with fear not for a day or two, which is scary but relatively easy, but for an extended period of months or even years.

You get rich by staying in the market through all its cycles, and long-term investing means being invested under just about *any* conditions. If you allow fear to force you to sell out in a bear market, or keep you from buying when it seems the bear is starting to turn around, there is no way you can be truly successful. The first principle is: *Stay in.* But when you're slumped in your chair and worried, like Ted Rorer's client, it's difficult to abide by this principle. All you want is to save "what's left," because you are convinced the end of the world has come. This is the total psychological reality of the moment.

Because this fantasy, and other manifestations of fear, can be so overwhelming — and so disorienting — you have to understand where they get their power. It may surprise you to learn that in the treacherous landscape of an established bear market, fear is not the only emotional factor, it is merely the master of ceremonies.

THE PSYCHOLOGY OF THE BEAR

Fear is the *obvious* emotion. Unlike greed, which tends to conceal itself from us, fear shouts, "I'm here," and a big part of an investor's job in a bear market is to quiet it down.

Undoubtedly, you've heard that injunction before, but many people find it difficult to live by, and they get angry with themselves if they fail.

Understand: It's not that you are weak, but that you are fighting a host of negative emotions working together *beneath the surface* to beat you down. In an established bear market you often have to cope with a depressive syndrome just as painful as that caused by other kinds of loss (and financial loss, like any other, *hurts,* emotionally). Let's examine how this particular syndrome — I call it Bear Market Depressive Syndrome (BMDS) — works.

On the conscious level, BMDS expresses itself as fear and panic. The other components are more difficult to recognize because they are often buried. It is these underground ideas and emotions that kindle the fires of fear and keep them crackling. And since fear can cost you a great deal of money, and keep you from recognizing the opportunity for potential gain, you need to understand what is going on.

Here is what you may be experiencing:

• *Loss of control.* Just as you felt totally in control during the last phases of the bull market, when you seemed to be making marvelous things happen to your portfolio, now you feel totally powerless, unable to stop the damage that is taking place. The panic you experience on the conscious level is a futile struggle to get back into control and impose your idea of order on a chaotic situation. Whenever I hear a client say, "It's simply *got* to get better soon," I know that person thinks he should have the power to do something about the market. That conviction only increases anxiety.

• *Shame.* In the bull market, when you were making money, you felt proud because you were living up to your ego ideals: taking care of yourself and your family, accomplishing what you expected of yourself. Now you're not meeting your own expectations and you feel diminished. You fear that the people you love may be disappointed in you because you've let them down. You feel ashamed that you have failed. Remember: The more greed you felt during the bull market, the more shame you are likely to experience now.

During the bear market of October 1987, Henry Sullivan, an acquaintance of mine, told me that he felt so ashamed of his losses that he couldn't face his wife. Henry, a forty-two-year-old television producer, had invested $50,000 in the market, watched it grow to $150,000 over four years, and then, within a few days, crash to $75,000. "I took too many risks," he told me; "that was our retirement money. What a dope I was."

When Henry did tell his wife, she was angry at first, because she hadn't known the speculative nature of the investments (and she should have), but she had perspective, and saw the glass as half full, rather than half empty. "We're still up 50 percent," she said, "and we have plenty of time until retirement." More important, she told Henry that she valued his efforts, even if they didn't always work out, because they showed such love for her and their life together.

• *Guilt.* You feel that you are responsible for the descending market; that you are somehow making bad things happen, and you say, "I should have known the market would go down the minute I invested," "What an idiot I was to invest in the first place," and other self-deprecating remarks, all ways of taking on blame.

Be aware that magical thinking — "If something's wrong, I must have done it" — tends to affect competitive, super-conscientious people who are demanding of themselves. They assume so much responsibility, at work and in their personal lives, that it seems natural to be responsible for the market, too.

If you blame yourself when things go wrong, if the word *should* plays a large role in your vocabulary — "I should have had those tires checked before we started out on the trip"; "I should have known the baby would get sick if we went to the country" — you may think that you "should" have done something about preventing a bear market, too, and "should" have sold earlier as well.

Subconscious guilt, besides making you unhappy, can cause you to punish yourself by selling at a market bottom or engaging in other self-defeating behaviors. (I'll have more to say about these in chapter 7 on the "I can't stop worrying" investor.)

• *Low self-esteem.* Your self-confidence goes down, along with the market. I remember a friend, a highly successful investor, saying during the bear market of the 1970s, "Every move I make is stupid." I was puzzled by the remark because it was so patently untrue, but over the years I have observed how easily self-esteem can erode as a bear market creeps along, like the steady drip of a leaking faucet.

This defeatism is the most dangerous aspect of bear market depression, because it *increases* your vulnerability to fear, just when you need to *decrease* it. When you're defeated, you can't accept that markets are cyclical, that this cycle, too, shall pass, that eventually you will restore your losses and make substantial gains, and that great opportunities exist in a bear market. Investors are often advised that the psychological "cure" for fear is to look at a bear market as a buying opportunity. But this is more easily said than done. When you are feeling defeated, that advice sounds very hollow, and you let opportunities go by because you've lost faith in yourself and the whole investing enterprise.

You cannot see reality, you cannot embrace opportunity, while you are under the sway of the Bear Market Depressive Syndrome. You cannot achieve long-term wealth if you allow BMDS to go on too long, so you must work to overcome it.

With my clients, I have been quite successful using cognitive psychological techniques to help correct the thoughts (and, therefore, the feelings) that characterize BMDS. You need to examine your thoughts, understand the distortions on which they are based, and replace them with other more realistic thoughts — because I can assure you, as I assure my clients, that the negative thoughts generated by a bear market are *not based on reality.*

It can be extremely worthwhile to examine these thoughts and how they can be altered:

BMDS-PROMOTING IDEAS	UNDERLYING DISTORTIONS	BMDS-OVERCOMING THOUGHTS
I feel terrible. I knew I would lose. What a jerk I was to invest!	*I shouldn't have to experience any pain in the market.*	*I know it hurts to lose, but bear markets come and go. Things will get better soon, and I'll be just fine over time.*
I'm a lousy investor. No wonder I messed up.	*I have to be perfect to invest.*	*No one is skilled enough to predict a market decline. Every investor is affected, not just me. I'll stay in because every bear market ends.*
I knew the market would collapse as soon as I started investing. Why did I invest? I'm to blame.	*My feelings control the market.*	*It's childlike to believe I'm responsible. The market is cyclical, and that has nothing to do with me. I invested to secure my future. I picked good companies and they'll do fine over the long haul.*
I've lost money, and I've disappointed my family. I'm a failure.	*My family's love depends on money.*	*My family loves me no matter what happens in the market.*
This bear market will never end. I'm going to lose every single cent I have invested. The world is coming to an end.	*Bear markets last forever.*	*The market will recover. If I examine my losses, I'll see that I'm far from losing "everything." In the future, I'll make up my losses and make new gains.*

You need to pay particular attention to the last depressive/defeatist idea, "I'm going to lose every single cent I have invested," because, as Martin Pring, noted investment adviser and financial writer, has pointed out, this is the *absolutely universal fantasy in a bear market*. Even the most sophisticated and experienced investors, people who have been through many market cycles, can have the nagging fear that maybe the world *is* going to end, because it certainly feels that way.

And for the ordinary investor, the fantasy can be overwhelming.

Some time in the early 1970s, when the market was in a decline, a stockbroker friend got a call from a client, who had bought Colonial Penn Insurance Company at 15. When it reached 80, he'd advised her to sell, but she demurred, saying she was making too much money. Now Colonial was down to 10, and as her feelings of panic grew, she'd decided she had to sell.

"This is the time to hang on, Gloria," my friend advised, noting that Colonial Penn was a solid company. "I can't," she replied, "I'm sure they're going bankrupt; the stock will go down to zero, and I'll be totally wiped out."

The great danger of the "world is coming to an end" fantasy is that it promotes irrational selling. Test the fantasy rigorously by asking yourself what it would *really take* for you to get "wiped out."

The answer is it would take an event that totally destroyed the U.S. stock market — a nuclear holocaust, a political revolution, or a Martian invasion. Even in the stock market crash of 1929, investors did not lose "everything" — unless they had bought on margin in a way that is no longer legally permissible.

Bear markets do not cause good companies to go bankrupt, as Gloria imagined. That's why it's so valuable to think like a business partner when you invest, because businesses exist independent of the market. No matter what the market cycle, good companies continue to be good, and if they get underpriced, as they usually do in a bear market, they are even better investments.

Finally, the most powerful back-to-reality facts to remember are these:

- Bear markets are a natural part of the business cycle.
- Every bear market in history has come to an end, usually within nine to eighteen months, and then a bull market starts to build.
- Bull markets tend to last twice as long as bear markets, the reason why long-term investing is such a good way to get rich, particularly if you can take advantage of the buying opportunities that occur when the bear market starts to turn around.

WHEN TO START BUYING

Deciding when to sell is the most difficult investing decision. The second most difficult is deciding when to buy in a bear market. In the depths of a bear, with doom and gloom all around, you don't even want to think about buying, yet this is the very time to start planning.

One thing that keeps me motivated is a "wish list" I have of good quality companies — Coca-Cola, Intel, Microsoft, Motorola, Wrigley, Kellogg, for example — that I want to buy if they reach certain prices or P/Es. I'll write down, "It would be great to get Kellogg at 50." Not only does the list help me prioritize, but also, on the psychological level, it reminds me that opportunities lie ahead, and it prepares me to act immediately when my target price is reached.

I got the idea from John Templeton, who years ago told me that he maintained such a list. During the one-day crash of October 1987, Templeton put in offers to buy large amounts of the stocks on his list at below market prices. Anyone can make a below-market bid, but it is rare for that bid to be successful, and usually only for a thinly traded stock when the seller feels pressured. But the crash was an extraordinary event, and Templeton exploited the panic by being a willing buyer when no one else was. While he didn't get all of his "wishes," he did finish the day with some handsome gains.

John Templeton didn't need a list, of course, to know what he wanted to buy, but psychologically, writing down your intentions can be valuable, since it encourages you to follow through. I advise you to keep such a list.

The first few months of a bear market is a good time to draw up a new list or revise an existing one in anticipation of the "selling climax" that often signals the end of a bear market. Intensify your study of these companies and begin buying when your "buy" levels are reached, even if the market as a whole is still declining.

The reason for analyzing companies is that the more you think like a business partner, the more easily you can separate yourself from the market's volatile emotions. In a fear-laden bear market, you very much want to achieve that separation. If you have overcome Bear Market Depressive Syndrome, it's far easier to have a positive outlook. That is why the techniques I described earlier are so important.

In a bear market, my goal is to buy solid companies when they are 50 percent undervalued, according to the net present value (NPV) method of evaluation (see Appendix B).

You can also employ the reliable measures I wrote about in chapter 3:

- A low P/E *relative* to the current average for stocks in the same category, as measured by the appropriate index — the Dow Jones Index for large capitalization stocks, the S&P 500 for medium-to-large cap stocks, and the Russell 2000 for small cap stocks. A relatively low P/E is one that is 70 percent of the average for the index or less.
- An absolute P/E of 10 or less.
- A price to sales ratio (PSR) of 1.5 or less.
- A price to book ratio of 0.75 or less.

That there are so many choices available should help to lift your spirits in a bear market. In October 1996, when the Dow hit a then new high of 6,000, there were only 24 companies that fit my buying criteria according to computer screening programs. But in the bear market of 1981, there were more than 130 companies that matched my standards. That was the year I bought IBM at $60. Two years later, I sold it at $140.

When a substantial number of the companies I've been watching have reached my levels, I start buying, because I have disciplined myself to do that. I need discipline because it is usually at a time when the market itself is the most pessimistic and reports in financial magazines are progressively more bearish. The general consensus is that the bear will last a great deal longer than could have been expected because of factors that apply now but didn't apply in the past. You have to be just as wary of the phrase "it's different this time" in a bear market as you do in a bull market.

As a long-term investor, I want to buy at the point of greatest pessimism, just as I want to sell at the point of greatest optimism. If I can accomplish this, I'm pretty sure to be buying low and selling high — every investor's ideal.

As a psychiatrist, I know how difficult it is for people to act in this way because of the group psychology I discussed in the previous chapter. What's most comfortable, what feels "safest," is to do what everyone else is doing and wait for assurance that the bear has "bottomed out," especially after the anxiety you've endured as the market descends.

If you wait for that assurance, you can be sure you will miss the boat, because by the time the media tell you that the bottom is near, it has most likely come and gone.

You need to motivate yourself to act in an uncommon way to buy when you *know* prices are good but *before* you are emotionally ready to take the step. Your actions need to be ahead of your comfort level.

Ask yourself what you are waiting for. If you are waiting for the very bottom — the lowest 1 percent of the decline — you have set an unrealistic goal, because there is absolutely no way to tell when such a bottom has been reached.

You can often identify the time when the market is in the lowest 25 percent of its decline, because, typically, that time is nine months into the bear market. A definitive sign is that the P/E of the Dow will be down to around 14 or so. (In 1974, it got down as far as 7.)

When you buy in the lowest 25 percent, you may be buying earlier than other investors, and can expect prices to go still lower, but in a year or two, you will certainly have above-average gains. *The psychological importance is that you will save yourself the anxiety of waiting for the absolute bottom that is impossible to identify.*

Since the market may go down further, protect yourself by making your purchases incrementally. My personal system is as follows: When I think the market decline is within 25 percent of its bottom or nine months into a bear market, whichever occurs first, I commit 50 percent of my available cash. Three months later, I begin to deploy the remainder. I make an exception for the stocks on my "wish list," which I purchase whenever they reach my target price.

Here's another approach: Six months into the bear market, reinvest a third of the cash you held aside. Two months later, reinvest another third. Two months later, reinvest the final third.

You're prepared for the market to continue to go down, but if it goes up, and you are unable to make all of your purchases at still lower prices, that's all right, too, since it's more important to have a plan and follow through than to be absolutely on target. I expect this plan to be imprecise. In investing, you get rich by being generally right most of the time — not perfectly right all of the time, since no one can accomplish that feat.

My goal in having a plan is to manage my fear and compel myself to invest at bear market prices which ultimately turn out to have been bargains. Notice that managing fear is the primary point. If I can do that, everything else falls into place.

But making that first reinvestment in a bear market is difficult, because you are still nervous. In August 1987, my timing happened to be very good. I increased my clients' cash allocations, expecting a correction, and in October, the market "crashed." When it had recovered about half its losses, which took a few days, I advised my clients that it was time to start buying.

I met with great resistance. "I just can't bring myself to do it, John," one woman told me. Another said, "I'm sure I wouldn't be able to sleep at night." And remember, these are people who had reason to trust me because I had already helped them make a great deal of money!

I know how hard it can be to get out ahead of the crowd, even when you have a money manager behind you, because you wish you could get a group consensus to confirm that you are on track. But you must realize that you are *not* going to get that approval.

What it comes down to is this: Decide whether you want the *illusory* security of acting like everyone else — or the *real* security of building wealth over time. When you think about it that way, I've found, it's really not too hard to choose.

PART TWO

THE PROFILES

CHAPTER 7

The "I Can't Stop Worrying" Investor

- Do you frequently start the day feeling anxious about your investments?
- Do you listen to the market news compulsively?
- When the stocks and funds you own go up, do you paradoxically find yourself feeling nervous?
- Do you sometimes get pleasure out of castigating yourself when your stocks go down?
- Do you need to check out information with your broker or mutual fund company at least once a week?
- Do you sometimes hang on to stocks you've decided to sell, only to feel bad about it later on?
- Do you feel that every market decision you make has to be the "right" one?
- Do other investors regard you as well informed, and even consult you for advice, yet you think you don't know nearly as much as you should?

Some people are avid investors, and hardworking, too, yet they make themselves miserable because they are always anxious. They think they have to worry in order to do well — a kind of price for success — when the very opposite is true. The more relaxed and confident you can be, the greater the likelihood of sticking to the discipline you have set up for yourself. Worrying is a form of mental sabotage because it can sink a portfolio.

Phil Anderson came to see me because he was "nervous" about investing, and he needed some advice. He wasn't making much money and he found it difficult to figure out why because he really "kept on top" of his investments. Phil was a gregarious and charming person, appealing in his earnestness, and I could see that he took his responsibilities as an investor seriously. "Not a day goes by that I don't spend time checking on my stocks," Phil told me.

When I reviewed his portfolio, I found the stocks he selected were sound. They had included Coca-Cola, Merck, and Philip Morris, all companies that were doing well in a market that was going strong, yet Phil's compound total return (capital gains plus dividends) over the past three years was only 7.5 percent, far behind the Dow or the S&P 500.

"I can't figure out what I'm doing wrong," he said, "and I can tell you that I feel pretty upset about it."

Phil read about the market a great deal. He subscribed to the *Wall Street Journal, Barron's,* and at least two online services. He enjoyed the challenge of learning about investing and selecting his own stocks, but he was never totally comfortable with his decisions.

"Even though I can feel pretty good about a stock, I always think there may be something I don't know, something that's going to mess me up," he told me.

Because the market was so "complicated," Phil spent a lot of time thinking about the various opinions he read and trying to "sort things out." Sometimes he'd wake up in the middle of the night, particularly if there had been such anxiety-provoking news as predictions of rising interest rates, and wonder if he should have sold some of his holdings. If the news had been promising, predictions of higher-than-expected earnings, for example, he'd wonder if he should have bought more. Several times a week, he'd find himself chatting with his broker about one thing or another, but basically because he wanted the reassurance of having someone to "check in" with.

"I just can't afford to make any mistakes," he remarked in a serious tone.

Phil, who was forty-seven years old, was counting on his portfolio to fund his retirement and, particularly, to take care of his wife, his partner in their computer consulting business, who was about fifteen years his junior. "I try to be careful about the stocks I buy," he said, "but obviously I'm not being careful enough, because I'm not coming out ahead."

Phil considered himself to be "disciplined." He bought stocks for the long haul, he told me, and his standard was to sell when a stock had gone up 50 percent, yet he frequently found himself abandoning his standard, for reasons that he couldn't quite fathom.

If a stock was going up, he'd start feeling nervous by the time it had reached 15 percent or so. Surely, he'd think, the stock must have reached a "top" by now and would soon be heading south. He'd ask himself why he should wait and lose part of the money he had made when he could consolidate his gains right now. It seemed to Phil that it "must" be time to sell, even though he had no particular evidence.

For a while, he'd vacillate, watching the stock closely, but as he watched, his feelings of discomfort mounted. Finally, when his discomfort was greatest, Phil would sell, and experience instant feelings of relief. "Thank goodness, I sold," he'd tell himself, "a person never goes broke by taking a profit," but such thoughts lasted only a short while. If the stock continued to go up, which in a bull market it frequently did, he'd castigate himself for having sold too soon, and even experience pleasure in putting himself down.

On the other hand, if Phil owned a stock that was doing poorly, and there seemed to be a good reason to sell, such as a negative change in management, or a market sector that seemed poised for a downturn, he often felt paralyzed. Since he was counting on his portfolio to fund his retirement, he told himself that he couldn't afford to lose money — the stock *had* to turn around — so Phil would wait anxiously for it to go back up. If he could only "hang on" for a while, he assured himself, he could avoid losing money altogether or at least lose less.

As he waited, Phil was on an emotional roller coaster, worrying about the stock and whether or not it would "make it." At a certain point, mental exhaustion would set in, and he'd sell, usually pretty close to what proved to be the bottom. Once the sale was complete, he'd go over every step of his decision making, and as the stock turned around, berate himself for having sold at all.

Phil also compared himself with other investors. If he knew that a friend owned a stock he owned, he'd try to find out if the friend was worried and was thinking about selling. If he learned that the friend had sold out, Phil would get agitated and wonder whether he should do the same. If the friend was hanging on and Phil had sold, he'd wonder whether he had done the wrong thing. So Phil was making himself mighty uncomfortable.

THE SELF-TORTURE ROUTE

Worrying about one's investments is common, and it's natural, because there's a great deal riding on the outcome, and it's impossible for even the most able investor to make the "right" moves all of the time.

But some investors feel unusually nervous. I once had a client who telephoned me every single day for three months. He was certain, he said, that he was going to lose all of the money he had invested, and calling me for reassurance made him feel better, but not enough better that he didn't call again the next day. Despite his obsession with losing everything, he knew that the market was the best place to make his money grow, so he stayed invested, but he was anxious all the time.

Investors like this client and Phil Anderson are hard on themselves. Generally, they're intelligent people and genuinely interested in investing; they enjoy learning about it, and they're actually optimistic about their chances of doing well. In fact, they usually have the feeling that they *must* do well.

But this powerful motivation also makes them anxious and competitive. Rather than seeing the market as it is — a place that offers investors the opportunity to make a profit by buying shares in businesses — they view it as an arena where they must meet a test of performance. The market's innate competitiveness encourages their own competitive instincts and heightens their need to measure themselves against other people. It fuels their obsessive aspects through the oversupply of information and opinion it constantly churns out. While the market itself feeds on this material and is able to deal with its inherent contradictions, an individual investor can become overwhelmed and increasingly anxious if he or she attempts to make sense of everything and find the "right answer," as worriers tend to do.

Often, the worrier's anxiety is linked to an upbringing in which very high standards were set and the child was often criticized. Even though the person may be competent, and is seen that way by everybody else, he or she remains fearful of encountering parental displeasure or disapproval.

One of my clients, Lois Albanese, is her aging father's partner in a clothing store. A few years ago, Lois took over most of the management from her father. Now every time she comes to a decision that would be counter to her father's opinion, she experiences a great deal of anxiety and is afraid of making a mistake. "I can just about hear Dad saying 'I told you so,' " Lois told me.

Lois, like many people who strive to do well, constantly questions her stock market performance: What if I buy when I should have sold? What if I sell when I should have bought? What if I miss the "signs" I should have seen of an impending upturn or downturn? What if I lose money and fail those who are depending on me?

Lois allows "what-ifs" to dominate her and to take the enjoyment and genuine excitement out of investing. She deserves a lot better, and if you think you're this type of investor — you do, too.

You're probably a worrier in other areas of your life, and you may be aware of this tendency. You are meticulous about your work, even obsessive about it, yet you frequently feel you could be doing better, and you invest a lot of time being concerned about problems or possible problems. You're sometimes nagged by guilt, and this is why you can even find gratification in berating yourself over an error. You think you deserve to suffer.

Friends and family may tell you that you worry too much, and quite often you may find that you worried about something but things turned out to be okay after all. *In the market, your worrying can harm you, because its obsessive nature causes you to make sell decisions that are against your best financial interests.*

PROGRAM FOR THE
"I CAN'T STOP WORRYING" INVESTOR

Worriers feel they *must* achieve perfection. Their goal is to understand the market so well that they can always come out ahead and never suffer any setbacks. When they learn how to do this, they tell themselves, *then* they'll be able to relax and stop worrying. In the meantime, they have to keep on worrying in order to avoid mistakes.

Remember that in investing, as in anything else, there is no perfection, nor is there the certainty that worriers seek. The best investment advice you can give yourself is this: "I can live with uncertainty and understand that I don't have to be perfect in order to relax. In fact, relaxing will make me a more successful investor."

For worriers, the idea of relaxing, especially about something as financially significant as investing, may seem impossible. But realize that letting go is not just something to consider, but something you must do. Only after you have relaxed a bit can you stand back from your portfolio and analyze what's going on.

A famous Wall Street maxim goes "Cut your losers short and let your winners run." But if you're a worrier, your tendency is to do just the opposite of what the maxim advises — to sell your winners too soon and your losers too late — because you need to seek relief from your inner agitation.

While you may be making some money on your winners, you're not making nearly as much as you could if you had the emotional ability to hang on to them longer. In a bull market, like the eight-year run-up we have recently experienced, a solid stock like Coca-Cola can go up four- to fivefold. But a worrier who bought the stock probably held on to it for only a few months or a year, thereby losing out on the full advantage of the bull market.

Your problem may be that you don't have standards in place for selling, or if you do, you allow your obsessive thoughts to override them. You may plan to sell a stock when it reaches a certain price or price/earnings ratio, or a certain percentage increase, yet you sell sooner because you get seized by the thought that you've made enough money and it's "time to get out." Or you may plan to hang on to a stock long term, over at least a three-year period, yet sell because you've heard some irrelevant bad news, such as rumors of difficulties with a product when the company has many other products that are doing just fine.

A final point: Because you react obsessively, your portfolio is far too active, with large costs in brokerage fees and taxes that are cutting into your profits.

YOUR TARGET: OVERCOME OBSESSIVENESS

Worriers tend to make decisions and then constantly rethink them, a process that is both debilitating and exhausting. They agonize over whether they bought at "the right time" or sold at "the wrong time." If you're a worrier, this habit is so ingrained that you may think of it as "natural" because you are used to it, and it gives you a certain amount of gratification. Some of the gratification, a kind of pleasure in castigating yourself, stems from guilt feelings going back to childhood because you weren't living up to parental standards.

If a stock goes down, instead of evaluating the situation, you focus on telling yourself what a dope you are, one reason why it can take so long for you finally to decide to sell. If you wait for the stock to turn around, you can avoid having made a "mistake," something you don't easily forgive yourself for. You are making yourself suffer in several ways, and this is a market "bonus" that you don't need or deserve.

Worriers are often so concerned about being found wanting that they ignore their strengths. If you're like many worriers, you are conscientious and willing to chart your own course. You enjoy a challenge and you can see yourself coming out ahead, if only you can allow yourself to do that. Most likely, you have demonstrated the intelligence and the persistence to pick winning stocks and funds. Now you need to do it in a way that will bring you pleasure instead of pain.

Your goal is to reverse the process by which you are turning your strength — your thoughtfulness and conscientiousness — into a weakness that defeats you. The weakness grows out of your tendency to over-intellectualize and obsess about your decisions.

You need to develop a system for circumventing your anxieties by making major decisions *once,* and only minor adjustments from then on. *Your Rule: Decide — and let it go.*

The strategy: To *use* your obsessiveness to *restrain* your obsessiveness. You can do this by creating a *written* plan for each investment you make that relies heavily on stop/loss orders — orders to sell if the price drops below a certain level. Once you have created the plan, you are going to follow it faithfully, making reassessments only when certain criteria have been reached. The idea is to transfer your punitive conscience, the mechanism that causes you to feel guilty and anxious, to the plan itself. Once you have created the plan — and accepted it — decision making is taken out of your hands and worry is curtailed. What serves to relax you is the idea that you have relinquished control to something else, the plan.

The plan depends on a method called "trailing stop/losses," a system for controlling loss by knowing exactly when you will sell. I don't always advise using stop/losses, but it is important for you because of your need to sell irrationally when the stock goes up and to hold on irrationally when it goes down. You may have tried stop/losses before, but found that you frequently called your broker and altered them because you were unaware of how important keeping them in place could be to you psychologically.

The strategy you must employ now is to write down your stop/losses as well as entering them with your broker, since writing will help you to regard your plan as fixed. Writing something down, as I noted in Chapter Four, is a form of psychological commitment, and this type of commitment is even more important for you than for other investors.

To begin, buy a notebook or create a computer file for your portfolio plan. For each stock you purchase, write down the reason for purchase and the exact stop/loss system. Although the system will be similar for all stocks, you *must* have the numbers in the plan for each investment. If you haven't got it in writing — you haven't got it. Repetition helps to control worry.

Let's imagine that, after researching the *Value Line Investment Survey* or the company annual report and 10K form (see chapter 3 for general information on researching stocks), you decide to purchase 100 shares of a company I'll call Acme National, a financial services firm with a percentage of overseas holdings. Your plan might look like this:

> Date purchased: October 22, 1996
>
> Cost: $20 per share
>
> Reason for purchase: An underrecognized, asset-rich, U.S. deal-making financial company, superbly managed, with stakes overseas; provides low-cost entree to an emerging market.
>
> Greatest loss I can accept emotionally: 15 percent
>
> Goal: To make as much money as possible by holding as long as the stock goes up. Minimum hold goal: Three years.
>
> Emotional goal: To reduce obsessiveness and increase patience.

On the day you buy Acme National, put in a stop/loss order at $17, 15 percent below your purchase price of $20. If Acme National is an over-the-counter stock, on which you cannot enter stop/losses with a broker, you must put in a "mental" stop/loss *and* honor it. (This is more difficult to do. If you cannot adhere to a mental stop/loss, I recommend that you restrict yourself to stocks listed on the New York Stock Exchange and the American Stock Exchange.)

With the stop/loss system in place at 15 percent, you are strongly defensive. If Acme National goes down immediately, you're out — and fast — so guilt feelings get minimized and perhaps even eliminated. You avoid the torturous scenario of waiting for it to go back up so you can feel less guilty about having lost money. You deprive yourself of the opportunity to twist the knife.

Many people are able to hang on to a descending stock or even to buy more shares when they have reason to believe that earnings and growth will improve or that the market doesn't reflect the stock's true value. But for you, it's *rarely* advisable to hang on, since you suffer too much on the downside, and your goal should be to experience no more loss than the amount you have decided you can accept. *Remind yourself that if you can limit your loss, you are actually coming out ahead.*

When a stock goes up, and you can be less defensive, the general rule is to "trail" your stop/loss so that it is always 25 percent below where the stock is until gains become quite substantial. For example, let's suppose that Acme National climbs steadily to $25. You raise the stop/loss from $17 to $18.75. At $30, your stop/loss should be at $22.50, at $35, your stop/loss should be $26.25, and so forth. With a stop/loss at 25 percent, you are forced to hold on to gains, to "let your winner run," and to allow yourself to enjoy feelings of gratification rather than question them.

(As you become comfortable with this system, you may choose different percentages. This is fine, as long as you put the changes down in writing.)

KEEP TRACK OF YOUR FEELINGS

You need to monitor your emotions closely, since they will probably try to undermine your resolve. As Acme National goes up, you can expect anxiety feelings to increase. Note these feelings in the plan, too. Writing can help to dissipate them, or force you to look at them and evaluate them rationally. For example, if you write, "Stock at $35; I feel like selling," you can demand of yourself a solid, economic reason for wanting to sell. If there isn't any such reason — what I call a "business reason" related to the company — hang on. Remind yourself that you are protected by the stop/loss order from any loss you cannot accept emotionally.

Remember, anxiety will always be there, ready to strike, particularly if your stock does extremely well in a short period of time. When that happens, you must take steps to protect yourself emotionally, and to protect your substantial financial gains.

Let's say that Acme National has a sharp rise and doubles to $40 within a few months. Amend your stop/loss to $36, 10 percent below

Acme's price, so that you guard most of the gain. If Acme triples, put the stop/loss at 5 percent below. Proceeding this way, you lock in a significant profit, while soothing your worry-prone psyche.

With this system, you don't ever have to think about when to sell Acme. The sell decision, one of the hardest things for you to deal with, is made for you by the plan.

What you must do is to remind yourself that although you can amend the stop/loss orders, you *cannot* remove them. If you do, it will be like eliminating your psychological safety net, and you are certain to founder.

Another thing you must not do, since you tend to obsess, is to play that deadly worrier game: "Did I do the right thing?" Let's say that Acme National goes down from $40 to $36 and you get sold out. A few weeks later, Acme National is back up, all the way to $50. If you berate yourself for having sold, instead of congratulating yourself on the substantial gains you achieved, you walk right back into the "I can't stop worrying" trap.

Remember that for you, the peace of mind and the long-term financial success you will achieve from sticking to the plan is more important than any immediate additional profits. Over time, this conservative approach will pay off more handsomely for you than more aggressive approaches and, at the same time, significantly reduce your anxiety so you can participate comfortably in the market.

You need to have a written plan for mutual funds, too. Write down the reasons for your purchase and what you expect the fund to achieve. Your criteria for a large cap fund may be that it do 3 percent better than the S&P 500 over a three-year period; for a bond fund, that it do 1 percent better than the Lehman Brothers Bond Index, the index that tracks various types of bonds.

Evaluate the fund every three months and no more than that. Write down the date when you will do the evaluation, and avoid the temptation to check before the appointed time.

If your evaluations show that the fund is doing better than your criteria, allow yourself to be pleased. If the results are moderately disappointing — after a year the fund is doing only 2 percent better than the S&P 500 or 1 percent worse — resolve to hold on for a while. Market cycles are usually about three years long. Give your fund manager a fair chance. On the other hand, if a fund is *seriously* underperforming — the S&P 500 went down 2 percent and your fund is down 10 percent — you *must* sell because you are unlikely to come out ahead over the three-year period.

You can alter your expectations for funds, just as you can alter the stop/loss orders for stocks, but you need to regard a plan as fixed in stone until you have put the changes *in writing*. The minute you deviate from what you have written down, anxiety and guilt will increase, and you will feel destructive impulses.

At all times, remember that your goal is to cut decision making down to a minimum. The more often you reassess what you have decided, the greater the danger of reverting to your original pattern of cutting your winners and letting your losers run.

THE DOMINANT THEME OF YOUR PORTFOLIO

Psychologically, your profile can benefit most from value-oriented stocks, defined as those with low price-to-earnings multiples, low price-to-book values, and other assets generally considered undervalued by the market (see chapter 3 for descriptions of investing styles).

The advantages of a value approach for your emotional style are:

- These stocks fall within established parameters. Working within parameters gives you a sense of security.
- You enjoy doing research, and value stocks are there waiting to be discovered.
- Your competitive urges are satisfied by discovering stocks that few people may know about.
- Value stocks are usually less volatile than growth stocks, so they keep your own emotional volatility under control.
- Value stocks require a longer time to pay off, and force you to be patient and to adjust to market fluctuations. As you learn this discipline, guilt and anxiety will both diminish.

You can include a certain percentage of solid growth stocks.

But you need to avoid highly volatile stocks — small capitalization or high tech — that experience sharp highs and lows. For you, owning such stocks is like putting yourself on the rack. If you find yourself considering one, remember it may be because you can derive *gratification* out of being on the rack. Limit your propensity to beat up on yourself by saying no to predictable volatility.

Restrict your equity investments to ten stocks, or a combination of stocks and funds. Remember, when you purchase too many investments and have too much tracking to do, you raise your anxiety level.

For each investment, stock or fund, keep a running record in your written plan, and proceed only according to plan.

Pay attention to the schedule of your buying decisions. Although you research stocks thoroughly, you are always anxious about whether this is "the right time" to buy. The best way to make purchases is through dollar cost averaging, which relieves anxiety about timing and spreads out your risk by making equal investments at regular intervals — alternating among your stocks and funds. If you have a portfolio of six funds, you can take 10 percent of your pay each month and invest in three of the funds one month, and the other three the next month; by rotating, you invest in each fund six times a year. Dollar cost averaging can substantially reduce risk, because you buy fewer shares when prices are high and more shares when prices are low, so you achieve an average cost per share that is less than the fund's average share cost.

Although dollar cost averaging is a good rule for every investor, it is particularly valuable for you (and for the "Make me safe" investor I will discuss in chapter 12).

The most important psychological benefit of dollar cost averaging is that, like your plan, it reduces decision making. Once you have decided to put a certain amount into your investments at certain intervals — *you've decided, you've written it down, and you can let it go.*

Dollar cost averaging, by encouraging you to remain in the market through fluctuations, also helps you to develop patience, discipline, and a long-term viewpoint, which you need in order to increase your level of profitability.

Every investor worries about a bear market, but worriers, of course, worry even more. Remember that if you follow your stop/loss program, you will avoid large losses in a bear market. If you make adjustments, alter the stop/losses or sell prematurely, you will only increase your natural tendency to suffer. The more bearish the market, the more you need to stick to plan, and that means continuing to invest through dollar cost averaging, even if you may feel like pulling back altogether.

PORTFOLIO FOR THE
"I CAN'T STOP WORRYING" INVESTOR

Following is a sample portfolio for John Evans, who is thirty-eight years old and an "I can't stop worrying" investor. This portfolio is a prototype, and not a set of current stock recommendations, since it was developed in the past. I present the reasoning behind the choices *at the time they were made.*

John, an advertising copywriter, and his wife, Susan, a real estate broker, have a joint take-home pay of $110,000. With two children in elementary school, their goals included saving for college and building for their own retirement, twenty-five years away.

My goal for John was to minimize his anxiety by emphasizing long-term holdings, stocks and funds with strong defensive qualities, and the need for long-term growth. The less John had to look at his holdings, the less anxious he would be. Using the trailing stop/loss system, he would not have to check often, and he would be forced to "let his winners run." I expected him to have many winners, thus encouraging long-term market participation.

The portfolio's total value of $70,000 was divided as follows:

VALUE STOCKS AND FUNDS: 70 PERCENT

STOCKS:

Leucadia National. Insurance holding company with diverse manufacturing interests. Leucadia's key executives, Ian Cumming and Joseph Steinberg, are known for their nose for value and their diligent investigation. Deal makers extraordinaire, they search the globe for value. Besides the company's well-run domestic insurance operations, it owned the second largest insurance company in Argentina, purchased for a steal, and also had extensive holdings in Russian stocks, including vast natural resources, and was in a joint venture with Pepsi in Russia and Kazakhstan. Leucadia had a Beta volatility rating of 1.0, meaning that its volatility was the same as the market's. However, Leucadia did well in bear markets, giving John anti-anxiety protection.

St. Joe Companies. Paper company, diversified into other industries. Formerly known as St. Joe Paper, this company has a fascinating history: It was created out of the estate of Alfred duPont, who left a trust of huge Florida holdings to benefit the crippled children of Delaware and Florida. As originally constituted, it held 3 percent of the land in Florida, mostly in timberland and sugarcane plantations. It owned a paper company, 65 percent of the profitable Florida East Coast Railroad, a couple of other small railroads, sugar mills, and some small telephone companies. While the company's stock was trading in the $75 range when I purchased it for John, I conservatively estimated underlying assets to be worth $165 per share. There were new pressures on management to maximize value. Regardless of market gyrations, John could sleep comfortably because of St. Joe's great assets.

Merrill Lynch. Financial services company. In the emerging global economy, Merrill Lynch was the closest thing to a world financial services company, unrivaled until the 1997 merger of Morgan, Stanley and Dean Witter, Discover. Soundly managed banks and financial services are good choices for worriers because they have a record of stability.

United Asset Management. A holding company of investment management companies. UAM had a winning formula for acquiring medium-sized money managers who wanted to cash out. The company's long-term growth prospects, with highly predictable earnings, made it a good choice for a worry-prone investor.

FUNDS:

Third Avenue Value Fund. (No-load. Not yet ranked by *Forbes*. Five-year annualized total return as of August 31, 1997: 22.45 percent. *Morn-*

ingstar rating: 5 stars.) This fund is managed by Yale business professor Martin Whitman, the consummate value investor. (Read Whitman's excellent book, *The Aggressive Conservative Investor,* to learn how a professional value investor can obtain above-average results while taking below-average risks.) Owning this fund allowed John to invest in bankruptcies and other special situations, yet maintain a highly defensive posture.

Mutual Series Qualified Fund. (Load: 4.50 percent. *Forbes* rating [August 25, 1997]: C for up markets, A for down markets. Five-year annualized total return: 20.93 percent; ten-year: 14.78 percent. *Morningstar* rating: 5 stars.) Since I bought the fund for John, manager Michael Price sold the Mutual Series funds to the Franklin-Templeton Group (1996), but he contracted to stay at the helm for at least five years. Price learned value investing from a master, Max Heine, Mutual's founder. In time, pupil surpassed master and Price sports a value record second to none. A *Forbes* rating of A for down markets should let John sleep well at night.

GROWTH STOCKS AND FUNDS: 20 PERCENT

(The following stocks and funds are more volatile, but they are not speculative. My assessment of John and Susan was that they could tolerate having 20 percent of the portfolio in more aggressive investments without undue anxiety. This is a decision that each "worrier" needs to make individually.)

STOCKS:

PepsiCo. Soft drink and food company. Not exactly a bold choice, and certainly one a worrier could live with. Second fiddle to Coke in soft drinks, Pepsi's Frito-Lay was the undisputed "King of Snacks." Pepsi also had a powerful set of restaurant franchises (Kentucky Fried Chicken, Pizza Hut, and Taco Bell) that it planned to spin off. The key to Pepsi's future success depended on the inspired vision of its CEO, Roger Enrico. Timing was the key for a "worrier," because when I bought the stock for John, it was highly undervalued, and therefore poised for growth. Coke was similarly undervalued in 1987 and 1988, but few professional investors, other than Warren Buffett, recognized it.

Amgen. Biotechnology company. Maybe risky for a worrier, but the company's long-range fortunes looked so good, I thought John should own it. I saw Amgen being where Merck was thirty years ago, and if John could envision it as a future blue chip, his anxiety would be relieved.

FUND:

Fidelity Blue Chip Growth. (Load: 3.00 percent. Not yet rated by *Forbes.* Five-year annualized total return as of August 31, 1997: 21.34 percent. *Morningstar* rating: 4 stars.) This fund gave John instant, widespread diversification in quality growth companies. It has the drawback of being a load fund, which I don't usually recommend, since there is almost always a suitable no-load alternative, but John planned to hold this fund for a long time, thereby amortizing the initial 3 percent load.

MONEY MARKET: 10 PERCENT

Should bonds be in a worrier's portfolio? An old rule of thumb is that the percentage of bonds in your portfolio ought to be equal to your age. If you are in your twenties, 20 percent of your portfolio should be in bonds. If you are in your sixties, 60 percent. The rationale has been that older people need the increased safety of bonds, and often the increased income as well, whereas younger people can afford to take greater risks in the interests of growth.

There are different schools of thought nowadays about that rule of thumb. My view is that, unless you need the income, you need not have bonds in your portfolio at all, if interest rates are below 8 percent, because historically you are likely to do much better with equities. If interest rates are above 8 percent, you may want to have a portion of your portfolio in bonds. U.S. Treasuries, reliable and liquid, are the best choice for all investors, and particularly those who tend to worry. (Corporate bonds are relatively illiquid for the small investor.)

Despite my belief that bonds don't belong in a portfolio when interest rates are low, a significant percentage of them can be calming for a worry-prone investor, *if* you find bonds less anxiety provoking than stocks. I say "if" because most worriers worry equally about all investments and some find bonds *more* worrisome because of their lack of growth. But if you look upon bonds as a form of security blanket, divide your portfolio this way:

Value stocks and funds	40 percent
Growth stocks and funds	20 percent
U.S. Treasury bonds	30 percent
Money market	10 percent

HOW TO STAY ON YOUR STOP/LOSS PLAN

- Keep your written plan where you can get at it easily.
- When you find yourself feeling anxious, reread the plan, check to make sure you are on target, then put the plan away.
- Ask your spouse, significant other, or a close friend to help you stay on plan. This person should require you to give a sound explanation for any change you want to make. Let's say you're nervous about selling Acme National, because you think it will climb above the stop/loss order you set. You fear selling at a good profit because you might lose out on a greater profit. Your anxiety becomes less compelling when you have to explain your reasoning to someone who knows your inclinations and can help you stick to your plan. And, if the stock continues to rise after you sell, this person can tell you that you locked in your gain and stuck to your plan.
- Join an investment club. For an individual who worries, being part of a group is a good way to increase your tolerance of uncertainty — which as a nervous investor you need to achieve.

OTHER HELPFUL STEPS

• *Cut back on the amount of checking you do.* Look up your stocks in the newspaper once a week at most. Checking more often increases your level of agitation and worry. Remind yourself that you don't *need* to check, because the stop/loss system protects you.

• *Limit your market reading and television viewing.* There is probably too much material coming through your pipeline, and you have to shut some of it off. Information overload paralyzes decision making, a problem for all investors, as I said in chapter 2, but particularly for you.

A dangerous aspect of the "information explosion" in financial publishing — there are currently more than 840 market newsletters — is that the divergence of opinion can produce anxiety. In investing, there are always at least two views. Restrict the amount of input to what you are comfortable with. Reading any financial newspaper every day — even if the paper is the *Wall Street Journal* — is not good for your investor profile. Stay away from television programs where panels of Wall Street experts offer opposing opinions. If you do watch, remember that many experts advocate a strategy that is not yours. Be sure you have established your own goals and philosophy (as discussed in chapter 3) so you won't become confused by the myriad opinions about the market.

• *Enlist your broker's aid.* Evaluate whether your broker is playing a negative or positive role in your investing life. Your pattern of selling successful stocks soon after you buy them may be generating lots of commissions, so a broker who is less than scrupulous will not encourage you to change. A broker who has your long-term interests at heart should advise you to do less nervous selling.

Tell your broker you are trying to worry less about the market, and arrange a meeting to discuss your psychological objectives. Your broker can help by reminding you of your plan if you try to alter a stop/loss order that the two of you have agreed on. Your broker can also help by limiting the number of calls he or she will take from you each week and by limiting to what is pertinent the information he or she will give you about your holdings, such as new products or changes in management, not general market "talk."

• *Compare less.* Make a concerted effort *not* to find out what your investing friends and relatives are doing. If a friend calls to chat about the market, steer the conversation around to another subject. You should tell the people who are close to you that you're reading and thinking less about the market and that it would help you to talk about it less, too.

• *Finally, be sure to let the pleasure in.* You deserve to get more satisfaction out of the effort you are putting into the stock market. Investing is meant to be emotionally as well as financially rewarding, but your tendency to overintellectualize is spoiling the fun.

You can get pleasure from thinking about what you are going to do with the money you earn and earmarking some of it — *in the plan* — for what excites you. If you're like most worry-prone investors, your investment goals are sensible (retirement planning, paying off a mortgage), and focused on others (your children's college education, setting up trust funds for them). But you also need to have goals that just plain make you feel good — a recreation vehicle, a second home, a special vacation — whatever you think would reward you for working on investing, sticking to your plan, and worrying less.

The biggest reward, however, will be your increased success over time. When Phil Anderson adopted the "write-it-down, trailing stop/losses method," his attitude toward the market became more relaxed and his portfolio blossomed. Over seven years, Phil achieved annualized total returns of 15.3 percent, far better than the 7.5 percent he was doing when he first came to see me.

Most investors don't realize the extent to which worry can damage a portfolio. But worrying isn't inevitable. It can be contained and curtailed — and lead to the winning financial results you deserve.

CHAPTER 8

The Power Investor

If power is important to people in their careers and personal relationships, it will take center stage in their investing life as well. Such people will be attracted to stock selection methods that they consider powerful and to stocks with reputations that reflect power.

To say, "I've got Microsoft," or "I've got Netscape," at a social gathering is an acceptable way to announce that you are powerful, and desirable as well, since power also enhances sexual attractiveness. The stock is code for the message you want to send; it becomes your ally in creating an image and it validates not only the intelligence of your choice, but your personal importance as well.

Power investors bring a genuine sense of commitment to the process; they put all of themselves into it. And they tend to feel confident about the stocks they pick, so they avoid the anxiety and guilt that plague some investors. Power investors have a good time in the market, and that is a wonderful aspect of their personalities.

Because of their high energy levels and lack of fear, power investors often do well in a strong market — particularly an outstanding market like the one of the past fifteen years. But in a market decline, they suffer disproportionately because they tend to be heavily weighted toward speculative and overvalued stocks, the stocks that collapse first and farthest. Their emotional suffering is disproportionate, too, because power investors lose self-esteem as their stocks fall.

In a decline, the pain can be so great that power investors sell out altogether, guaranteeing a loss. And they may stay out of the market until it has completely recovered, thereby losing out on the buying opportunities of the early recovery.

You can't make money over the long term if you don't participate in every kind of market. So, if power investors want to do well, they need to protect themselves against the market's mood swings and their own by putting more balance into their investing style.

ATTACHED VS. HIGHLY ATTACHED

The central emotional issue is their attachment to their stocks.

While all investors get attached to their stocks, power investors get *highly* attached, and this attachment can distort their vision and hamper their judgment.

Wall Street has a maxim for this situation — "The stock doesn't know you own it," meaning that an investor's narcissism, the need we all have for self-love, can cause us to become blind to the company's faults or to ignore times when the market may seriously overvalue the stock.

There's no reason to feel uncomfortable about narcissism. It is a nearly universal characteristic, and identification with our investments is universal, too, as I wrote in chapter 3. It's natural to want to feel good about ourselves and one way we achieve that is through the things we own, houses, cars, boats.

When you buy a stock, and it does well, you feel great because it is validating your intelligence. The better the stock does, the better you feel, particularly when you buy a stock early and it takes off.

I bought Berkshire Hathaway on "the ground floor," and I know I have a strong narcissistic connection to that stock, and so do other investors who bought it early on. Every year, I attend a meeting of the "Omaha Club" — my name for a group of investors with a substantial Berkshire stake — and there I've observed that people who bought fifteen years ago when Berkshire's price was less than $1,000 a share (it is now more than $44,700 a share) feel euphoric about the stock and themselves for having bought it. It's hard not to be euphoric about Berkshire, but euphoria is one of the signs of overidentification that make it difficult to sell when a situation calls for selling, so I become wary when I realize I am experiencing this very natural feeling.

People who invest for power have a strong tendency toward euphoria, since they merge themselves with their stocks. This is one type of merger that should never be consummated.

Because overidentification is a common problem, and can affect any investor on occasion, let me give you some examples of how it influences behavior and of the problems that can develop.

TWO INVESTORS ON THE "CUTTING EDGE"

About a year ago, at a national medical meeting, a man came up to me who, I later found out, was a highly regarded neurosurgeon. Walter Swanson had a reputation for daring in the operating room and for taking on cases that others thought inoperable.

In his late forties, Walter was tall, slender, and elegantly dressed, but what impressed me most about him was his beaming smile and open manner. He shook my hand firmly and complimented me on my newsletter, which, he said, he had read at the home of a friend who was "a bit more conservative about the market than I am." Although I was talking with some other people at the time, Walter, with his easy conversational manner, had no trouble becoming part of the group.

After the others had left, Walter asked a few perfunctory questions about producing a newsletter, but it was clear that he really wanted to discuss his own portfolio. This is an occupational hazard for me, and usually what they want is to get some tidbits of advice.

Walter's purpose was different. He simply wanted to share with me his sense of excitement about investing, which he enjoyed so much, he said with a smile, that he had come to think of himself as a market "insider." His account was valued at about $800,000, and his broker often told Walter that he was a very special client, so special that he let him buy 200 shares of America Online when it came out as an initial public offering. Brokers had extremely limited supplies of this IPO, and very little was sold outside of "the business," so Walter was as thrilled as if he had bought the first edition of a book that might become a classic.

He talked on and on with great enthusiasm about America Online and other stocks. He had been in the market for about four years, he told me, and he'd been fortunate enough to choose quite a few "winners."

Walter was heavily invested in the internet stocks, Netscape, America Online, and Spyglass, and the biotechs Agouron, Centocor, and Autoimmune, companies that invent new products by combining the most recent advances in biology with advances in computer science and radiology.

For Walter, biotech was attractive because he "knew the terrain," and indeed, it did seem reasonable for a medical professional to buy stocks in a field related to his own work. An excellent principle of investing is to stay within your sphere of competence. He also had stock in a company that was developing a new type of laser that would undoubtedly turn out to have surgical uses.

At first, I was impressed as he talked about the laboratory processes involved in creating the laser, since it was clear that he had used his intellectual narcissism — his love of science — to identify an appropriate investment. But as he went on talking, waving his hands for emphasis, I began to worry about the extent of his involvement with the stock. When I heard him say, "This laser will put us up on top," I knew that Walter's enthusiasm had led him to blur the line between himself and his investment.

In an effort to focus Walter on the business fundamentals of this company, I wondered aloud about the financials of the company and whether it had the ability to survive years of research and development without having a product on the market. Walter admitted that he had paid little attention to this issue, since he saw himself as a "momentum player."

In momentum investing, as I said in chapter 3, a stock becomes desirable because unexpected accelerations in earnings or other exciting factors have caused the price to start rising more than the prices of other stocks. Once this trend gets established, the price tends to rise ahead of the pack, so a reason to buy a company is that its price is moving unusually quickly; that it is doing unusually well is a sign that it will continue to do so. In short, the stock has "momentum."

Many investors find momentum exciting, particularly investors like Walter Swanson. In the last two to three years, momentum seems to have produced the best results of any investment technique, and power investors are drawn to spectacular success.

With this kind of payoff, it's easy to understand why Walter Swanson had become so overly enthusiastic about his investments. But this enthusiasm, I knew, put Walter in extreme danger should his investments fall, taking his self-image along with them.

Years earlier I had treated a woman for depression who was similar to Walter in her investing style. Meredith Johnson, a svelte redhead in her late forties, was the owner of a florist shop that specialized in unique wedding arrangements.

Meredith's business was good, but not as good as she had hoped it would be, since her husband was disabled and she was the family's sole support.

At first, I thought that our treatment issues would center around Meredith's struggle to come to terms with her business disappointments, but after a while, I learned that investing also played a significant role in the depression.

A few years before she became my patient, Meredith had decided to abandon her dream of expanding the business and focus, instead, on retirement planning. Gradually, she shifted money out of CDs into a portfolio of $200,000, invested mainly in bond funds and such conservative stock funds as Fidelity's Puritan Fund. But as she began to read the financial news, she developed an interest in stocks, particularly those that had exciting "stories" attached to them.

She read about a company that was working on a process to be used in genetic engineering of plants, a subject that seemed to be closely related to her own business. She bought $10,000 worth of the stock, which had been at $6 for more than a year, and almost immediately, it started to take off.

Every time the stock went up a few points, Meredith was gratified, and when, at the end of eight months, it had risen to $14, she moved from gratification to euphoria. The stock's success made her feel more successful than she had in years and, for the first time in a long time, she felt good about her florist shop. It occurred to her that perhaps she could make enough money in the market both to fund her retirement and to revive her dream of expanding her business.

Meredith began to invest in an aggressive way in the bull market of the late 1980s, and, bit by bit, she found herself cashing in her mutual funds and buying stocks, particularly IPOs, that were increasingly risky. The "newer" the company, the more "exciting" its story, the more powerful it made Meredith feel. These IPOs represented the way Meredith liked to see herself and her business — both could become "new" again through the stocks.

By the time the bull market reached its height, Meredith had turned her $200,000 into $500,000, and she and her husband were talking a great deal about her success. "Meredith and her stocks" were much admired within the extended family, and particularly by a cousin with whom she had long had an intense rivalry. And Meredith's own admiration of her stocks continued to grow.

But in the course of all this excitement, Meredith abandoned the standard for selling she had set for herself. In chapter 4, I discussed the importance of setting at least one such standard, and how standards can vary from investor to investor. Meredith's intention was to sell half of any stock that had gone up by 50 percent, so she would at least protect her original investment. But as the bull market continued, applying this standard seemed foolish. Why sell even half of a winner, when her stocks were making her feel so powerful?

By the time a downturn began, and several of Meredith's favorite stocks started to lose ground, she was poised to react in the disastrous way that is typical of power investors. The first response is to feel totally perplexed, since this scenario is not "supposed" to happen. The power investor is totally unprepared for bad news, and responds with a denial stronger than most investors experience. (See chapter 6.)

The common psychological sequel to denial is the belief that things will turn around soon. Instead of reappraising the situation and asking such vital questions as "What's the problem?" or "What moves should I make now?" the individual falls back on such reassurances as "My gut instinct is never wrong" and "Nothing to worry about; it'll get back up there."

Sometimes these thoughts seem to do the trick; the stock goes back up, perhaps even higher than before, and the power investor feels a renewed sense of power and energy.

Inevitably, a stock or group of stocks is hit hard and the illusion that things are getting better becomes difficult to preserve. As denial shatters, the investor experiences an overwhelming threat to his or her sense of identity, and either sells everything, without evaluating each company on its merits, or holds doggedly on to the power dream.

Let's imagine an investor owns a stock he bought at $17 on the recommendation of a famous newsletter that predicted that within three years the stock would be worth $52. It is enormously exciting to own a stock that will triple in three years, and he talks about the stock so much that several friends buy it on his recommendation.

If the stock starts down, and continues to fall, even after the investor has done his best mentally to "get it back up there," he tells himself, "Well, the newsletter said it was volatile; I'll hang on." As the stock drops further, he thinks, "There's probably some organized short selling in the picture; I'll hang on." The rationalizations continue, even in the face of revelations about serious problems with a product or management, because the investor is *still* getting those power feelings from the idea of tripling his investment. This fantasy he absolutely refuses to give up.

Meredith Johnson hung on to her power feelings until her portfolio had gone from $500,000 to $150,000, leaving her with $50,000 less than she had when she started. With her portfolio went her dreams for the flower shop, her hope of a comfortable retirement, and much of her self-esteem.

An investor who loses esteem when the market is the very place she had hoped to find it can experience strong feelings of disintegration because the self gets shattered. This disintegration is different from the reaction when you lose money because of greed. Then you certainly kick yourself for being a dope, and you can feel rotten, but you tend to recover quickly. It takes much longer to bounce back from a blow to one's narcissism, as Meredith Johnson's long-standing depression showed.

ARE YOU A POWER INVESTOR?

Power investing is a double-edged sword. When things are going well, as for Walter Swanson, the emotional payoff is terrific. When things are going badly, as in Meredith Johnson's case, the emotional toll can be excruciatingly painful. I've never met a power investor who had been through the downside who thought the tradeoff was worth it.

The first step toward protecting yourself, and also the first step toward building long-term wealth, is to recognize the symptoms of power investor behavior. If you think you may be a power investor, consider whether you are doing the following things:

• *You buy on the excitement of "the story."* You choose a stock not on the basis of company fundamentals, but because it has an intriguing concept, a "story" that makes you feel good and that you know others will find impressive. Although you may skim a number of financial publications, you're looking for "hooks" that will excite you, rather than solid information that might cause you to investigate a company further, the way I talked about in chapter 3. Typical hooks include sky-high estimates of future earnings and promises of a new discovery "too hush-hush to talk about" that may revolutionize the industry.

• *You fantasize quick gains.* Because the concept is so compelling, you dream of making a "big score." I have seen power investors become disenchanted with stocks that had doubled in price in three months because they didn't double again in the next three months.

• *You think you can keep the stock "up there."* You get so connected to a stock that you believe you can make it go up. Many years ago, a close friend persuaded me to invest in TWA. We each purchased 200 shares at $12. Within a few months, the stock had risen to $18, a handsome short-term profit of 50 percent. Then the price stalled for some time.

The next time I saw my friend, he said, "Don't worry about your TWA. We'll soon have it over twenty." The minute I heard that crucial word *we*, I knew my friend was overidentifying with the stock, since the collective clout of our 400 shares was invisible.

• *You make excuses for the stock.* Once you have "merged" with a stock, you try to avoid listening to news that reflects badly on the company's management. If there's a problem, you look for something else to blame.

A medical colleague bought stock in a company that was developing a process to extract oil from oil shale and oil tar. She bought 200 shares at $12 and, as the stock rose to $36, she became excited about it. Then a story came out in the newspapers saying that the company and its process might be fraudulent, and the price plummeted to $6.

I offered to look into the facts for my colleague, but she was insistent that "her" company was doing nothing wrong. "I'm surprised at you, John," she said. "Can't you see that the big oil companies are spreading those rumors? They've probably organized short selling as well. The last thing they want is for oil to be extracted from shale."

I don't know whether the rumors were true, but I know that any investor should get to the bottom of a negative story. If you don't believe that, if you're making excuses, it's because a blow to the stock would be a blow to your ego.

• *You feel increasingly grandiose about the stock.* As your fantasy of immediate gains is fulfilled, you begin to feel there is no limit to how high the stock can go. I warn my clients that grandiosity builds on itself and that they should be very wary when they are feeling euphoric. Watch out for grandiose dreams of flying or swimming on top of the water. If your stock is soaring, the dreams may refer to the market, and it is time to be very careful indeed.

PROGRAM FOR THE POWER INVESTOR

The power investor's portfolio is usually weighted toward speculative stocks, often 100 percent. Your goal is to develop a more balanced portfolio, while maintaining your wonderful sense of enthusiasm and excitement about equities you own. Let me assure you that this is possible, if you will agree to *limiting* your excitement in the interests of *expanding* the long-term gain, and *protecting* yourself from extreme danger in a downturn.

First, *determine the risk vs. emotional reward of the "concept" stocks you love.*

Concept stocks tend to get overvalued — far ahead of growth in sales and earnings — and become risky because the efficiency of the market will, at some point, bring down the price in order to reflect the actual value or something close to it. When that happens, you stand to lose disproportionately. In one month in 1996, America Online went from a high of 71 to 39⅞, and Iomega Corp., another high-concept stock, went from 55⅛ to 30⅛. Nevertheless, you really enjoy owning concept stocks, and for you, the market wouldn't be the same without them, since they add significantly to your investing pleasure.

You need to analyze what this psychic value is worth to you, since you are paying a price for it in increased risk.

I ask my clients to write down the emotional payoffs they get from these stocks. Typical answers are "feeling smart," "feeling successful," "having the fun of talking about them," "knowing I'm on top of a trend," "having people come to me for advice." Write down the payoffs that apply to you, in order of importance. Once you've listed them, assign each a "pleasure value" on a scale of 1 to 10, 10 being the highest and 1 the lowest. When you add them up, you can get an idea of how significant these feelings are to you.

Then you can evaluate what the feelings are worth in terms of risk. Are they worth owning stocks that are 25 percent overvalued? Thirty percent? Forty percent? Try to arrive at a percentage you find *emotionally valid,* and make it the yardstick for when you will sell an overvalued stock, even if it's a stock that you like a great deal. (To calculate the actual value of a stock, see the discussion of net present value in chapter 3 and Appendix B.)

By doing this exercise, you create a discipline for separating yourself from a stock you are identifying with strongly.

I plan to sell when a concept stock is 25 percent overvalued, although I'll admit that it can be a real wrench when you are attached to it. A while ago, a stock I've owned for a long time, a venture capital company, had a big price run-up that had nothing to do with the value of the company. This company still had all of the things I liked about it — high-quality management and a splendid long-term record — yet I sold when it was 25 percent overvalued, planning to buy back if the price went down. It has not happened yet but I feel confident that it will.

Once you have set your "overvaluation" level, take these steps:

• *Decide on the proportion of overvalued stocks in your portfolio.* I feel that they should constitute no more than 10 percent, but this number can vary according to your risk vs. emotional reward ratio.

If you are going to allow individual stocks to get overvalued by no more than 10 percent, you can have more overvalued stocks in your portfolio; if your overevaluation level is 35 percent, you should have fewer of them.

You can also change the percentages according to market circumstances, *if you will commit the new percentages to writing when you do this.* Suppose your standard is the 10 percent I recommend. In a strong bull market, that 10 percent can easily increase to 20 or 25 percent as prices rise. If that happens, say to yourself, "I'll hang on, but I won't buy anything more that's overvalued."

It's important to write down new percentages because, in a bull market, you will want to buy more overvalued stocks, and you can easily go beyond the percentage you have allotted for yourself.

• *Raise your safety level by choosing stocks that have crossed the line from speculative to growth.* You always need to think, "How can I get security along with the excitement that makes me feel so good?"

Stick to companies that have a product on the market — and thus a record of profits, predictable earnings, and a rate of growth. Most biotech companies do not have products as yet, though some do, including Amgen, Chiron, and Genzyme. These companies have crossed the line from speculative stocks to solid growth. *This is the line where you want to focus your attention.*

If you want the excitement of being in a new "hot" area, try to do it in the safest way possible. It is likely that the regional phone companies or cable TV companies will ultimately control the internet industry. Many speculative "net" stocks will vanish, so if you want to "play the net," a safer way to do it is to buy the stable companies that may well emerge as the true winners. This does not mean you cannot make *small* bets on some of the emerging companies and the highly specialized products for the net, but the emphasis is on the word *small.*

• *Love the "story," but probe beyond it.* Spotting a stock with a "story" and allowing yourself to be seduced by it is, for you, part of the fun of being in the market, so don't stop being on the lookout for intriguing possibilities. But, to protect yourself, make it a rule to investigate a stock as thoroughly as possible before buying. This caution is important for all investors, but it is particularly important for you, because you don't want to investigate. As I said in chapter 3, every investor should obtain a copy of the annual report and the 10K form required by the Securities and Exchange Commission. Look at sales, earnings, book value, cash flow, return on equity, and growth. If the company does not yet have a product, examine the amount of financing budgeted for research and development, determine whether the company has partnerships with established companies, evaluate its potential for creating spin-off companies. You want to know whether this company has the clout and the financing to see it through several years without a product on the market.

Another way to get information that most power investors find compatible with their need to be on the cutting edge is through a news service, like the Dow Jones News Retrieval Service, which, as I said in chapter 3, provides all the news that has been reported about a company for the past three months. You may find the details of a change in management, reports of an SEC investigation, or information about the activities of competitors that may be relevant. The more you know, the more objective you can be about the stock, because you become aware of its warts as well as its beauty spots.

• *Start with your own area of expertise — then analyze.* If you can't resist buying companies in their formative stages, you can protect yourself by sticking to areas that you know about — drug companies, if you're a physician, personal care products, if you're in the beauty industry, telecommunications, if you're in the communications industry. Having an insider's view of an industry gives you an idea of a new company's chances of success.

But beyond that, you need an intelligent forecast of future earnings. One method is to average all of the analysts' forecasts about the company. The greater the number of forecasts, the more accurate the average is likely to be.

Or, as I do, you can do some forecasting yourself. Let's say I'm investigating a company that's developing a new drug for gram-negative septicemia, a form of blood poisoning. I want to find out if the drug will be an improvement over existing drugs, how many cases there are of the disease each year, and how many treatments each patient will need. If there are 400,000 cases annually, I figure that about 75 percent of patients might need the drug and that the average patient will need twelve treatments. The first year the drug is on the market, one-third of potential patients will be getting it, the second year, one-half, and so on. Then I'll ask the company how much it costs to manufacture the drug — $2 per treatment, let's say — and what they are going to charge for it — $50, let's say. Now I can estimate that in the first year, the company will have earnings of $57,600,000, and in the second, $86,400,000. You may not want to do all this research, but *any* investigation you do gives you a yardstick for judging a start-up. Although you may not be able to find out everything you should know, you may find out enough to keep away.

• *Make your stocks stand up for themselves.* Every stock in your portfolio needs to justify your holding it. Evaluate it periodically, as I explained in chapter 4, to see whether it is still meeting the expectations you set when you bought it.

If you are a power investor, you may resist this process because judging your stocks seems to you like judging yourself. But unless you evaluate, you cannot determine whether you own the stock because you are attached to it or because it is still a good investment. As I said, I identify with Berkshire Hathaway, and it's hard for me to believe that anything could ever go wrong with that company, yet annually I sit down and write an evaluation of Berkshire and each of its thirty-four subsidiaries because I know I need to be objective about every stock, and this stock in particular. It's always important to remind yourself that you have invested in businesses, and the value of your portfolio will depend on the businesses' success.

• *Understand that the next trend is more important than the current one.* If you like "trend surfing," and most power investors do, the only way to play is to look at what you think the trend will be two years from now — you have already missed the trend of the moment, even if you are currently excited about it.

Figuring out what may be next is not an exact science, of course; it comes from intellectual awareness, of thinking about changes in technology, in our society, and in the broader world — something you enjoy doing, and that can really pay off. One trend that aware investors spotted was how the fall of communism would benefit such companies as Coca-Cola, PepsiCo, and Gillette that have international brand recognition.

One good way to spot a trend is to listen to the signals sent out by the money management community. Each quarter, *Barron's* prints the Lipper Company's reports on mutual fund transactions. By looking at these transactions, you can get an idea of professional investor sentiment about companies and industry groups. When IBM reported business troubles and an earnings decline in 1991, funds began to unload into a declining market for IBM. By mid-1993, fund sales and purchases balanced out, signaling an end to professional negativism about IBM.

Another route is to be aware of new legislation, since each piece of major legislation creates some business opportunity. The Kennedy administration's space program spurred enormous growth in the aerospace industry in the 1960s, and the Clinton health plan proposals in 1993 drove down the prices of such great drug companies as Merck and Johnson & Johnson, creating wonderful buying opportunities.

• *Be aware of the dangers of "stock talk."* For many power investors, talking about their stocks is one of the great pleasures of investing. You probably don't want to give this up, but you do need to heighten your awareness of the effects. Talk not only gives you social gratification, but also increases your emotional investment and causes you to think even more highly of the stock. I know how powerful this effect can be because it happens to newsletter writers, myself included.

In 1996, as part of an SEC investigation into the possible manipulation of Presstek stock, the agency reviewed the activities of Carlton Lutts, publisher of the *Cabot Market Letter,* whose stories about the small printing company in New Hampshire had helped to make it a "hot stock." Under consideration was the allegation that Mr. Lutts had issued overly rosy earnings predictions. I don't know what Mr. Lutts's intentions were, but I do know how easy it is to get carried away emotionally when writing about a stock — and the effects are even greater when you talk about it. It's okay to chat, but you need to recognize the psychological transaction that is taking place.

• *Avoid putting all of your eggs in the "momentum" basket.* We have seen that power investors are attracted to momentum investing — buying stocks that are rapidly rising because statistics show that they are likely to continue to rise. What attracts momentum investors to these stocks, beyond their recent record of success, is that they are exciting, and since price tells the story, theoretically, no research is needed. Just follow the numbers and plan to sell on those first downward blips.

This strategy is particularly dangerous for a power investor, because you are so attached to your stocks that you hang on even after you spot the blips. *Your emotional style, the same style that attracts you to momentum, may make it difficult for you to move quickly enough to get out in time.* Make sure you also practice other investing styles — growth and value investing, where you don't have to move so quickly to preserve your investment. Or, if you play the momentum game, establish rules for exiting the stock before the market turns sour on it. As I said in chapter 4, you *must* sell the minute the stock drops out of the top 5 percent of performers for its index or industry group. (You can find this information in *Investor's Business Daily.*) Another criterion is to sell the minute the stock fails to meet analysts' expectations.

• *Hold off for at least twenty-four hours before buying a stock.* Just as power investors tend to be slow to sell, they are often quick to buy.

But the more quickly you buy, the more attached to the stock you will be. No matter how excited you are, make yourself wait. With rare exceptions — in potential mergers or speculative deals you should avoid — there is no reason to buy a stock quickly. Take the time to stand back, investigate, and put some emotional distance between you and the stock. Don't let anyone, particularly your broker, pressure you into moving faster.

PORTFOLIO FOR THE POWER INVESTOR

Following is the portfolio I developed for Terri and Richard Blaine, a couple in their midforties, who run a catalog company that sells home-decorating products. They have a net income from their business of $175,000. The Blaines, who married in their late thirties, have a five-year-old son. They are both power investors who love to take "flyers" in the market, but they realized they needed to invest more cautiously in order to provide for their son's private school education, and to meet their five-year plan for expanding the business. Their portfolio is worth $280,000.

Before coming to me, 70 percent of their portfolio was invested in speculative stocks. They decided to limit them to 20 percent. I advised the Blaines to pair their least profitable speculatives and their losing speculatives and sell them off at the same time, to reduce the tax consequences of the sale. The money was reinvested in blue chips.

The goal of restructuring was to continue the Blaines' strong sense of identification with companies, while reducing their speculation.

The portfolio was divided among blue chips, quality growth stocks, and some speculative stocks. Among the stocks were several I recommended, not only because of their good records, but also because they are established "power stocks" in a psychological sense, and power investors find them *almost* as exciting as speculatives.

An established power stock is one already at the top of its field, but which continues to generate excitement. It has image as well as power. In the computer field, Microsoft and Intel are such stocks, in the drug field, Merck, and in food franchising, Coca-Cola.

Again, what follows are not current stock recommendations, which I do not make in this book, but the reasoning employed at the time selections were made.

BLUE CHIP STOCKS: 40 PERCENT

(These selections, with one exception all household names, increased the stability of the Blaines' portfolio.)

Coca-Cola. Soft drink manufacturer. In the soft drink industry, the world's leader, which the Blaines saw as reflecting well on them. Coke's worldwide distribution network, built up over generations, would require billions of dollars for a competitor to duplicate.

IBM. Hardware and software manufacturer. Although it wasn't what it used to be, IBM was still "king of the hill" with an undisputed franchise in mainframe computers.

McDonald's. Food service retailer. The Coca-Cola of fast food. A solid power stock with appeal to a power investor.

ServiceMaster. Professional cleaning services. Cleans hospitals, industrial sites, and homes and through subsidiaries — Terminix, Merry Maids, ChemLawn, American Home Shield, and Furniture Medica — offers lawn services, pest control, and home maintenance. The trend toward working couples would create growth in the service industry, and power investors like to be on top of a trend.

QUALITY GROWTH STOCKS: 40 PERCENT

(Although these stocks are aggressive, they emphasize quality over speculation. They require more careful monitoring than the blue chips, but power investors can learn to enjoy such monitoring.)

Intel. Microprocessors manufacturer. Microprocessors will drive the world of the twenty-first century (an appealing image for power investors), and Intel dominates microchip development and manufacturing. Over the next fifty years, Intel could be to the world economy what General Motors was to the U.S. economy from 1920 to 1970.

Microsoft. Software manufacturer. Absolute king of software, with designs on the satellite communication of data. Headed by the driven genius of Bill Gates, the world's richest man, Microsoft was the power investor's dream.

Circuit City. Electronics and appliances retailer. Rapid growth and sexy products appeal to the power investor, yet the company's real success stemmed from basic retail skills and its excellent reputation for service.

Markel Corporation. Insurance company. This small insurer arrogantly patterns itself after Berkshire Hathaway and might just pull it off. If it does, there will be much emotional gratification for the power investor. Markel family members, who run the business well, have an investment ace in my friend Tom Gayner, who is in charge of investments.

Amgen. Biotechnology company. As the sexiest of the biotech companies, this one has great appeal to the power investor, yet its long-range growth prospects made it viable even for a worrier. (See the portfolio for the "I can't stop worrying" investor, chapter 7.)

SPECULATIVE STOCKS AND FUND: 20 PERCENT

STOCKS:

Cisco Systems. Computer internetworking systems. This high-quality, high-tech company — the major supplier of internetworking products for linking local area (LAN) and wide area networks — gave the Blaines the clout they seek, yet is also an industry leader. However, I emphasized Cisco's speculative nature; its franchise is not immune to competition from a new product.

Hughes Electronics. After GM acquired Hughes Aircraft, this company was for a while known as General Motors "H" stock. It's important in defense electronics, auto parts, and satellite communications — the DIRECTV satellite dish. When I selected this stock for the Blaines, its diversified business buffered the volatility of satellite communications, but a year later the company sold off a few other businesses to become a "pure play" in satellites. This delights Mr. Blaine, who loves inviting friends to watch sports on his DIRECTV satellite dish, but although the stock fuels his "power juices," I wouldn't purchase it for him today.

U.S. Surgical. Surgical staples manufacturer. From 1988 to 1991, a popular growth stock; then business problems and world-class competition from Johnson & Johnson knocked it for a loop, and back into the "speculative" category. When I bought it for the Blaines, business was coming back, and a first-rate management team showed promise of good long-term growth.

FUND:

Robertson Stephens Emerging Growth Fund. (No-load. *Forbes* rating [August 25, 1997]: A for up markets, D for down markets. Five-year annualized total return: 19.42 percent. *Morningstar* rating: one star.) A superb performer in bull markets, a laggard in bear markets, but long-term performance should please the Blaines — as should the amount of "action" generated by this fund.

THE MARKET, POWER, AND SELF-ESTEEM

Everyone who invests is vulnerable to the power appeal of the stock market because, in our culture, money and power are so inextricably linked. If you ask the average American what money means, nine times out of ten he will say that citizens with money can play at being gods and do anything they wish. Money has the power to buy prestige, luxurious living, a "trophy" car, and maybe even a "trophy spouse." Just make a wish, and money appears to grant it.

Since power is exciting and sexy, even conservative investors — people who have always stayed with blue chips, for example — can get drawn in. The investor starts out buying AT&T, goes from Merck to Motorola, then to a stock like Intel, and then jumps into something risky.

Justin Mamis, chief of equity trading at John Hancock, has likened this pattern to a middle-aged man having affairs. He tires of the stocks he's married to, and winds up having a crazy fling, with each purchase becoming ever more dangerous and exciting. When Mamis presented this analogy at the Congress of the Psychology of Investing, he was criticized for being sexist, but I have seen investors of both sexes get seduced by power, just as they get seduced by greed.

The power-money linkage seduces because it raises self-esteem. *The greater our quest for esteem, the more likely we are to become power investors.*

According to the theory of self-psychology proposed by Heinz Kohut, self-esteem relates to the amount of "mirroring" we get from our parents. "Mirroring" is projected by admiring parents who derive pleasure from watching their infant grow and achieve mastery, and reflect the pleasure back to the child. This positive message gets integrated into the sense of self and the child becomes a whole person.

If parents fail to provide an admiring reflection, or if they ignore or denigrate the child, the self fails to achieve cohesion, and the individual suffers keenly from a sense of being incomplete. In Arthur Miller's *Death of a Salesman,* Willy Loman, the tormented salesman, says that he feels "kind of temporary about myself," a succinct description of what it is to lack a strong sense of self.

When we carry this burden, we seek completeness in the pursuit of power and the admiration that it produces. Even though we may be successful, likable, and seemingly self-confident, like Walter Swanson, the surgeon, bubbling beneath the surface there can still be issues of esteem that make us vulnerable.

Power investors are vulnerable to manipulation by others, self-interested brokers, for example, or opportunistic financial advisers, who know how to capitalize on our need to feel good about ourselves.

Brokers are not always good advisers for power investors, but power investors are very good clients for brokers, because they respond to statements like "I've only got five hundred shares of this great new issue, and I'm putting them aside for you," or "Not many people would appreciate how big this company can become, but I know you really understand investing." Notice that the appeal is to our narcissism —

"You're a savvy investor, practically a colleague of mine" — rather than to greed, and so it can be more difficult to recognize as a sales pitch.

Power investors are more vulnerable than others to the growing number of unmonitored "postings" about stocks on internet bulletin boards, because the internet itself appeals to the need to be on the cutting edge. To say to a friend, "I found this wonderful stock while I was surfing the net," elicits admiration and enables you to tell a story, two motivations that you find quite tempting.

There are several things you can do to counter your vulnerability.

Make sure the stock market does not become the main area in your life for building self-esteem. Your reinforcement should come from such other areas as family, work, friendships, and community ties. Don't allow investing to become an emotional substitute for them; stocks can't carry this weight.

For Meredith Johnson, the flower shop owner, her stocks served as compensation for a business career that she regarded as "second best." Because she hadn't met the high expectations she set for herself, Meredith looked for her stocks to do the job, and experienced crippling disappointment when they failed.

As Meredith and I worked together therapeutically, I tried to get her to appreciate her accomplishments — she had a successful business and a loving husband — and to allow herself to gain self-esteem from them, rather than turning to the market.

It is valuable for power investors to broaden their view of the meaning of money. Many people see money as a symbol of status and our society, of course, encourages this. Remember, though, that status is only one of the three basic reasons for our interest in money. The other two are instinct — our fascination with money goes back to infancy — and rationality — we need money in order to survive and be comfortable.

It can help to visualize money as the bedrock of three geological layers — instinct, rationality, and status. If you are like most power investors, when you close your eyes and try to do this exercise, you find that the status layer is prominent and the other layers practically invisible.

Don't worry about instinct; it's always there, whether you see it or not. Your need is to increase the size of the rational layer, to bring it into your consciousness, because this is the layer most critical to successful investing.

Like everyone else, I sometimes fantasize about how a certain investment will gratify my sense of power, will impress the media with my brilliance — but every time I find myself falling into this reverie, I remember that a dollar is for buying a loaf of bread and a stock is a percentage of ownership in a business, not an esteem builder. I try to concentrate on the rational layer of money, because it keeps me in balance.

Investing concerns the rational uses of money, to ensure and increase our physical comfort. When we think of investing in this way, power issues shrink. In the market, the less powerful we try to be, the more successful we can truly become.

CHAPTER 9

The Inheritor

A person who inherits money from a parent, a spouse, or someone else whom they were close to may be surprised by the amount of emotion the money evokes. Grief, confusion, guilt, a sense of distance from the money itself, and helplessness at the thought of managing it are all common reactions. And the less experience one has with money management, the more pronounced the helpless feelings are likely to be.

Wendy Tremaine, a hospital administrator in her midforties, slumped in her chair as she told me her story. Three months earlier, she had inherited $2 million from her widowed mother, most of it in bonds and blue chip stocks.

Wendy had been raised in comfortable circumstances, but no one in the family had ever hinted that she would come into such a large sum of money. Now Wendy was faced with investing decisions she never expected to make, with constant feelings of anxiety, and with jokes from friends who told her that if the money was making her uncomfortable, well, they would gladly take it off her hands.

Wendy said that I must find her emotional reactions very strange, since the inheritor of money is usually regarded as fortunate. I assured her I did not. I work with a great many people who have inherited money, and I know that there can be problems, whether one inherits $3 million or $30,000, though the larger the sum, the greater the likelihood of psychological difficulty.

Until recently, only the rich passed substantial wealth to their children, but today's older middle-class generation has accumulated significant wealth, not only through the inflated value of real estate, but also through participation in the stock market, so more and more middle-class children are becoming inheritors. Researchers at Cornell

University report that over the next forty-five years baby boomers may eventually inherit an estimated $10.4 trillion — the largest amount of money ever passed from one generation to another. Consequently, inheritance-related psychological issues are increasingly important and will be even more pressing in the future.

Many inheritors have absolutely no problems. They accept the money, feel comfortable with it, and are grateful. Clearly this discussion is not for them, but for the others who, like Wendy, find themselves troubled.

I have one client, an academic, who inherited a fortune from his grandfather, a survivor of the Armenian holocaust. When I started working with this man, he could not touch the money at all. "I'm afraid I'm going to break the nest egg," was the phrase he used when I suggested various investment ideas. Yet this client had little difficulty investing his "own" money, so I was sure that the problem was emotional, related to the inheritance.

If you have inherited money, *in any amount,* you can experience this fear of "breaking the nest egg" along with other reactions:

- Not feeling entitled to the money.
- Being embarrassed, perhaps even ashamed, to tell anyone about the money.
- Wishing that someone would take the money off your hands.
- Thinking that the person who left you the money is looking over your shoulder.
- Being resistant to learning how to manage the portfolio.

YOU INHERIT MORE THAN MONEY

The emotion beneath all these reactions is often unconscious guilt. When you inherit money, you also inherit the relationship you had with the legator. If you had an embattled relationship, that conflict attaches itself to the money. It lives through the money.

I have a patient who admits to murderous wishes toward his father, a man he also admires and cares for in many ways. But my patient has financial difficulties, and on a fantasy level, he thinks the problems could be solved if only he could get his hands on his father's money. Were the father actually to die, my patient would experience intense guilt as punishment for his greedy, murderous wishes.

The more ambivalent the relationship you had with the legator, and the more greedily you wanted the money, the more guilty you are likely to feel. Surprisingly, relationships that were either mainly positive or mainly negative evoke far less guilt. Ambivalence creates the strongest feelings, and since ambivalence is common, especially in child-parent relationships, guilt about inheritance is also common.

My client who inherited from his Armenian grandfather had felt close to him, the family patriarch who inspired him in his scholarly pursuits. As the most intellectually gifted of the grandchildren, he was his grandfather's favorite. But my client also was intimidated by his domineering grandfather, and resented his control. He felt that he couldn't measure up to the bravery his grandfather had shown as a mere boy in rescuing his family from the Turks. The fragility he felt in the relationship was reflected in the "fragility" he assigned to the inheritance.

Another cause of guilt is family conflict over an inheritance. If you were left more money than your siblings, or if you feel that you were favored unfairly, you may well develop inhibitions about handling the money.

When I was ready for college, my well-to-do grandmother put a large sum of money into an account in both our names to cover my college and medical school expenses should anything happen to my father, an alcoholic with an erratic income. But she opened no such account for my brother or any of her other grandchildren. As it turned out, my father was able to pay the bills, and after my medical school graduation, my grandmother began to use our joint account for her own living expenses. Upon her death four years later, $600 remained in that account. I found that I simply could not write the final check to close the account, even though I was handling millions of dollars as a money manager and had considerable sums of my own. Finally, I realized that my inhibition was caused by guilt about my special treatment.

People who inherit from a spouse have a different problem. They are usually not as troubled by guilt, because the money was most likely accumulated jointly, and they see their own labor as having contributed to it. Instead, as I will discuss later, their identification of the money with the spouse becomes part of the grieving process.

For other inheritors, the inheritance can engender a sense of shame, because in our society, people are expected to work for their money, and money that is acquired without work has a certain stigma attached to it.

When one inherits a large amount of money — today $2 million or more would certainly qualify as a "large sum" — the shame can be intense. Some inheritors disassociate themselves from the money by adopting an antimaterialistic point of view — "Money isn't the important thing in life. I have more spiritual values. I can't be bothered with it."

They recognize subconsciously that even though money is highly admired in our society, it is also associated with dirtiness. Too much money, money that we didn't earn, is considered to be unclean and embarrassing, and should be covered up. Yankee families with "old money," the Cabots and Lodges, downplay their wealth by decorating their houses and dressing in a deliberately understated manner. Money — particularly lots of money — is taboo, more taboo than sex, as Sigmund Freud pointed out decades ago when sex was taboo also.

Inheritors are often unprepared for the sheer amount of envy they encounter. When Wendy Tremaine's friends told her that they would gladly "take the money off her hands," they were expressing envy, not a desire to be helpful. The "official" position of the culture is that they are fortunate to be members of what Donald Trump called "the lucky sperm club," so they are confused at finding themselves feeling embarrassed and burdened instead.

When inheritors are uninformed about money management and

investing, if they got parental messages earlier on that they weren't "good at handling money," if there are other factors that might cause turbulent feelings, they may feel they should give the money away.

This inheritor thinks, "Why should I have all this money when other people are living in poverty?" and comes up with a solution — "I need to do good with it." He has a strong impulse to give money away, to create a charitable foundation, or to invest only in socially conscious companies or funds.

I tell my clients that if they feel these impulses soon after coming into an inheritance *of any size,* they need to hold off decisions for a while. These impulses are not as altruistic as they might seem on the surface; initially, they are almost always related to guilt and shame.

There is certainly nothing wrong with doing social good with one's money, or with being a socially conscious investor, but you want to make the decision on the basis of personally held values, *not* because you feel an irrational impulse. Almost always, the clue to irrationality is that the amount of money you want to give away is out of proportion — half of your inheritance, for example, or even all of it. The rule is: *Be wary of a need to do good. Concentrate on getting guilt under control.*

A WAY TO DEAL WITH GUILT

Guilt can often be relieved by working at learning about investing and working at managing your portfolio. If you have neither the time nor the interest for this, you need to *work* at finding a manager, as I will explain later in this chapter. Then you have to devote the time and *effort* to understanding the choices the manager is making on your behalf.

The reason I emphasize the words *work* and *effort* is that if you put labor into investing, you assuage some of the guilt over having money you did not labor to acquire. It helps to remember that when you invest, you are investing the fruits of *someone's* labor, generally someone who wanted you to share in them.

Through my grandmother, in addition to the remainder of the joint account she had set up for college costs, I inherited a substantial sum of money that she had inherited from her husband, my grandfather. He had inherited some of this money from his father, but he had also built up, through hard work, wealth of his own invested in the stock market. I knew that my grandmother wanted me and my children, yet unborn, to benefit from the money and to achieve a connection between the generations in a loving manner — a positive way to view inherited money.

Looked at in this way, a primary responsibility of someone who inherits substantial wealth is to conserve the money and pass it along. *Ideally, you want to increase wealth, but conservation must be your major concern, and seeing yourself in a caretaker role can help relieve guilt because you are not acting in your interest alone.*

Like any other investor, you need to assess such factors as your age, marital status, degree of aggressiveness, and your goals. The first use for any inheritance, large or small, should be to pay off credit card and other debt. The inheritance may put you in the fortunate position of being able to meet personal goals — to fund college educations, buy a vacation home, or finance a comfortable retirement. Wendy Tremaine wanted to help her twenty-two-year-old son start a computer services business.

The portfolio we worked out for Wendy's $2 million was based on her need both to be a conservator and to have sufficient income to meet her expenses and help her son. The stock portion of the portfolio she had inherited from her mother was invested in the blue chips of the 1950s. (If Wendy had inherited a portfolio that was all in bonds or cash — not likely, but it happens — I would have told her, as I advised beginning investors with large sums in chapter 3, to make her stock purchases over a three-year period, so that she would not risk committing everything to a falling market.)

Preservation of capital is the guilding principle for inheritors of substance. The first task is safety, the second, maintenance of buying power. These goals are achieved by focusing on quality and by creating a diverse portfolio that protects against bear markets.

AN INHERITOR'S PORTFOLIO

VALUE STOCKS, A VALUE FUND, AND GROWTH STOCKS: 33⅓ PERCENT

VALUE STOCKS:

Chris-Craft Industries. Television broadcasting service. Through its majority interest in BHC Communications, Chris-Craft owns eight TV stations and a very valuable stake in United Paramount Network (UPN). The company's chairman, Herb Siegel, has one of the best track records for media industry investing. At the time Wendy bought the stock, I calculated the stations' market value to be greater than the company's market value, so Wendy bought her interest in the stations at a discount, and got UPN thrown in for free.

Exxon. Oil company. Exxon gave Wendy the prospect of solid, if subdued, growth, along with the likelihood of future dividend increases, making it the best "widows and orphans stock" available.

J. P. Morgan. Banking. An outstanding commercial and investment bank with a rich history and an excellent international franchise. With the growing global economy, J. P. Morgan promised to outperform the banking industry as a whole.

St. Joe Companies. Paper company, diversified into other industries. The darling of value investors because its market price was far below underlying assets. This made St. Joe a good bet both for worriers (see chapter 7) and inheritors, who also need solidity. When Wendy purchased St. Joe at $55 a share, I calculated the value of its real estate holdings at $135, its percentage of Florida East Coast Railroad at $20, its paper business at $24, its sugar business at $4, and other subsidiaries at $8, adding up to a total value of $191 a share. Even if I was wrong in some of my evaluations, St. Joe would still have been very undervalued.

VALUE FUND:

Tweedy-Browne Global Value Fund. (No-load. Not yet rated by *Forbes*. Three-year annualized total return as of August 31, 1997: 14.40 percent. *Morningstar* rating: 5 stars.) Foreign holdings diversify a portfolio, since they do not mirror U.S. market performance, but there are only a handful of countries (other than Canada) where U.S. investors can get enough information to purchase individual stocks intelligently. The best solution is a well-managed international fund. I chose Tweedy-Browne for Wendy because of my admiration for Christopher and Will Browne and their partner, John Spears, all adept value practitioners.

GROWTH STOCKS:

AirTouch Communications. Telecomunications services. AirTouch, created by Pacific Telesis to spin off its cellular communications business, is one of the world's leading wireless telecommunications companies, serving over 3.6 million customers worldwide. Although a growth stock, AirTouch was at the lower end of its historical ranges for P/E and dividend yields when Wendy bought it, making it a good value as well as growth play.

Hewlett-Packard. Hardware and printers. A great growth company, with a unique corporate culture that rewards employees who help to sustain growth.

Intel. Microprocessors manufacturer. The dominant company in what will be the dominant industry for the next twenty-five years. (See the portfolio for the power investor in chapter 8.)

Merck. Drug company. In my opinion, the best managed company in the world, and the world will always need the pharmaceutical industry, making for a potent long-term investment. When Wendy purchased Merck, its price was depressed because of investor worries over the Clintons' proposed health care plan — a good example of opportunity created by market psychology.

BONDS: 33⅓ PERCENT

U.S. Treasury bonds, "laddered" over a ten-year period. (A ladder is a mixture of short-, intermediate-, and long-term bonds. Since the bonds have different maturities, the risk is spread out and the investor achieves a blended yield, greater than short-term bonds alone.) Individual investors are best served by Treasuries, which offer the greatest level of safety and liquidity. High-grade corporate bonds are fairly safe but are relatively illiquid and have substantial "friction" costs, which are the commissions and "bid-ask" spreads (the bid is the highest price a prospective buyer is prepared to pay, the ask is the lowest price acceptable to a prospective seller). The slightly higher yield of corporates is not worth the additional risk. I advise investors to stay away from "junk" bonds (bonds issued by companies that don't have substantial track records of earnings and sales or by those whose credit strength is questionable). It's not worth taking equity level risks for a couple of extra interest points. These bonds aren't called "junk" for nothing. Warren Buffett had it exactly right when he said, "Never buy junk bonds on a day ending in Y."

REAL ESTATE: 33⅓ PERCENT

REITs (Real Estate Investment Trusts):
   New Plan Realty (on New York Stock Exchange)
   Bradley Realty (on New York Stock Exchange)
   Washington Real Estate Investment (on American Stock Exchange)
   or
   a real estate mutual fund, e.g., Cohen & Steers Realty Shares (No-load. Not yet rated by *Forbes.* Three-year annualized total return as of August 25, 1997: 18.3 percent. *Morningstar* rating, 4 stars.)

REAL ESTATE AS AN INVESTMENT

Real estate is particularly appropriate for an inheritor or for any conservative investor because it is strongly defensive. *From the psychological point of view, real estate creates a feeling of solidity and a link between past and present.*

Through the centuries, real estate has been an excellent investment, with returns comparable to the stock market. Like stocks, real estate goes through ups and downs, so it is by no means a sure thing, but if you choose wisely and you can wait, it is a good investment. Will Rogers made the point when he said, "I always like to buy real estate. They aren't making any more of it, you know."

The surest way to make money in real estate is to hold property over a long period, as the person who inherits substantial money is often in a good position to do.

Real estate differs from most other investments because you can borrow up to 80 or 90 percent of the value of the property, so by putting up a small amount of money, 10 to 20 percent, you can purchase a much larger investment. If the value of the property goes up, leverage works for you; but remember, if it goes down, leverage works against you. In your role as an inheritor/conservator, you want to avoid highly leveraged real estate situations where there is a great deal of risk.

One thing that does work for you is that appreciation compounds tax-deferred as long as you own it. If you sell, you can still avoid paying taxes by exchanging your property for a similar type of property — another shopping center, let's say — that is just as valuable or more valuable. And in addition to appreciation, you collect rent, and rent will increase with time and inflation.

If you haven't the inclination or the time to find your own properties, you can invest in real estate through limited partnerships. Locate real estate professionals in your area who put partnerships together and have a good track record. What you're looking for is a situation in which there is modest leveraging and no sales commissions. As a limited partner, you want to get a return on the same level as that of the general partners, who develop the deal but generally put in less or no capital. Avoid limited partnerships that are sponsored by brokerage firms, because they charge substantial up-front fees and commissions and, often, are structured to give the general partner a disproportionate share of the capital gains.

An easier way to invest in real estate is to purchase shares in REITs (real estate investment trusts) that invest in different kinds of real estate — apartment buildings, commercial buildings, shopping centers, and health care facilities. REIT managers purchase the properties and handle the management. Over the past twenty years, REITs have produced annual compound returns as high as 19 percent. REITs trade as securities on the stock exchanges and, unlike limited partnerships, are liquid. To find out about a REIT's record, look at *Value Line* or *Standard & Poor's*. The REITs I recommended for Wendy's portfolio are companies that I have owned.

There are also real estate mutual funds which own REITs or real estate development companies and offer excellent exposure to the real estate market. In 1997, funds with good three-year records, as reported in the *Forbes* magazine mutual fund survey, were CGM Realty (23.2 percent, no-load), Cohen & Steers Realty Shares (18.3 percent, no-load), Columbia Real Estate Equity (20.6 percent, no-load), and Fidelity Real Estate Investment (17.1 percent, no-load).

THE SOCIALLY CONSCIOUS APPROACH TO INVESTING

Inheritors sometimes want to make socially conscious investments. But any investor who is socially oriented might consider that course. As I suggested earlier, you should decide on the basis of principle, not guilt-inspired impulse, and approach the decision with a degree of flexibility.

I once had a client who didn't want to buy any stocks that were related to tobacco, alcohol, gambling, weapons, nuclear power, support of foreign dictatorships, or animal testing of cosmetics and drug products. She did want to invest in companies that were friendly to the environment, had good labor relations and affirmative action programs, promoted women equally, and did not discriminate against gays.

If you are looking for total "purity," which usually reflects a very strong subconscious desire to "clean up" your money, you must realize that you are not likely to meet your goals completely, because there are gray areas in the social records of most companies, including companies that are ethical and well managed. It's easier to avoid the "bad" than to seek only the "good." Identifying the devils is a simpler task than finding the angels.

There are thirty-three "socially responsible" mutual funds (less than one-half of one percent of mutual funds) that won't invest in such industries as tobacco, alcoholic beverages, and gambling, and which seek out socially responsible companies. You can add some of these funds to your portfolio, bearing in mind that the record of returns of the "socially responsible" sector has not been outstanding. According to an article in *Mutual Funds* magazine, no socially responsible equity fund has topped the S&P 500 over the past ten years and only one has in the last three and five years. In addition, many of these funds have substantial loads and expenses.

There is a price for being socially conscious, and you should take that into consideration. If you find that you *want* to pay and think you *should* pay *a lot* extra for doing good, you haven't dealt with the issue of your guilt.

Here are six socially conscious funds, selected by *Forbes* magazine in 1996, and having no sales commission and expenses of no more than 1.9 percent. With three-year annualized total returns updated as of 1997, they are Aquinas-Equity Growth (23.4 percent), Citizens-Emerging Growth (22.2 percent), Domini Social Equity (27.5 percent), N&B Socially Responsible Fund (24.0 percent), Parnassus Income-Balanced (16.6 percent), and Pax World Fund (17.91 percent).

To create a socially conscious portfolio, you can combine these funds with companies that are both ethical and well run. Some companies that I believe meet these criteria are ServiceMaster, Berkshire Hathaway, Johnson & Johnson, Ben & Jerry's Ice Cream, and Energy Conversion Devices.

There are several other ways to be socially conscious. You can set up a charitable trust, with the help of an attorney who specializes in these matters. You can donate regularly to charities that reflect your values, a surer path to furthering your goals than socially conscious investing.

If you continue to be uncomfortable about your money, there are a number of self-help groups for people who have inherited substantial wealth and are experiencing difficulties. Working with a group can be psychologically useful, because an inheritor can often feel isolated even from old friends and family members. A support group is a good way to connect to people who are in the same situation. One such group is The Impact Project, 2244 Alder Street, Eugene, OR 97405, (541) 343-2420. The Project publishes a newsletter, "More than Money."

LOYALTY AND AN INHERITANCE

Another emotional issue for inheritors is their reluctance to alter an existing portfolio; or, if the money was left in cash, reluctance even to think about investing. A spouse, in particular, is likely to view changes of any sort as disloyalty to the deceased partner. The emotional message is: *The way things were left is the way they ought to be.* This stems from normal grieving, in which denial is an important coping mechanism. The survivor acts "as if" the spouse were still alive.

Adam Smith, in his book *The Money Game,* called enshrining the portfolio "IBM as religion," and tells the story of the husband who instructs his family, "Whatever you do after I die, never sell the IBM." The family is forever loyal to IBM and to every other stock in the husband's portfolio and the portfolio becomes engraved in stone, an extremely poor idea because inevitably circumstances change.

Sometimes a spouse will say to me, "Let's leave the portfolio alone. After all, everything is in blue chips." But blue chips are not necessarily blue chips forever. When Charles Dow created the Industrial Average in 1896, it consisted of a dozen stocks. Of that original dozen, only one, General Electric Corporation, is in the average today. The others were absorbed by other companies, went out of business, or became less important because their industries became less significant to the economy. Railroads and steel were the backbone of the nation's economy at the turn of the twentieth century, but at the turn of the twenty-first, they have only minor significance.

Not only spouses are loyal to the stocks they inherited. I have a friend and client whose father, a vice president of a blue chip company, left him a portfolio, 90 percent of which was in that company's stock. This client needs to diversify, but the thought of selling so much as one share of Dad's company is too painful to consider. "The company was good to my father," he says, "and I'm not going to turn my back on it."

Children may be loyal, but generally spouses are even more so, particularly if they did not participate in the building of the portfolio and aren't knowledgeable about investing. *By holding on to a partner's choices, a spouse attempts to hold on to the person, delaying completion of the grieving process.*

If you are reluctant to change a portfolio, you need to consider the emotional factors that may be holding you back — denial, loyalty, lack of confidence in your ability, an understandable desire to keep your spouse or parent with you, and even fear at the thought of surpassing a parent or spouse. Some children who inherit money aim to "show" their deceased parents that they can do better. Others believe they can never do as well and will be punished if they try. Spouses sometimes try to keep investment results the same, since they feel that to surpass a partner is to express a lack of love.

A forty-eight-year-old widower became my client after the death of his wife, who was the family money manager. One day he telephoned to ask why his taxes were so high for 1995. I explained that it had been a banner year and that he had made 45 percent on his money. There was a moment's silence, and then he chided me gently, saying, "Well, 12 percent was good enough for Anna." It was funny, but I knew he would rather have Anna with her 12 percent than me with all I had done for him.

An inheritor must remember that there can be severe financial consequences from wanting to keep a portfolio or its results the way they were. If you want to preserve and increase wealth and pass it along to your heirs, you cannot afford to practice "IBM as religion."

I have worked with a great many families, and have experienced their sadness at selling stocks that the deceased selected. I know it can be like packing the deceased's clothing up for Goodwill — an acknowledgment of loss and of a significant life change.

But portfolios often need to be restructured to adjust to the inheritor's new status, goals, and income. With the death of a spouse, alterations are called for, because there are new practical and psychological requirements: the practical requirement for greater investment income because there are no longer two salaries in the family; the emotional requirement to maintain or increase the feeling of security. The two don't always jibe, but they can be managed. Let's see how, by looking at three spouses, their portfolios before and after their partners' deaths, and the psychological as well as financial reasoning that took place.

1. MYRA CATANIA

Myra, forty-five years old, is a freelance graphic designer. Her husband, Evan, a magazine art director, died in an accident at age fifty. The Catanias had no children. Myra's goal was to maintain her lifestyle and save toward a comfortable retirement. Before Evan's death, the Catanias had an income of $110,000 a year, which included Evan's salary of $70,000 and Myra's income of $40,000 from freelance work. They had assets of $200,000, excluding their primary residence. Myra's income level was variable, but she thought she would need $24,000 a year from investments in order to be secure and make up for the loss of Evan's salary. Evan left $200,000 in life insurance. Before his death, the Catanias' holdings were $30,000 in cash; $40,000 in CDs; $90,000 in stocks, divided approximately equally among IBM, New England Electric Company, Digital Equipment, Polaroid, Merck, Mobil, Microsoft, Intel, Netscape, and America Online; and a $100,000 condo on Cape Cod with a $60,000 mortgage and $40,000 in equity.

The restructured portfolio invests Myra's $400,000 to yield 6.7 percent, giving her the additional $24,000 she will need in annual income. Forty thousand dollars is invested in each of three corporate preferred stocks, which collectively yield 8.4 percent. Twenty-eight thousand dollars is in each of eight common stocks and two REITs, which collectively yield 4.91 percent. The common stocks are all of high quality and have a history of consistent dividend increases outpacing inflation. *The central theme of the portfolio is balance: not only creating the income Myra needs, but also providing emotional stability.*

Myra's restructured portfolio:

Corporate preferred stocks: 30 percent

Chase Manhattan pf A

MCI quips cap

Morgan Stanley 8.20 percent

Stocks: 60 percent

Alltel — telephone and information services

Duke Power — utility company

Oklahoma Gas & Electric — utility company

Exxon — oil company

Mobil — oil company

Mid Ocean Ltd. — property catastrophe insurance

National Presto — appliances manufacturer

General Mills — cereal maker

Real estate: 10 percent

New Plan Realty (REIT, on New York Stock Exchange)

Washington Real Estate Investment (REIT, on American Stock Exchange)

Myra could have invested her $400,000 in one or more mutual funds, with the emphasis on balanced funds. Although not all the following are balanced funds, good selections for Myra would have been Vanguard Wellington (No-load. *Forbes* rating [August 25, 1997]: A in up markets, C in down markets. Five-year annualized total return: 15.83 percent; ten-year: 12.04 percent. *Morningstar* rating: 4 stars); Fidelity Equity Income II (No-load. Not yet rated by *Forbes*. Five-year annualized total return as of August 31, 1997: 18.46 percent. *Morningstar* rating: 4 stars); Fidelity Puritan (No-load. *Forbes* rating [August 25, 1997]: B for both up and down markets. Five-year annualized total return: 15.96 percent; ten-year: 12.25 percent. *Morningstar* rating: 4 stars); AIM Balanced (Load. *Forbes* rating [August 25, 1997]: A+ in up markets, D in down markets. Five-year annualized total return: 18.32 percent; ten-year: 11.73 percent. *Morningstar* rating: 3 stars); and IAI Growth & Income (No-load. *Forbes* rating [August 25, 1997]: D in up markets, B in down markets. Three-year annualized total return: 21.7 percent).

None of these funds would have provided Myra with all the income she needs, and she would have had to dip regularly into capital gains. John Templeton and many other professional managers advocate a strategy in which both income (dividends) and a portion of capital gains are used for living expenses. Over the last century, this strategy would have worked for Myra unless she had started in 1927–1929 or 1970–1972.

2. TOBY WINTERS

Toby, forty-four years old, is a former teacher and the mother of two young children, ages seven and twelve. Her husband, Carl, a lawyer friend of mine, died suddenly of a heart attack. Toby's goals were to stay in their home, to provide for her children's college educations, to maintain the couple's beach house, and to leave an estate for her children. She did not want to take a job immediately, but in four years, when the children were older, she planned to return to teaching or to open a small business.

Before Carl's death, the Winterses had an income of $175,000 a year and $100,000 in U.S. Treasury bills. Fortunately, Carl left $700,000 in life insurance. Toby believed she could maintain a comfortable lifestyle if she could achieve an annual income of $82,000 from her $800,000.

Toby's friends advised her to put all her money in U.S. Treasury bonds, since she needed income she could count on. But at that time, fall 1993, long-term bonds were yielding just under 7 percent, so the bonds would have produced $56,000 annually — $26,000 shy of Toby's goal.

Toby had to make choices, balancing her need to feel secure against her confidence in the future. She decided to take more risk and to put the money into mutual funds instead of Treasuries, since she is basically an optimistic person and optimism and the ability to take risk are related.

The plan was to develop a portfolio from which Toby would withdraw $82,000 annually.

We began by investing $400,000 divided equally among three mutual funds: Mutual Series Qualified; Lexington Corporate Leaders Trust;

and Third Avenue Value Fund. We put $200,000 into one-year T-bonds and $200,000 into two-year T-bonds. As the bonds matured, they were invested among the three funds with the addition of a fourth fund, Guardian Park Avenue.

As it turned out, Toby would have fared better had we immediately committed the entire $800,000 to the market, but hindsight is always twenty-twenty. By investing the money incrementally, we avoided risking the entire amount to a down market, which can be psychologically devastating.

With this portfolio, Toby has maintained her standard of living by selling equal dollar amounts of shares of the mutual funds and drawing dividends from the T-bonds as they came due. As the market rose steadily from 1994 to 1996, the net asset value of the portfolio, despite the annual drawdown, managed to grow to $1.2 million by the end of 1996.

When Toby returns to work part time, earning another $20,000 or so annually, she can begin to build the growth stock portfolio that interests her. For the present, however, her conservative fund portfolio, while restricting Toby a bit more than she might like, gives her the long-term emotional security she needs.

3. BOB JENKINS

Bob is a fifty-five-year-old civil engineer whose wife, Sandra, an accountant, died of breast cancer. Sandra's first husband, Edgar, left her a substantial portfolio, which she managed successfully. Sandra left all of her assets, $350,000, to Bob, who earned a salary of $70,000 a year. He wanted to take early retirement, which would give him a pension of $35,000 a year, and supplement his pension with money from investments. His goal was to buy a boat and to travel. Sandra did not leave any insurance.

Sandra's portfolio before her death consisted of long-term U.S. Treasury bonds (maturing in 2012), and a large number of stocks, including AIG, Merck, Johnson & Johnson, IBM, Motorola, Honda Motors, Barrick Gold, AT&T, Aetna Life & Casualty, Heinz, Hershey, Philip Morris, Polaroid, Sears, MCI, Caterpillar, and Viacom.

Sandra had done a first-rate job of stock picking. Her results were so good that Bob was awed by them, feeling he couldn't match her ability. And missing Sandra, he found the thought of selling "her" stocks disloyal.

I encouraged him to review the portfolio with me, because I wanted to demonstrate to him, psychologically, that circumstances change with companies as they do with human beings. I encouraged him to do more selling than I normally do. Among the sales, we decided that IBM's heyday might have passed, and sold it. We sold Honda because we thought the end of a market cycle that favored automobile manufacturers was in sight. We sold Aetna because I believed that Markel would be a better insurance bet. Polaroid and Sears were sold because they were "tired franchises." We sold half the Caterpillar shares because they constituted more than 10 percent of the portfolio, which needed to be gotten back into balance. We debated selling Philip Morris (Bob is a smoker) and, after some indecision, decided to keep it.

At that time, the oils were underpriced and I suggested he buy Royal Dutch Petroleum and Exxon, as the bluest of the blue chips, plus Texaco, which is more highly leveraged and was apt to be the biggest gainer from the higher oil prices I expected. (All three oils turned out very well.)

We added three banks — the blue chips J. P. Morgan and Barnett Banks, plus Corus Bankshares, a well-managed, medium-size bank in the Chicago area — and also two companies that are long-term favorites of mine, Berkshire Hathaway and United Asset Management.

Being involved in the decision making showed Bob that he could make sound judgments and that he was capable of altering the portfolio. After our initial work together, he developed an interest in investing, and at his insistence, we bought Amgen, even though I thought it was overpriced at the time.

I suggested that he research companies in his "circle of competence" as an engineer. I suggested California Energy, Duke Power, and Stone & Webster. He decided to add all three to the restructured portfolio.

Bob's restructured portfolio:
Stocks: 70 percent
AIG — insurance Company
Amgen — biotechnology company
AT&T — telephone, wireless communications
Barnett Banks — bank, financial services
Barrick Gold — gold mining
Berkshire Hathaway B — holding company
California Energy — utility, power plants
Caterpillar — earth-moving equipment manufacturer
Corus Bankshares — bank
Duke Power — utility
Exxon — oil company
Johnson & Johnson — drug company
Markel Corporation — insurance
MCI — telephone, wireless communications
Merck — drug company
J. P. Morgan — bank
Motorola — wireless communications
Philip Morris — tobacco/food company
Royal Dutch Petroleum — oil company
Stone & Webster — management consulting
Texaco — oil company
United Asset Management — holding company of investment firms
Bonds: 30 percent
Long-term U.S. Treasury bonds (2012 maturity)

Bob's stocks, bond interest, and early retirement provide him with income of $55,000 a year, which is ample since he has no mortgage to pay and few expenses other than his boat. Bob might have opted for a higher-income-producing portfolio, but at fifty-five he needs a long-term outlook, and considers growth of principal more important than current income.

I think Bob's portfolio contains too many companies for an individual to follow, but he disagrees. He likes the diversification, and he wants to emulate Sandra, who in my opinion also owned too many stocks. I've decided it's best psychologically to leave the issue of numbers alone.

Most important is that Bob is enjoying retirement and now has a fifty-two-year-old widow as a "significant other," who loves sailing, too. On land, Bob enjoys following his investments, and makes a point of attending the annual meetings of a number of his companies.

WORKING WITH A MONEY MANAGER

As you can see, restructuring a portfolio can be a new beginning, both financially and emotionally. But inheritors who are not experienced at money management, or have no interest in it, hesitate to take on the job themselves, at least at the beginning.

If you feel reluctant and have inherited a substantial amount of money, you may be best off finding a good money manager. You should look for an independent financial adviser who gets a fee for services, rather than a sales commission, as brokers do. You can work successfully with brokers, and many brokers are good, but when you are taking on investing responsibilities for the first time, choose someone who has no conflict between his interests and your own.

Since a manager can be very important to you emotionally, you need to be aware of both psychological and financial issues. Let's consider the practical issues first. There are currently more than 21,000 firms registered as investment advisers with the Securities and Exchange Commission. The quality of these advisers varies widely; as yet, there are no uniform standards.

A money manager should meet the following qualifications:
- Have at least a six-year track record available to you in writing.
- Be registered with the Securities and Exchange Commission and show you copies of the required forms that were filed.
- Be licensed in the state where he or she practices, if licensing is required.
- Be willing to provide references.

Ask the manager about the various services available. One method is to work with you to prepare a financial and investing plan, review it with you at intervals, and update the plan as needed. You do the investing yourself. Usually, you pay a flat fee or an hourly fee for this planning.

Another option is total management of the portfolio, making all of the investment decisions, and taking a percentage of the portfolio as a fee. This fee is negotiable, but typically it is 1.0 to 1.5 percent for the first $1 million, 0.75 percent up to $3 million, and 0.5 percent or less above $3 million.

In addition to fees and services, you should discuss the investment style the manager favors — value, growth, or a combination of the two.

You are looking for someone who will be a good psychological fit *for you*, who projects empathy, warmth, and dependability. These qualities are more important than finding "a star," i.e., the lead manager at a billion-dollar firm.

Pay close attention to the emotional vibrations you feel during the interview. The manager should be listening to your concerns and talking about your goals, rather than trying to impress you. You want someone who is open and willing to do some hand-holding, because, at least at the beginning, you may need it.

Accessibility is a central psychological issue. Ask how often the manager plans to meet with you, when he is available by telephone, and whether your calls will be answered promptly. Some managers have special hours for telephone consultations, as some doctors do.

If you feel a need for reassurance, make this clear. An empathetic manager will be willing to meet with you more often at first — every few months, perhaps — and will assure you that your questions will be answered.

Make certain that the person you are interviewing is the person with whom you will have the relationship. If you hear something like "I'll be managing your account, and I'll meet with you once a year, but in between, Ms. Brown will be your liaison," that may work out, but first you have to meet Ms. Brown and make certain you're comfortable with her. If you get the sense that you are going to get shunted aside, look elsewhere. At this point in your emotional life, you should not have to endure the feeling of being abandoned.

If the parent or spouse who left you the money was already using a money manager, you will probably continue with that person. While he may be appropriate, you should evaluate that manager as you would a new one. You, and not the legator, are going to be working with the manager, and you have to test for a good fit.

If you find that you would rather use someone else, be frank about it. Sometimes an inheritor is inhibited about making a change, not wanting to hurt the manager or be disloyal to the loved one who chose him, and thus feels trapped and uncomfortable. The psychological mechanism for not wanting to change is projection of the bereaved's feelings of abandonment onto the adviser. This feeling needs to be recognized and dealt with.

A few years ago, I began to work with a recently widowed woman whose deceased husband had been with another manager for twenty-five years. This manager had not done a very good job. He had lost money for the couple during a very strong market, yet the woman told me that she found it very hard to sit down and write a "farewell letter." If you feel that way, remember you have to do what's best for you and not for the manager — and managers are usually professional enough not to take such matters personally.

The opposite of switching managers is to become dependent on the current manager — in psychiatric terms, to make an immediate "transference" — from the parent or spouse to the manager. While it can be positive to depend on someone, it's destructive to become *so* dependent that the inheritor feels no need to be aware of what the manager is doing.

At a dinner party, I met a young man, a writer, who told me that the money his father left him was being managed by a "wonderful" adviser, the same woman who had handled the father's investments when he was alive. When I asked what investing style the manager favored, the writer smiled. "I don't know; we meet for lunch once a year,

I tell her how much money I need, and she comes up with it for me."
Perhaps the money he needed was coming out of capital, perhaps it
wasn't, but the writer never asked.

I could tell this man was frightened by responsibility for the money
and was handing it over to somebody else completely. Such an attitude
can turn out to be very dangerous and financially costly as well.

No matter how much you want a manager to take charge, a responsible manager will always insist that your understanding of his or her
investment decisions is a crucial part of the management process.

THE "WINDFALL" INHERITOR

People who inherit smaller amounts of money — from $10,000 to
$50,000 — can have problems similar to those who inherit large
amounts of money — guilt, family conflict, and inhibition — but in
one way, the emotional response is different.

This inheritor regards the money as a "windfall" — a one-time-
only affair, like winning the lottery — and is inclined to devote it to a
single use, a form of mental accounting I call "sequestering." The
thought is "The money that Dad left ought to go for something special,"
and the family will use it for a down payment on a house, for a car,
for a terrific vacation, or some other goal — *but for one thing only.*

The psychological reason for sequestering is to memorialize the person, to make the money more important than it would be if it got spread
out over a series of investments. *Just as money lost is more valuable than
money gained, the emotional principle is that inherited money kept separate is more substantial than inherited money that gets mixed in with other
funds.*

Unfortunately, sequestering avoids using the money for "non-
memorializing" projects, such as paying off credit card or other debt.

"Windfall" inheritors also avoid investing altogether because they
fear they will be told to diversify (the standard advice for new investors).
If they put the money in a bank, it won't be thought too strange if they
open a separate account for it. Not investing is a great loss, because

one of the best ways to memorialize someone you love is to make the money grow and become more useful.

For a long time, I was puzzled by sequestering and wondered, "Is this good or bad?" but now if I see it's emotionally important to a client, I suggest ways of investing the money so it can be kept separate. One way is to put the money in a specialized fund that invests in only one sector of the economy, such as natural resources. If the person who left the money worked in a special area, health for example, you might invest in a fund in the health care industry.

The Granger family made a "sequestered" decision about $30,000 they inherited from Tom Granger's father, using it to support both their goals and a special dream. Tom, forty-two years old, is an automotive engineer; Evelyn Granger, thirty-nine years old, is an administrative assistant. The Grangers have two teenage children, and a joint income of $85,000 a year. Before the inheritance, they already had $50,000 in five different mutual funds, earmarked for college expenses.

Tom wanted to use the windfall to make a down payment on a vacation property he had long coveted in New Hampshire, a dream inherited from his father, who had a similar longing. However, Tom felt the college funds might be insufficient, so he chose to put the entire $30,000 into a single fund — Fidelity Contrafund — sequestered for the *ultimate* purpose of the New Hampshire property, but only after college funds were secure.

BEFORE MONEY IS INHERITED

Many of the difficulties I've discussed in this chapter can be avoided if the person who is going to leave the money discusses it with the heirs beforehand. This primary responsibility of a legator all too often is not carried out, as in Wendy Tremaine's case. Even extremely large amounts of money can come as a surprise to an inheritor, because the subject of the inheritance was a closed one.

For couples, the ideal is to share decision making about investing and other major issues as well. And increasingly, among younger and middle-aged couples, that is the case. But in a marriage, one spouse is often more skilled at handling money or investing than the other, and that person tends to take over the investing decisions. When this happens, "the major money person" must keep the spouse informed about what decisions are being made, the assets invested, where important papers are located, the name and phone number of the broker or money manager, and other pertinent information. The couple should talk about the adjustments that might have to be made in lifestyle *and* in the portfolio when one of them dies, so that the paralyzing message "This portfolio is engraved in stone" is not transmitted.

I know it can be difficult to talk about these matters. Even in this enlightened time, when I lecture to groups on investing and estate planning, I am sometimes met with resentment. Remember: Planning ahead, and talking about those plans, is one of the most loving things a couple can do.

I believe that adult children should always have a clear idea of parental assets, how they will be divided, and — most important, if there are going to be perceived inequities — *why*. Some parents decide to leave a greater amount of money to a child who will never have the earning capacity of the others, as is often true of special needs children. Although it's likely that siblings will understand, it's better to air suppressed resentments in order to prevent future guilty feelings.

Unfortunately, parents hesitate to talk about estate planning issues with their children, either because they don't want to give up control or they fear they will create conflicts. But conflicts are more likely to arise from *lack* of discussion.

In the Boston area where I live, it is customary in Irish families for one of the daughters to take care of her aging parents, sometimes remaining in the parental home to do so. In return for her sacrifice, the "understanding" is that she will be left the house in addition to her share of investments or other money. Unhappily, the "understanding" isn't always understood, and often ill feelings develop after the parents die.

Finally, though, the most important "estate planning" parents can do is to raise children who have an understanding of the practical meanings of money. When I first meet with new clients, I usually ask questions about childhood experiences. Did you have an after-school job? Did you put money in a savings account? Were you expected to save for major items you wanted to buy? Did you contribute to the household in some way?

If I get affirmative answers, I know my new client has a good chance of becoming a successful investor, someone who is likely to be realistic about money and not attach fantasy expectations to it.

ARE WE HAPPY YET?

Realists tend to be successful inheritors because they avoid the fantasy that can accompany a large inheritance — "This money is going to buy me happiness."

Certainly, money is important. Clearly I believe it is important or I wouldn't devote so much of my attention to it. Money enables us to meet and go beyond basic needs, creating options for ourselves and our families. Money is empowering and also, frankly, is one of the ways in our society we keep score of an individual's accomplishment. But happiness is another matter. Although in our fantasies we link material wealth and happiness, an actual relationship between the two has never been established. And the amount of money that's required to produce happiness is also elusive.

Harper's magazine editor Lewis Lapham, himself born into an oil fortune, asked people how much money they would need to be happy. Most said they needed twice the amount of money they presently had, whether that amount was $15,000 or $1 million. Other studies show that people believe they need about 20 percent more. Happiness always seems to require more money than we've got, and that stems from the nature of greed itself, which, as I wrote in chapter 5, cannot be satisfied psychologically.

In regular surveys by the National Opinion Research Center of the University of Chicago, the same number of Americans report that they are "very happy" as in 1957. The "very happy" share of the population has remained at one-third since the mid-1950s, though both gross national product and personal consumption expenditure per capita have doubled, even when adjusted for inflation.

An old saying goes "Beware of getting what you wished for." Because I am sometimes known as "the money doctor," I have attracted a number of patients who have won the Massachusetts lottery, and so I believe I have gained more insight into the psychological impact of having one's money wishes suddenly granted than most therapists.

All these winners were, of course, thrilled to have the money, but soon afterward, problems set in, like those experienced by inheritors but more severe. Friends and relatives either became distant or expected more of the money if it was shared with them, or demanded a share if it was not. Bitter family disputes became unavoidable. And the changes in status could be disconcerting and painful. One family found that their old neighbors avoided them. Another bought an expensive house in an expensive neighborhood and found that their new neighbors did not accept them.

The common denominator was that the money did not produce the happiness they expected. This "betrayal" was at the heart of their emotional distress. If you have emotional problems that you thought would be "cured" by money, and the money doesn't do the job, it only makes the problems all the more painful.

Therefore, I always warn clients, and inheritors in particular, against strongly linking money and investment success with happiness. Inheriting money can be wonderful; making money investing can be wonderful. But they are not a guarantee of happiness. The basic elements that create happiness — love, self-esteem, fulfillment through work, close relationships — can be nurtured by money, but they do not stem from it. For these things, the true "fortunes" in our lives, we need to look elsewhere.

CHAPTER 10

The Impulsive Investor

In the past two decades, we've learned to trust our feelings more and more, and release of emotions has become a guiding star for many people. Compared to the time when repression of feelings was the norm, we are certainly better off. Being expressive can be valuable in many areas of life — in love and friendship. But for the investor, feelings can be extremely hazardous. All too frequently, they block intellectual analysis.

Impulsives are people who are intimately in touch with their emotions. They tend to lead with their feelings in all aspects of their lives. As investors, they'll buy a stock because something about it resonates emotionally. They connect and they buy.

Often, impulsives make the right choice because they have a keen instinct for spotting what's going to be successful. But over the long term, that instinct is not accurate enough to bear the entire weight of decision making.

Instinct and image tend to be highly linked. People who are impulsives find image *very* appealing. They are particularly attracted to companies that appear glamorous because of their sleek advertising or because they are in the news.

The impulsive style of investing is on the increase and there are two basic reasons for this: the prolonged bull market of the 1980s and 1990s, which has attracted people of all personality types to the market, and the explosion of media information about the business community and investing.

Although the information is intended to inform, it also incites greed and contributes to the creation of image. Image was once reserved for movie stars and sports heroes, but it now includes top business "personalities," their skyrocketing salaries and dazzling compensation packages. Even mutual funds capitalize on this trend by marketing such superstars as Peter Lynch. Impulsives are drawn to celebrities, and since the business world now boasts many celebrities, it follows that a growing number of impulsives are attracted to investing.

NAVIGATING BY EMOTION

Impulsives fall in "love at first sight," and when they do, they idealize the people they love and are intensely loyal to them. But if the lover disappoints them, the impulsive may break off the relationship because he or she feels so deeply hurt. Impulsives are devoted to their work, put in lots of effort, and are strongly attached to the company. But if they start to feel unappreciated or pushed aside, they may leave because the idealized image of the employer crumbles.

I have a patient who left a job he often told me was "wonderful," because his supervisor turned down his request for two extra vacation days. "She owed it to me," he said, "after all I've done for the company and all the extra time I've put in." I knew that my patient had an exaggerated view of how "wonderful" his company was and, most likely, his sense of betrayal was equally exaggerated.

Impulsive investors act the same way because they tend to idealize their stocks and that exposes them to extreme disappointment.

THE IMPULSIVE AS INVESTOR

Olivia Pierson fit the pattern of the impulsive investor.

Olivia, an attractive forty-two-year-old single mother of two young children, was a buyer for a Boston lighting store and had an income of $54,000. She told me she'd started investing two years earlier, when she got a divorce settlement of $200,000 from her second husband, the father of her younger son. The settlement required the sale of the family's house.

The second husband paid child support, but only for his child. Olivia provided the entire support for her older son, Tom. His father, her first husband, was a "deadbeat dad," a would-be writer with no steady income. "He's an absolute, total disaster," she confided, "I don't know what I could have seen in him."

Olivia's investment goal was to create a college fund for Tom and to save enough money to buy another house that would be "even better" than the house that circumstances had forced them to give up.

She and her second husband had bought the original house one day when they were out for a drive and saw the "for sale" sign. They stopped the car, went through the house, and put a down payment on it right away. "I had to have the house," Olivia recalled. "I saw that it was just right for us, even though we hadn't quite figured out how we could afford it."

The house *was* too expensive, and making the payments was a financial stretch, but it was the fulfillment of a dream, since Olivia had grown up poor. "Ever since I was little I've wanted nice things," she told me, "and when I see something that's going to be right for me — I know it."

Olivia had picked stocks the same way. One Saturday while shopping in a mall, she went into an Ann Taylor store, tried on a few things, and decided that the fashions were "wonderful." On Monday, she called her broker and bought Ann Taylor stock. She'd bought the Bombay Company because she liked the furniture she saw in the catalog.

On Bombay, Olivia turned out to be right; on Ann Taylor she was not so lucky: The company experienced management problems and the stock went down by more than 50 percent.

A typical impulsive, Olivia was buying far too many stocks and selling them far too quickly. When I looked over her portfolio, I found that it consisted of twenty-two stocks, including Microsoft, Netscape, Cisco Systems, and America Online. Over the past year, she had sold ten stocks. Her portfolio also lacked diversification — almost all of the stocks were concentrated in two areas, retailing and computers.

Worse than the concentration, which exposes one to risk, the rapid turnover was the absolute killer in Olivia's portfolio, since brokerage fees and taxes on gains eat away short-term profits. Moreover, on dips Olivia had sold several stocks which later recovered. She bought Genzyme at a split-adjusted price of 24, sold it at 18, and on the day of our consultation, the stock was at 39.

Olivia's portfolio had a total annualized return over two years of 8 percent — at a time when the return on the S&P 500 was over 22 percent. My estimate was that Olivia could have done about as well as the S&P 500, if she had simply hung on to every stock she had bought.

Olivia came to see me because she thought she needed help choosing companies that would perform "better." Actually, what she needed was to slow down, buy less, and hold on longer, because her impulsive style was reducing profits. If the market had been less good, her style would have produced substantial losses.

I told Olivia that unless she was willing to make changes in her approach, she would neither be able to fund her son's college education nor afford another house that met her standards. *The impulsive approach to investing, though it feels exciting, always turns out to be disappointing because there is not enough analysis to create stability. By centering so completely on the feelings of the moment, the style virtually forecloses long-term gains.*

The impulsive investor is not aware of the mechanisms at work. All the person knows is that there is an alternation — sometimes rapid — of enjoyment and disappointment. If this is the pattern you experience, you need to think about whether you may be an impulsive investor.

ARE FEELINGS PARAMOUNT WITH YOU?

If you are highly influenced by feelings, you probably know it. Perhaps you've been told that you "wear your heart on your sleeve"; perhaps you've been hurt a lot in love and job relationships. You frequently may be disappointed by the people close to you, since you idealize them and expect a great deal of them. You may have a history of "falling in love" at first sight and regretting it later on.

What you may not realize is that you can be expending the same sort of intense emotional energy on your stocks.

Ask yourself these questions:

- Do you ever buy stocks because you have a "feeling" they will do well?
- Have you ever bought a stock because something undefinable about the company excited you?
- Do you occasionally find yourself buying a stock because it simply came up in conversation with someone you admire?
- Are you inclined to buy on "tips" from people who are close to you?
- Do you often sell a stock *as soon as* it experiences a dip?
- Have you ever sold a stock because you didn't like the looks of the company's new products?
- Do you sometimes sell a stock because the company does not excite you any longer?

If your answers are in the affirmative, you probably know the reasons why you buy — attraction, excitement, and an instinct that many impulsives seem to have, which often serves them well.

But, most likely, you are unaware of the psychological reasons you sell, and since selling too frequently is costing you profits, or causing you to lose money, you must look hard at this.

All investors personalize their stocks to some extent — we endow them with human qualities because we identify with them. When we visualize blue chip companies, we see them as Dutch uncles, dependable and solid. We can imagine them sitting in front of the fireplace smoking their pipes.

But impulsives anthropomorphize their stocks more than any other type of investor. And it is the human aspect they attribute to the company that attracts them. When Olivia Pierson had an "instinct" at the mall to buy Ann Taylor it was because she saw the company as a fashionable, chic woman who would continue to be in the forefront of fashion trends, a woman with whom Olivia would want to be associated.

Because impulsives view stock personally and give themselves to the stock, they expect, in return, that the stock will reward them with quick gains. The underlying fantasy is "I've loved the stock, the stock must show that it loves me back by showering me with wealth."

On the conscious level, every investor understands that no company can meet emotional demands; but on the unconscious level, for the impulsive, the fantasy is powerful.

When a stock goes down, or a company does something that seems like a betrayal, the impulsive investor feels keenly disappointed and sells, just as he or she bought, without investigating too closely.

Usually when people sell hastily, the dominant emotion is fear: "Oh my God, the stock is going down, I'm going to lose, I better get out." For an impulsive investor, the feeling is "The stock is starting to let me down. I'm going to walk out because the stock is walking out on me." In short, "I'm getting out of this relationship first." This act is an unconscious retaliatory abandonment.

If you've ever been deeply hurt in a real relationship, you'll recognize the feeling. You need to connect that feeling to your investment behavior. In the market, hurt and disappointment can be more difficult to control than fear because fear comes and goes, while disappointment is a constant motif and more consistently fuels impetuous selling.

PROGRAM FOR THE IMPULSIVE INVESTOR

If you know your investment pattern is to react emotionally, if you are currently losing money or not making as much as you had hoped, there are several steps you can take that may well guarantee you better results.

What's losing money for you is a tendency to buy and sell quickly. *Therefore, your goal is to restrain that impulsiveness by allowing for a vital period of investigation and reflection between your feelings and your actions.*

You should continue to value your heightened emotional awareness — an important asset — but to regard it as only *one aspect* of investment success. This "feeling quality," which is actually intuitive inductive logic, can be useful in spotting good investment ideas, but it must be tempered with a hard look at the facts.

In his excellent book *One Up on Wall Street,* Peter Lynch tells of being inspired to buy Sara Lee stock for the Magellan Fund after seeing L'Eggs panty hose (a Sara Lee company) in their clever egg-shaped containers in a supermarket. Don't be lulled into thinking that Lynch bought on instinct alone. You can be certain that he thoroughly investigated Sara Lee before investing millions of dollars of shareholders' money.

You are fortunate to have a strong intuition, as Lynch does, but like Lynch, you need to combine that *inductive* awareness with more *deductive* investigation. By making a moderate shift in your behavior, you can accomplish a great deal.

Let's imagine a typical scenario that might get an impulsive investor involved with a company, typical because the setting is glamorous and is likely to open up an impulsive investor's "investing pores" and unleash inductive powers.

On a family trip to Las Vegas, you notice a number of hotels with entertainment "themes" — Excalibur, where the theme is King Arthur's court, and the Luxor, where the theme is a step back in time to ancient Egypt. The hotels are crowded, and you see families enjoying themselves. You think to yourself, "This theme idea is great. And it's probably just at the beginning. People love gambling and they love family entertainment. Combining the two things is brilliant. I'm going to buy Circus Circus Enterprises, the company that owns these hotels."

Your usual pattern would have been to call your broker as soon as you returned home (or maybe even from the hotel) and make the purchase.

But now you say to yourself, "It's exciting to feel this way, and maybe I'm on to something, but what do I know about this company?"

When you ask this question, you immediately limit your idealization of the stock, because you opened yourself to the idea that there may be more to the company than the image it projects.

The rule is — you can fall in love at first sight.

But you can't buy at first sight — not ever.

First, you have to come up with solid information.

Impulsive investors are reluctant to investigate the companies they want to buy; research isn't conducive to the feelings of loyalty they value, and it tends to temper the excitement. But tempering is exactly what you want to do.

If you feel a strong aversion to investigating, remember that there are ways you can limit how much you have to do and still be effective.

In chapter 3, I suggested several resources for investigating companies and how they might be used. A major resource is the *Value Line Investment Survey,* which is published weekly. Its combination of comprehensiveness and historical depth cannot be equaled, and the *Value Line* ranking system for stocks — one is the highest ranking, five the lowest — has proven to be very accurate. The *Hulbert Financial Digest,* a newsletter that ranks newsletters, has often rated *VL* as first or second for long-term results.

For impulsive investors, an effective approach is to go to the library, locate the stock in *Value Line,* and look at three things alone: earnings, sales, and cash flow. Invariably, I have found, you will then go on to read the rating and commentary. The commentary is the current story of the company from a business point of view, so when you read it (and it's usually pretty interesting), you get a picture that may be quite different from the image you have in your mind, and you bring yourself closer to the reality of the company.

Next, contact the company for the annual report, but don't feel that you have to read it thoroughly; thumb through to get a better feel for the company. As with *Value Line,* I've found that people become interested and read parts of the report. With experience, immersion grows. And the process not only educates, but enforces a discipline that puts time between the impulse and the actual purchase. *The more quickly you make a purchase, the more quickly you are going to be disappointed, so the introduction of time is a very important element for the impulsive investor.* A good rule is don't buy until you have at least looked over the annual report.

The report will give you practice in understanding that there are two parts to a company — the image and the actual business. The image gets promoted by glossy photographs, a sleek design, often expensive paper, and by the narrative which strives to present the company in its best light. But the narrative also deals with such business aspects as profits, assets and liabilities, and sales data. In the narrative, you can see the two aspects of the company coming together, and you can bring them together in your own mind. The annual report also contains valuable business statistics.

A business-oriented investigation of Circus Circus Enterprises would find that it has an excellent growth record, a reputation for sound management, and has captured a major share of gamblers who travel with their families.

If you decide to buy a company, write down your business expectations for its performance over the next year and your standards for selling, as I outlined in chapter 4. You are going to review these standards regularly, every month or so, so you can remind yourself that you have them.

The reason to review so often is that you are highly vulnerable to feelings of disappointment, feelings that can lead you to abandon your standards and sell precipitously if the stock goes down or doesn't produce high returns quickly.

If you can prepare in advance for these feelings, you can learn how to handle them.

Let's say you bought a stock I'll call Acme National at $40, and within three months or so, the stock goes down to $32. You had great expectations for Acme — a conglomerate of chemical, manufacturing, and retailing enterprises — because of a new process it has developed for the manufacture of perfumes.

You are disappointed at the downturn, and probably angry as well, so the first thing is to tell yourself, "Well, I expected this to happen. I'm feeling annoyed at the stock. I wanted quick results, and I'm not getting what I wanted."

Next say two words: *"Nothing personal."*

The stock is not deliberately disappointing you, because, as the Wall Street saying goes, "The stock doesn't know you own it." Or in your case, "The stock doesn't know you have emotional expectations of it."

When you have this thought, you stand back from your feelings, like counting to ten in an argument with a loved one. This "time out" diffuses your emotions and allows you to consider what's relevant — why is the stock going down?

- Perhaps the stock was overpriced and is now correcting to a fairer value.
- Perhaps there are production problems with the company that have temporarily dampened earnings.
- Perhaps the entire industrial sector is undergoing a correction.

You need to give yourself time to investigate, and you are not inclined to do that when feeling intensely.

As I explained earlier, my philosophy is that you should not sell a quality stock that you selected carefully until you have given the stock at least a year to meet your business expectations. Unless there is a disturbing development in a company, a shift in the technology of the industry that will affect it adversely, or serious long-term management problems, you are going to hold on.

WALKING THE LINE

While you work at becoming more objective about buying and selling your stocks, you need to think about ownership as well.

When impulsive investors own a stock, it's not just a piece of paper; they identify closely with the company. Rather than feeling "the stock is me" as the power investor does, they feel "the stock is mine." Impulsive investors show great loyalty to their companies. An Exxon stockholder will drive miles out of the way to fill up at an Exxon station. And impulsive investors enjoy getting special attention from "their" companies. They love the feeling of being wooed (as who doesn't?).

Many corporations make a regular practice of sending gift packages to shareholders who hold the stock certificates themselves. These gifts can be impressive. For example, Disney Corporation sends out discount certificates to Disney World, Hershey sends chocolates, and the 3M Company sends a wonderful box of tapes at Christmastime. The railroad CSX Corporation hosts a discounted shareholders' weekend at the magnificent Greenbrier Resort, which it owns. Getting packages and perks can make an impulsive investor feel great.

For emotional reasons, such investors enjoy attending annual shareholder meetings. At these meetings, they are made to feel special in a glamorous atmosphere where they get to rub shoulders with top management.

It's all right to relish the feeling of being courted, if you can remember that your wooer's objective is to attach you to it. You need to *avoid* becoming overly attached, since that can result in extreme disappointment and a quick sale should something go wrong. For your own protection, be aware of the dynamics and walk the line between feeling good and being wary. If you can say to yourself, "I love getting gift certificates, but I'm still going to pay close attention to this company's business record," you're on target. But if you find yourself using the gifts and tossing the annual reports aside, you have strayed too far off the line.

PORTFOLIO FOR THE IMPULSIVE INVESTOR

The following portfolio, the one I worked out for Olivia Pierson, provides her with diversification and limits her holdings to nine stocks.

Note that the list contains several solid consumer goods companies, which make products that are familiar to everyone in the country and are so down-to-earth — soft drinks and breakfast cereals, for example — it is difficult to idealize them and endow them with romantic qualities, as impulsive investors tend to do.

Impulsive investors should stay away from companies whose products are a mystery to them, because this mystery is part of their fatal attraction, as with Olivia and computer companies. Although she used a computer in her work, and she understood the difference between hardware and software, that was all she cared about. We decided to sell off — gradually — Olivia's computer stocks, with the exception of Microsoft, her biggest gainer and a company that owns an extraordinary franchise.

Olivia's highest priority was funding her son's education. She projected total college costs of $110,000, of which she could provide $5,000 annually from earnings. I urged her to accumulate at least $125,000 by buying $55,000 worth of Treasury "strips" or zero coupon bonds. These would yield about 7.1 percent over the twelve to sixteen years involved. (A "zero" does not make regular interest payments but sells at a deep discount from the face value of the bond. The rate of return comes from the gradual appreciation of the security, which is redeemed at face value at maturity.)

Olivia considered the option of gifting all or part of these bonds to Tom so that when he reached age fourteen, her income taxes would be lower. She decided against the gift because college financial assistance formulas require a higher percentage from student assets than parental assets in determining family ability to contribute to college costs.

We chose zero coupon bonds for Olivia, even though history suggests that she could have done better totally in equities. There were two reasons: Olivia wanted absolute safety for Tom's education, and U.S. Treasuries come the closest to providing that. The other reason was that with zeros there is a psychological lock-in — though completely liquid, investors "feel" they have to hold to maturity — and that guards against impulsiveness.

The rest of Olivia's portfolio is invested in high-profile, high-quality companies, with the goal of growing her principal so that in six to ten years she can buy her dream house. (Olivia is providing for part of her retirement through an employer matching plan.)

The goal was to select companies with excellent records as long-term holds, to counterbalance her impulsiveness.

Following is her $220,000 portfolio and the reasons for the selections that were made at the time.

GROWTH STOCKS: 75 PERCENT

International Flavors & Fragrances. World leader in the production of cosmetic and food essences. An international company, with manufacturing facilities in Europe, South America, and Asia, IFF had crossed the line from go-go growth stock to slower, long-term growth stock, yet it retained the image of glamour so appealing to Olivia. With more and more products using fragrances, from toilet paper to cleaning products, this is an area of great growth. IFF had the potential to surprise periodically with better than expected earnings.

Nordstrom, Inc. Retailer. Olivia picked Nordstrom, a chain with eighty-three stores in eighteen states, as a replacement for the more speculative start-up retailers she owned when we first met. Since Nordstrom is regarded by many as the best-managed upscale department store, I thought it offered long-term safety, while allowing Olivia to continue to identify with fashion.

Walt Disney. World's largest entertainment company. Disney combines magic and creativity with down-to-earth profits — a long-term hold. Assets include theme parks, film and television studios, cable networks, newspapers, Disney stores, and even a hockey franchise, so it's well diversified, and into areas that reflect Olivia's love of media. Although the choice was mine, she enjoys owning the company and talking about it with her sons.

Microsoft. Software manufacturer. The power investor's "dream stock" (see portfolio, chapter 8) also works for an impulsive investor because it combines image with an outstanding record of success. Because the company dominates software, it is unlikely to disappoint, and Olivia should have no trouble hanging on. The fame of Bill Gates — who some think is going to wind up owning the world — was part of the thrill for Olivia.

Coca-Cola. Soft drink manufacturer. Coke has a great consumer franchise and a powerful international distribution system. Add to that solid management and the watchful eye of Warren Buffett and you have a recipe for long-term growth. At the time I recommended Coke to Olivia, its P/E was very high, but worth buying, in her case, because of the emotional pluses.

Johnson & Johnson. Drugs and health care products. J&J has great products and, also, a wonderful corporate culture and effective decentralized management. Again, the stability of a long-term hold would guard against her impulsiveness.

Charles Schwab. Financial services. Schwab had become the most innovative and strongest retail broker. Two trends — the aging of the baby boomers and self-directed retirement planning — augured well for its future. Schwab increased Olivia's diversification, and also forced her to become familiar with financial planning issues. Although I made the choice, I was concerned about the cyclical nature of the brokerage business, although Olivia wasn't much concerned, since she focuses in the present. At the next downturn, she may panic and sell Schwab, but she'll rationalize holding Disney, Coke, and the others because she identifies highly with them.

Kellogg. Cereal company. Another great franchise and, therefore, another great defense against impulsiveness. Kellogg is to cereals what Coke is to soft drinks — pretty impregnable. Still, Kellogg was having some trouble (which I didn't think would be permanent) when Olivia purchased it, and she got a relative bargain.

Berkshire Hathaway. Insurance conglomerate. Berkshire is the personal vehicle of Warren Buffett, the company's greatest asset. The insurance division gives Buffett a "cash float" to invest in thirty-four diverse subsidiaries, including shoe manufacturers, candy makers, and an encyclopedia. His own portfolio includes significant chunks of Walt Disney, Coca-Cola, Wells Fargo, PNC Bank, McDonald's, and the *Washington Post.* Berkshire provides diversification and permanence with a capital "P." Olivia wasn't familiar with the company when I bought it for her, but I explained how it works, and she loves it, because of a growing identification with Buffett. She is learning more about investing from reading its annual reports.

BONDS: 25 PERCENT

Zero coupon (maturing over four years, coincident with son's college education).

ADVISERS AND OTHER PEOPLE

If an impulsive admires a close investor friend, the impulsive is likely to think highly of the friend's stock selections, too. That is the reason impulsive investors often buy stocks they hear about from a confidant or a lover. This is akin to buying on a tip, but with a difference, because what's valued is not the information but the individual providing it.

When you buy on your own impulse, you are acting on your instinct about the company, even if you don't know it very well. When you buy because you admire someone else, you are demonstrating your affection for that person, not a conviction about the stock itself. And should your relationship falter, you may be tempted to sell precipitously.

I once had a client who was deeply attached to an old school friend, a woman whom he described as his "closest confidant." In college, they had been members of an amateur theater group, and they continued to share cultural interests — theater, books, museums. They also advised each other about their personal relationships, and she had helped him through a difficult divorce. Occasionally, my client's friend would talk about her investments, and my client purchased a number of "her" stocks.

Sadly, this woman was not a very good stock picker and was attracted to very speculative stocks, with the result that my client lost a great deal of money. This was why he came to see me.

A money manager or financial adviser can be extremely helpful to an impulsive investor, provided the relationship can be kept objective. If it gets too close, the investor becomes overly reliant on the adviser, idealizing the person as Prince or Princess Charming of Wall Street, so that ultimately, the adviser is certain to disappoint. (Often it's a good idea for an impulsive investor to choose an adviser of the same sex so that the romantic element is downplayed.)

You want a money manager to help you set up a long-range investing plan and keep you on track. You need someone who will remind you, kindly and frankly, that you tend to be too impulsive.

When I get a call from an impulsive client, telling me about a stock, I ask the person to talk to me about the company in business terms. I want to know what the person has read in the annual report or *Value Line*. Descriptions like "marvelous," "wonderful," "exciting," and "sure to take off" are not good enough. Indeed, they should be seen as red flags — danger signs of impulsive judgment.

I have one client, a widow with young children, for whom I developed a conservative investment plan that includes a substantial proportion of bonds, since she must have a guaranteed income each year. My client knows that she is not in a position to speculate, yet she loves excitement, and she sometimes calls with ideas for high flyers that might add "some spice" to the portfolio. I believe she now phones because she knows I can help counter her impulses, not because she really wants to convince me that it's a good idea to buy.

The ideal money manager can help you curb impulsiveness, while not getting too close to you personally. Explain your needs to any potential adviser. For many investors, it is valuable to have a supportive relationship with a money manager. For you, emotional distance is important. With an adviser, as with your stocks, you have to be able to think, "This is business."

LOVE AND MONEY

Money is a totally neutral commodity; it has no meaning of its own, except as a medium of exchange, yet we endow it with every emotion imaginable, and two of the most primary are love and security.

There are no clear psychological explanations why some people become so intensely emotional about life and relationships. We do know that for these people, money is symbolic of love and security. Perhaps, in childhood, money became a substitute for parental affection. Whatever the source, impulsive investors express, through investing, their need for love and security.

Expressiveness is a wonderful trait, but not in the stock market, because it is the last thing the market rewards — and the first thing it punishes. Whenever you are "expressing yourself" in the market, you are in danger of financial loss, so by loving less, you can virtually assure yourself of gaining a great deal more.

CHAPTER 11

The Gambler

Every investor has the gambling instinct because we all harbor the hope of controlling fate, and to some degree, we all feel entitled to the things we desire. If we take a gamble, and pick a stock that pays off big, we get the thrill of feeling that we are at the center of the universe.

In the market, the gambling urge lies along a continuum. At the less hazardous end of the high-risk scale is the power investor, whose gamble consists in buying stocks "on the story" rather than in investigation, and the impulsive investor, who "falls" for a stock. At the most dangerous end is the addict, who bets compulsively on stocks, just as in a casino or at the track.

The investor I'm describing in this chapter is an enthusiastic person, in love with the sheer thrill of playing the market (notice how the word *playing* reflects the gambling roots of this form of investing). These avid "players" see themselves primarily as traders, buying stocks on price alone and turning them over quickly.

Gamblers are not addicted to the market, but they have an obsessive connection to it, magnified by the prolonged bull market of the 1990s and its speculative excess.

Intensifying the speculation is the vast amount of market information available online. Net "chat sites" stimulate market gamblers and increase their numbers. My estimate now is that as many as 10 percent of investors may be market gamblers; just a few years ago, I would have estimated 2 to 3 percent.

More and more in recent years, these traders have turned to options for their "action." As you probably know, an option is the right to buy or sell an investment at a certain set price called the "premium" for a specific time period. A put option is the right to sell; a call option to buy. If you believe the price of an underlying stock is going to go down, you might buy a put or sell a call. If you believe the price is going to go up, you might buy a call or sell a put.

Call and put options are rarely exercised. Traders buy and sell the options before expiration, trading on the rise and fall of premium prices of the options. Because an options buyer has to put up only a small amount of money (the premium) to control a large amount of stock, there is a great deal of leverage in options trading. Sometimes such trading can prove highly profitable, but more often, it is not, as you can lose more money than you put up if the stock rises when you bet that it would fall or falls when you bet that it would rise. There is also significant "friction" — the brokerage fees and the difference between the "bid" and "ask" spread, which is paid to the firm handling the trade. The costs and high risk make options trading inadvisable for the individual investor. Many people stop when they realize how easy it is to lose.

Gamblers, on the other hand, keep on trading because they focus on the wins and mentally bury the losses. The result can be an investing career that burns up, rather than builds up, money.

Even when gamblers make money, as many did in the strong bull market of 1995–1997 when it was nearly impossible for any investor *not* to do well, they usually think they are doing a lot better than they are.

But even in extremely favorable markets, *gamblers often lose*, because they take extreme risks, and they don't cover those risks sufficiently, as I'll explain. Gambling or speculating is very different from investing. The gambler operates on hunches and bets on a specific time frame. The investor acts like a co-owner of a business with a long-term stake. Time is the enemy of the gambler, but the friend of the investor.

COLD, IN A HOT MARKET

Darryl Watson, client, came to see me because he was worried about the money he was losing, about $10,000 over the previous year. For some reason, things had "gone cold" for him, even though the market was hot. His wife, Penny, was worried. The Watsons, with annual income of $72,000, were starting to get into debt in order to make up Darryl's losses.

Darryl, a thirty-eight-year-old merchandising manager, described himself as an "avid trader" who relished being in the market. On a second honeymoon in the Caribbean, he'd taken his laptop computer along in order to keep trading.

"I once made 600 percent on a single trade," he boasted. "And when Boston Chicken went public in 1994, I grabbed 100 shares at $24. I sold three days later at $42. On certain trades, you have an instinct that it's going to work out, and when it hits, you get a terrific high," Darryl told me.

When I gently pressed Darryl to talk about other feelings — as I always do when I think someone is telling me only one side of the story — he admitted there was a downside: the remorse he felt over each loss, much more remorse than he would admit to Penny or, until our conversation, had admitted to himself. It was not only his losses but his remorse that had driven him to see me. His insight was a very good prognostic sign for one who has a gambling problem.

Although he wanted my advice, Darryl was still convinced that better times *had* to be just around the corner. "The great thing about the market," he told me, "is that you can always recover your losses if you keep investing."

In Darryl, I observed the magical conviction — "I can make things come out my way" — that feeds the gambling instinct and makes it so compelling. The stock market is a respectable place to pursue this belief, whereas the racetrack and the casino are not. The market is also exciting, and the more exciting a "game," and the more control he thinks he has over the outcome, the more attractive it seems to a gambler.

Since the market offers so many opportunities for "action," since all of us are subject to the gambling instinct, and particularly, since the level of denial among gamblers is high, we all need to be aware of the signs that this instinct is dominating our investing strategies.

The most obvious sign of a gambling problem is a primary focus on trading, on taking opportunistic risks in the hope of quick profits, rather than investing — building up a solid portfolio of quality companies to be held over the long term.

If you are preoccupied with trading, you need to look for the signs of gambling behavior:

- You're focused on a "big win."
- You're taking bigger and bigger risks.
- You experience a tremendous "rush" when a trade pays off.
- When you lose, you feel extreme remorse.
- You rationalize your losses, telling yourself, "I'll win next time."
- After a loss, you step up your trading activity so as to make it up.

If this describes you, you may be getting some thrills out of the market, but you are very likely experiencing extreme lows as well, because you are on a roller coaster, and you certainly need to evaluate your investment policy.

EXAMINING THE FIGURES

When I work with a gambler client, I'm very frank because I'm aware of the enormous damage stock market gambling can do. I have one client who lost his appliance store because he had borrowed heavily to make a big bet on a small biotech company. Although his case is extreme, it's not unique. I've never known a single market gambler who came out ahead in the long run, although many can remember some great trades. But are such memories enough to make up for the losses, and the feelings of frustration?

A predilection for thrill-seeking is a serious matter because gambling inevitably grows more intense and can become an addiction. This is why up markets, which encourage gambling behavior, can be so dangerous. *In an extraordinary bull market, like the one of 1995–1997, it was possible to take extreme risks and still make money, and this can lead a gambler to believe that his trading is successful and increase the danger of addiction.*

Even when gamblers *are* making money, they exaggerate their winnings, projecting their big wins — like that 600 percent on a single trade that Darryl Watson made — onto their entire record, because gamblers have a strong inclination to think magically, as I'll discuss further.

If you suspect you may be a gambler, appraise your long term gains realistically. I always ask: "What is your *annualized total return* for the past three years?"

When I hear figures like "100 percent" or "200 percent," which are highly unlikely for anyone, I first ask if they include the "friction," an absolute killer for anyone in the trading game, because even if you're a skilled professional trader, doing everything right, friction drastically cuts your gains. These costs can reduce what you think you are making on a trade by 6 to 10 percent. Add to that the taxes on short-term gains, and a 30 percent profit quickly becomes a real return of 15 percent or so.

For psychological reasons, a gambler will resist figuring friction costs and taxes, since they are mentally counted as losses. Add to this a tendency not to remember losing trades at all, and you can see why gains are never as large as the gambler thinks, and compared to other investing styles, they are small.

One client estimated her three-year return at 60 percent, when it was actually 15 percent. While 15 percent is an excellent return, my client could have achieved it with far less psychological strain by investing rather than trading. She worried her husband about both the amount of emotion she expended on every trade and the considerable risk she was taking with money they earned jointly.

If you discover that you are losing money, or making less than you thought, if you or your family is disturbed by your style of investing, you may be motivated to alter your approach. I use the word *may* because change is difficult when you relish the thrill of "living for the trade" and when you are rationalizing your behavior as a defense mechanism *against* change.

A NEW VIEWPOINT

What attracts gamblers to their style is the stimulation it provides, but a really successful investor knows how to limit stimulation. As I wrote earlier, successful investing is about doing less, not more, about being extremely centered in oneself and on the portfolio. Gamblers engage in so much activity that they become overstimulated, making it impossible for them to establish focus.

Investors whose styles create problems can make moderate changes and still achieve the psychological rewards they get from their approach. A power investor can still achieve a sense of excitement from a portfolio that is less reliant on concept stocks, because he gains excitement from superior long-term results and the knowledge that his family is being provided for.

But gamblers must change their behavior "cold turkey," because thrill-seeking, their emotional objective, must be eliminated entirely, not simply reduced.

As I said, *all* investors have the gambling instinct, but successful investors defend against it — they protect themselves — by behaving in ways that run *exactly counter* to the demands of the instinct. This behavior characterizes conservative investing, and is why acquiring long-term wealth is so firmly linked to a conservative approach.

If you are a gambler, suffering financially or emotionally, you need to defend yourself by acting like a nongambler. You owe this to yourself because you deserve to do well, without suffering. Cognitive psychology sets forth the principle that if you "act as if" you believe something, and take small steps toward it, your actions will eventually create the new reality.

I tell my clients that if they "act as if" they are more conservative investors, they will become conservative investors. By opening the door

ever so slightly and giving yourself the chance to try something totally
new, you may find excitement, maybe even a thrill, in the idea of the
newness. If not, simply "act as if" you can. The goal is to put aside all
of the preoccupations that are so important to a gambler — the big
win, what's hot, the next trade — and act differently, following the
program I outlined in chapter 3 of building a long-term, diversified
portfolio of ten quality core stocks or a combination of stocks, mutual
funds, and bonds. How you allocate your portfolio will depend on your
income, savings, goals, and age.

Tell your broker or adviser that you are going to convert your trading account into a true investment account. Remember, the more transactions you make, the more money your broker earns, so if your broker
seems disappointed by your decision, or encourages you to keep on
trading by telling you that he or she has always been impressed by your
ability, get another broker, someone who will help you "act as if" you
are an investor.

I hesitate to suggest sample portfolios for gamblers because I believe
it is important for them to learn that they can make investment choices
on their own. Unfortunately, many gamblers don't have investment experience, since the compulsive nature of the gambling urge limits their
horizon. A gambler has to get used to the idea of exploring the wide
world of conservative investing options.

Remember the general rules about building up a portfolio incrementally, investigating companies, and selecting them for their quality
and prospects. As an investor, you are interested in the current and
future value of the company, rather than stock price alone, as traders
are. Put your considerable energy and enthusiasm into investigating
company fundamentals, rather than acting on tips or playing hunches.

There is one goal you should pursue in constructing your portfolio — *make the portfolio as difficult or expensive to alter as possible.* When
you get the urge to make an options trade, you will want to cash in
stocks or fund shares, and the harder that is to do, the better off you are.

Here are some investments that make portfolio changes difficult:

• *A variable annuity.* A life insurance annuity contract whose value
fluctuates with that of an underlying securities portfolio or other index

of performance. (Unlike a fixed annuity, which has a constant rate of return, a variable annuity has the potential to provide some protection against inflation.) Most annuities offer you a variety of portfolios, ranging from conservative to aggressive, so you exercise the important element of choice.

While the initial investment is made with after-tax dollars, a variable annuity compounds tax free until you draw on it (you must by age 70½, but can elect to do so earlier). Tax-free accumulation is an advantage, especially if you are in a high income bracket. But the major benefit is that although it's possible to cancel the annuity, you can't get your money out as quickly as you could by simply selling a stock. With some variable annuities there are cancellation fees, and adverse tax consequences. An annuity ties you up to some extent, and tied is what you want to be.

Because of the management fees and other costs associated with variable annuities, you must investigate carefully before you buy. The one I recommend to clients is Vanguard, which has an excellent record and low costs.

• *Real estate.* There are several valuable psychological aspects of real estate for the investor with a gambling proclivity. Properties appreciate over time, so to make money, you are forced to hold on; real estate is concrete — not numbers on a ticker tape — so it fosters the sense that money is being used for a real purpose, rather than for gambling. It is essential that you select sound properties, *not speculative ones,* such as raw land. A good guide to real estate as investment is *The Complete Real Estate Adviser* by Daniel J. DeBenedictis. It tells you how to evaluate a property, secure financing, and the other aspects of real estate investment. Because evaluating real estate takes time, it gives you less time to think about trading. (For more on real estate, see chapter 9 on the inheritor.)

• *Load mutual funds.* The added costs of a load fund create a psychological contract that makes you reluctant to sell. Two load funds with excellent records are Guardian Park Avenue (Load: 4.50 percent. *Forbes* rating [August 25, 1997]: B in an up market, C in a down market. Five-year annualized total return: 24.02 percent; ten-year: 15.37 percent) and Davis New York Venture (Load: 4.75 percent. *Forbes* rating [August 25, 1997]: A in up markets, B in down markets. Five-year annualized total return: 22.75 percent; ten-year: 17.48 percent. *Morningstar* rating: 5 stars). Remember — you don't want a "gambling fund" that is highly leveraged in speculative stocks.

Gamblers are reluctant to build a conservative portfolio because they don't want to own "boring" stocks — blue chips or quality growth stocks. They are hooked on their daily "fix" of checking stock tables to see what their high flyers have done. Anyone who has owned a stock that doubled or tripled in a few weeks understands the exhilaration produced by looking up the numbers. This thrill is particularly intense for a gambler, and because it is so pleasurable, it is difficult to give up.

It is a challenge to learn to value exhilaration less and "boring" more. Remember, your goal is to level the peaks and valleys and achieve a level plateau of reliable returns. If that plateau spells "boring," ask yourself this:

- What's boring about the certainty of a steady return over time?
- What's boring about giving my family peace of mind?
- What's boring about putting an end to my feelings of remorse when I lose?
- What's boring about being able to look in the mirror and feel good about myself?
- What's boring about definitely getting rich?

If you include in your portfolio some investments you consider boring, such as insurance companies and banks, you may find yourself loving them. I do. What's great about them is that they grow just as well as "sexier" companies (although people think they don't) and they are a good deal safer, because consumers always need them. They can't possibly go out of style. And, psychologically, they are about as far away from gambling as you can get, exactly why you want to own them. Some of my particular favorites have been Bank of Granite (North Carolina), Corus Bankshares, Wells Fargo Bank, Leucadia National, Markel, and Progressive Insurance.

A TRADING PORTION OF THE PORTFOLIO?

I believe you should give up trading altogether because it is so difficult to establish limits if you have a strong urge to gamble.

If you think you can establish limits, a matter you need to consider carefully, limit the trading portion of your portfolio to no more than 10 percent. Tell yourself that a trading portion is forever an experiment. If you find you are unable to stick to the limit, if trading starts to dominate your portfolio, you have to quit.

The basic rule is that the money you set aside for trading must be money that you can afford to lose, for psychological as well as practical reasons. If you have a strong gambling instinct, you believe that you are *always* going to win. If you limit your trading to money you can afford to lose, you introduce the idea that loss is *always* a possibility.

Have your broker set up two separate accounts — one for trading and the other for investment. Keep the two absolutely separate, mentally and physically. Use two separate folders for the records and put them in different places to establish firmly in your mind that there will be no mixing of investing and trading — and, also, no mixing of trading and gambling.

I've been using the term *trader* as synonymous with *gambler,* but there are significant differences between professional traders and gamblers.

A professional trader tries to make money quickly while curtailing risk. A gambler tries to make money while embracing risk, because, subconsciously, the thrill is in the risk. *The gambler thinks magically. The professional trader thinks protectively.* (This is a generalization, of course; there certainly is a degree of overlap between the two.) Your goal in managing the trading portion of your portfolio is to act more like a professional trader, and less like a gambler. Here is what you have to do:

• *Figure the odds carefully.* Professional traders analyze the probabilities by finding out everything that is known about a situation — a possible takeover, the influence of the weather on a crop. If they figure there's less than a 50 percent chance of a trade working out, they usually don't do it. Gamblers act on little information and pay less attention to the odds. Their magical thinking is "I'm going to win no matter what."

• *Cut your losses.* Professional traders don't like loss, but they accept it. If a trader buys a stock at 25 looking to get out that day at 28 or 29, and the stock goes to 23, he will sell, thinking, "Either I'm wrong or somebody knows something I don't." Gamblers will hold on. Their magical thinking is "The stock is sure to go up tomorrow."

• *Be wary of time.* Professional traders know that in speculation, time offers both opportunity and risk. If, on a Friday morning, a professional trader buys a position in corn, he will want to be out by the end of the day because things can go sour over the weekend. The growing season so far may have been dry, but if there are heavy rains on Sunday, corn could open limit down (the maximum price movement allowed for the day) on Monday morning and the contract would become impossible to sell. Gamblers feel less subject to the urgencies of time. Their magical thinking is "Nothing can go wrong so fast."

• *Stop trading during "cold time."* Professional traders recognize that there are certain times when things aren't going well for them. They'll try to figure out why they're stuck, but if they can't, they'll step back for a while. Traders value their intuition, but understand that it isn't magical. They know intuition comes from experience. When they get "out of synch," they take a vacation. Gamblers keep going. Their magical thinking is "All I need is that one winner. I can turn cold time 'hot.'"

• *Protect yourself.* Options traders can write either covered options, in which they own the underlying security and will at least retain its value, or naked options — obviously far riskier — for which they do not own the underlying security but are paying to borrow someone else's stock. Gamblers buy naked options; traders rarely do. Traders realize that they may lose premiums on many unsuccessful options trades before they make a successful trade, so they have to have protection. Gamblers are attracted by the enormous profit potential in naked options, and they eschew the possibility of loss.

Traders always use stop/losses in commodities trades and often stock trades as well. Gamblers rarely do. The magical thinking is "I'm going to win, so I don't need protection."

In short, a major difference is that traders try to cover themselves or work things so that they can win both ways.

One method of winning both ways is a "straddle," buying both a put and a call on the same stock. This may seem like a neutral or even self-defeating strategy, but it is applicable in special situations when, because of a particular set of circumstances, the market believes a stock may go either up or down by a large amount, as the following story illustrates.

In 1985, Texaco and Pennzoil were locked in a legal battle over the acquisition of Citgo. Pennzoil had entered into an acquisition agreement with Citgo when Texaco made a better offer. Citgo broke off the deal with Pennzoil and Pennzoil sued Texaco.

As the trial date approached, I saw a good opportunity to buy straddles in both Texaco and Pennzoil. My reasoning was that if Texaco won, Texaco stock would rise and Pennzoil would fall. If Pennzoil won, the reverse would occur. The potential existed for two of the four options to be big winners, more than offsetting the two losers.

As it turned out, the trade was spectacular because Pennzoil won an all-time record judgment of $13 billion, bankrupting mighty Texaco. (The judgment was reduced by more than 50 percent on appeal, and Texaco subsequently emerged from bankruptcy to flourish again.)

My Pennzoil calls went up thirteen times in value (the puts were worthless), while the Texaco puts rose almost 50 percent in value. Meanwhile, as it became clear that Texaco would not be seriously damaged, the Texaco calls regained enough value to be sold at only a 50 percent loss. The final outcome of my trade was a gain of 850 percent.

I tell this story not to point out how brilliant an options trader I am (I very rarely do such trades), but to demonstrate how complicated hedging can be and how much investigation it requires. Yet, unless you're willing to practice hedging, you limit your ability to do well, so you need to devote some effort to mastering this skill.

If you have a strong gambling instinct, however, you will resist hedging because inevitably you will lose one side of the bet. The magical thinking is "I don't need to hedge because I am going to win it all."

CUTTING THROUGH THE MAGIC

Unless you can counter this magical thinking, it will undermine any "act like a trader" measures you put in place. Tell yourself this:

- I am human and no human being can control the market.
- I cannot count on my hunches to be accurate.
- I have no special powers that will "make" me win.
- In fact, I am *more likely* to lose than other people because, although I'm not conscious of it, I may be harboring a deep wish to lose.

If you focus on these thoughts, particularly the last one, you will find that they diminish the sense of omnipotence fostered by the gambling instinct.

Once you accept that you are vulnerable to loss, just as everyone else is, you can establish rules for protecting yourself by hedging your trades. The parameters are something you have to decide for yourself, based on your knowledge of how likely you are to follow through.

Here are some examples:

- I am going to hedge every trade I make.
- I am going to hedge 50 percent of my trades.
- I am going to hedge two trades out of three.

There are various ways you can set this up, but you have to set something up because you badly need a discipline for limiting risk.

One way to limit risk is to have a "market buddy" — a friend or family member who is knowledgeable about investing and whose style is naturally more conservative than yours. You can review proposed trades with this person.

If you're thinking of something that's highly risky, the buddy can "talk you down," that is, suggest safer alternatives or persuade you to give up the trade altogether. You need someone who can focus on whether you've investigated enough and what the odds of losing are, since you are likely to be hiding that knowledge from yourself.

I once had occasion to "talk down" a friend, Ron Gilbert. Ron was trading silver, had successfully built a position of six silver contracts sold short, and had a paper profit of $18,000.

Ron called to say he was convinced that silver prices were going to tumble further and was considering either shorting six more silver contracts or buying six puts.

When I asked what made him sure that silver prices would go down, he gave me an answer that relied entirely on intuition and made no reference to facts of production, consumption, industrial uses, or existing market conditions.

When I pointed out that if he added six contracts and silver rose $.45 in price, he would lose $9,000, Ron was stunned. He thought that if he lost money, he would still have a profit of $4,500, since he reckoned his loss only on the second set of six contracts.

Ron had given in to the gambling instinct, although he is not a gambler; he was using magical accounting peculiar to the gambler, a special form of compartmentalized thinking married to denial, and one of the things that a good "buddy" can point out to you.

A broker can play this buddy role if you have confidence in him or her. Although brokers get a great deal of poor publicity, many do succeed in steering a fair-minded course between the client's interests and their own, generally people with a good deal of experience and clout within their companies, so that they are relatively free of pressure. Seek out this kind of broker, if you haven't got one already.

A converse of the "get a buddy" concept is to pay less attention to those gambling buddies you already have. If you are spending a great deal of time with an online "chat group," you should go online less frequently, because the dynamics of these conversations can encourage risk-taking through group consensus.

Here's part of a chat group conversation in which participants discuss whether they should continue to buy a stock that has been going down. (Once again, I'll call the stock Acme National.)

"I rode Acme from 9 to 39½; the only thing visibly wrong is their

PR." "You've done nice work mining the peaks and valleys, but this sucker can only continue to soar." "That's what the chart shows. It can only go up." By the end of the conversation, most of the participants have decided to continue buying a stock they all agree is overpriced and experiencing "trouble" of an undetermined sort. That's a gambling decision, not a trading decision, and certainly not an investing decision. (Remember that the internet is an unregulated medium, and that stock promoters are unquestionably using it manipulatively. Be very cautious.)

Follow these rules about the trading portion of your portfolio:

- No matter how much money your trades make, the trading portion of your portfolio remains limited to 10 percent. Profits above that amount go into the investing portion of the portfolio.
- If trades lose money, you do not replenish the trading account with profits from the investing account. If the trading account goes below 10 percent, so be it.

Traffic is one-way only, *from* your trading account *to* your investing account. If you can't control the temptation to take from your investing account — because you will most certainly experience this temptation — give up trading all together. Many people have gained great relief when they do give it up, because they acknowledge their powerlessness over their gambling instinct — and a great deal of tension gets resolved. One woman who lost $1 million in a trading account over a one-year period was able to experience such relief. Although she could afford to lose the money (obviously, she is very wealthy), needless to say she wasn't happy about it. Ultimately, she told me, she got a bigger thrill out of being able to stop trading than from trading itself.

AFTER THE TRADES

When you do stop trading, you may encounter troubling feelings of loss because you are giving up grandiose fantasies of fortune and the self-aggrandizement that accompanies such fantasies.

You may also feel deprived, because you are losing an activity that has been meaningful and has occupied a great deal of your emotional energy. If you got a "really alive" feeling from your trades, as Darryl Watson did, you need to look for challenges elsewhere.

Sports that test the individual: Learning to sail or ski or even fly an airplane are good alternatives, activities that involve new skills and *controlled* risks (not bungee jumping). Almost any situation where you test yourself and get a thrill out of accomplishing something new can fill the bill — participating in a theater group or getting involved in local politics. You want to expand your focus, to let in other, less risk-oriented sources of stimulation to take the place of your concentration on the market to the exclusion of other excitements.

If you're feeling deprived, think about the psychological mechanisms behind the gambling instinct and understand why you are better off getting them under control.

While power investors want to be reflected admirably by their stocks, and impulsive investors bask in the reflected love of theirs, gamblers are looking for a lot more — to be loved by fate itself. The idea is "If I can magically make a trade come through for me, it demonstrates that I am the favored one."

Fate takes on the guise of a giant parent, indulgent when the gambler wins, punishing when the gambler loses, and this punishment is what accounts for the remorse many gamblers feel when trades "go down."

Sometimes people pursue fate this way to make up for unhappy childhood experiences, for feelings of being unloved, unworthy, or unsuccessful, even if they are successful as adults and very much loved. Whatever the reason, the goal of being fate's most favored investor is absolutely impossible to achieve. It is just as fruitless as the search to satisfy greed, discussed in chapter 5. All of the thrill-seeking, the "rushes," the search for the big hit, are ultimately frustrating because the real payoff can never be achieved.

If you think you've crossed the line from a gambling style to a gambling addiction — an insatiable compulsion to bet — think about getting help. The signs are that you can't stop trading, or set limits on the amount you lose, or reveal losing trades to your family.

One of the resources is Gamblers Anonymous, a confidential support group based on the twelve steps of Alcoholics Anonymous. It has 1,038 chapters in the United States. To locate a chapter near you, call (213) 386-8789. Your state medical or psychiatric association may also be able to direct you toward a therapist who specializes in treating gambling disorders.

Remember — you deserve more, emotionally and financially, than being on a merry-go-round. The real thrill in investing is having a portfolio that performs for you, in a dependable way, making you rich over time. And despite what some people may believe about the market, that is closer to a certainty than a gamble.

CHAPTER 12

The "Make Me Safe" Investor

Sensible investors are wary of taking too much risk, particularly when a bull market appears to be topping out or the descent into a bear market has begun. But there are some people who are *extremely risk averse* at all times. The whole idea of investing makes them nervous, yet they think that they *want* to invest, because they know it's the best way to make money over time. Therefore, they ask, "John, can't you find me a stock that won't go down?"

Usually, the words are said with a smile, because the person knows that they're asking the impossible, but on the emotional level, the message gets across — "Make me safe."

I hear this request both from people who are just "thinking" about investing (usually, they've been thinking about it for quite some time), and from people who have been in the market, but are always fearful of loss.

Several years ago, I took on Marge Cosgrove as a client. She is in her middle thirties, has been investing for several years, and constantly needs reassurance. She has a reputation for calling her broker every other day, rehashing each decision, and often not taking any action at all because she fears "taking a chance." She told me, "I think Mr. Jones just got tired of me. That's why he recommended you. You know, I'm one of those people who just can't stand to lose."

What is behind this extreme risk aversion?

Well, you can take it at face value — losing money causes real pain, and so it's reasonable to have a real fear of it.

But not everyone is equally risk averse because not everyone feels the pain equally. Some people are particularly vulnerable.

Often "Make me safe" investors have experienced losses early in life, usually the loss of a parent, perhaps through death, perhaps through divorce or some other form of separation. Or maybe there was some family trauma, or a deeply entrenched anxiety, that inflicted great pain and insecurity. Sometimes, they are people who have undergone more recent losses, such as the death of a spouse.

Whenever a person asks for a safety guarantee, I tell them I understand that they have suffered losses and that they want to avoid loss now, since they have already experienced so much pain.

Highly risk-averse people need this kind of support because they feel out of place among other investors, who tend to view risk more calmly.

Most investors *overestimate* their risk tolerance by about a factor of two. "Make me safe" investors, on the other hand, tend to *underestimate* because they suffer from what behavioral psychologists call "myopic loss aversion." Their investing horizon is extremely short, extending only to the pain of the first loss. As a result, they are unaware of the other side of the picture: *If you select quality stocks and hold on to them over the long term, losses always become less significant, because they are less frequent than gains.* With time, losses diminish emotionally as well as financially, and this assurance is the greatest certainty you can achieve in investing.

When people express fear that their stocks will go down, I tell them they need not worry, because, at some point, their stocks *will* go down, and probably sooner rather than later. As I explained in chapter 4, this is because we tend to purchase stocks at the point of greatest optimism, when they are most likely to be overpriced and due for a correction.

So you need to be prepared to endure the pain of short-term loss, because this is one pain you will most assuredly experience. But you also have to remember that you have an excellent "analgesic" at your disposal, and that's the knowledge that your pain will almost certainly be replaced by the pleasures of long-term gains.

RISK AVERSION AND PERFECTIONISM

For the risk averse, investing is beneficial on a psychological level, because it gives the opportunity to deal with some of the issues surrounding risk aversion — a low level of self-confidence (which is why you can't take a chance), and the feeling that you are not allowed to make a mistake because you have to be perfect (another reason why you can't take a chance). Risk-averse individuals feel that if they're not perfect, people may leave them, as they have, perhaps, left in the past. (This perfectionism is similar to that of the "I can't stop worrying" investor, and you can understand how the same anxiety can produce both worry and risk aversion.)

To deal with risk aversion, remind yourself that you don't need to be infallible. The famous child psychiatrist D. W. Winnicott coined the phrase "the good enough mother," meaning a mother who is capable and caring but not anxious because she doesn't try to be perfect. There is also the "good enough investor," who is generally competent, but not in need of total safety, because he or she isn't always looking to be perfect or to "beat out" everyone else's results.

"Good enough" is a reassuring concept that can help you to become more risk tolerant (not "risk embracing," just more tolerant) and that should be the objective of the risk-averse investor. If you are like most highly risk-averse people, you are most concerned about "taking care" of your money. You need, instead, to develop the perception that, over time, your money can take care of you — if you put it to work for you.

THE CLASSIC "RISK-AVERSE" APPROACH

Extremely risk-averse investors are often advised to follow an approach that provides greater safety, perhaps, but at a substantially lower level of return with no significant growth. They may be told to put their money mainly into U.S. Treasury bonds, the safest of bonds, or perhaps into an asset allocation mutual fund, which shifts allocations among cash, bonds, and some stocks, according to the fund manager's view of market conditions. Asset allocation is sound in principle, but less so in practice. Studies show that while it can be determined, retrospectively, which allocations would have been successful during certain time periods, it is not possible to predict what will be successful in the future.

Even understanding intellectually that risk-averse portfolios have a lower rate of return, investors can still long for high returns with little risk — an impossibility. Their wish is not so absurd as it sounds. Wanting a good return is a sign of healthy greed, a sign that it is possible to expand the risk horizon, a development that should be encouraged.

The biggest problem with the totally risk-averse route is that it can freeze you forever into an attitude that will prevent investment success.

If you currently see yourself as extremely risk averse, and you don't even want to think about stocks at first, it's fine to *start out* with all of your assets in U.S. Treasury bonds. But keep in mind that your goal is to expand your risk horizon by gradually moving some money into equities or equity funds.

If you have $100,000 or more to invest in bonds, purchase a ten-year "ladder" of T-bonds. A ladder is a mixture of bonds of different maturities, in this case, $10,000 a year for ten different years, so that you have bonds maturing at regular intervals. Laddering is an excellent approach for a risk-averse person because it is a conservative way of spreading out risk and achieving a yield higher than short-term bonds would provide.

What's *psychologically important* is that you reexamine your goals as each bond matures. Ask yourself, "Am I going to buy another bond, or am I ready to put the money into equities?" Thus, the possibility of crossing the "great risk divide" is always in view.

When the first bond matures, for example, you can buy shares over the course of the year in one of the mutual funds on the *Forbes* Honor Role (see chapter 2 for a discussion of the Honor Role), since you will be more comfortable, at first, with funds than with stocks. When the next bond matures, you can start another mutual fund or buy one or two stocks over the course of the year.

With each maturity, you can move another 10 percent of your money from bonds into stocks or stock funds (or with every other maturity, or every third one).

What usually happens is that with even a small amount of money in stocks, people become gratified by the growth, and are encouraged to add more. If the stock portion falls, they have the stability of the bond income to fall back on, so the shock is not so great, although it may delay their adding more equities for a while. Psychologically, the bonds provide a secure base from which to get your feet wet in equities.

An extremely risk-averse person should work toward a mix of 60 percent in bonds, 40 percent in equities. Or he can follow the rule that when interest rates are at 8 percent or above, you will be 60 percent in bonds, 40 percent in equities and the reverse when interest rates are below 8 percent. (Historically, this has been a sound approach but, of course, history does not always repeat itself.)

I advise investors to purchase individual bonds instead of bond mutual funds, since fund management costs, and the shifting of bond maturities within the funds, generally result in poorer performance.

"NORMALIZING" YOUR INVESTING

In chapter 2, I suggested that, psychologically, the best way to get started is to view investing as a "normal" experience, rather than one that must be anxiety producing. (In a long-term, growing economy like that of the United States, the bias in equities is always up, especially if you pay attention to value.)

People who are highly risk averse need to focus on the idea that they can be as "normal" as other investors, and by "other investors" I mean my ideal investor — conservative and investigative.

There is not a great distance between extreme risk aversion, that demands stocks with a "no-loss guarantee," and healthy risk aversion that seeks to minimize loss, but the difference between the returns from being *highly* risk averse and *prudently* risk averse can be substantial. With a highly risk-averse portfolio, you could expect, historically, an annualized total return over the long term of 6.5 to 7 percent, but with a portfolio that's 60 percent bonds and 40 percent quality stocks, you could expect 8.2 percent. Over a twenty-year period, these few percentage points can significantly improve your results. (You'd probably do even better with a portfolio that's 100 percent in equities, since historically, such portfolios have returned 9.5 to 10 percent.)

Instead of thinking "safety," you need to think "spreading out the risk," four words that are psychologically very comforting to risk-averse people.

To spread risk, you need to be diversified and to make a religion of dollar cost averaging, which, as you know, means investing the same number of dollars on a regular basis regardless of how many shares of stock those dollars buy. This strategy forces you to buy more shares when prices are low and fewer shares when they are high, so you achieve a lower overall cost than you would by buying a constant number of shares at set intervals, or simply buying when you "feel like it."

The dollar cost averaging theory makes sense and is much admired by investors — but sometimes more in the breach than in practice. Psychologically, in a strong bull market (the time of greatest optimism), you may feel like investing more than the set amount, and in the throes of a bear market (the time of greatest pessimism), you may not feel like investing any money at all, so the discipline is ignored.

Remember — for highly risk-averse people, dollar cost averaging is a lifeline, so protect that lifeline by creating a situation in which you rely on dollar cost averaging and *the structure* it builds. A number of mutual fund families will arrange to have a set amount of money taken directly out of your paycheck each month. Or, you can set up a schedule for making mutual fund or stock purchases yourself. Or, you can arrange with your broker to invest the same amount on a schedule — every month or every few months.

TAKING CHARGE

Spreading out the risk is important for you.

So is acting as independently as you can. Many extremely risk-averse investors, since they lack confidence and want to make each move "perfectly," think they need a great deal of "hand-holding" from their broker or investment adviser, and even their friends. They think, "I'll get to feel more secure eventually, if I have someone I can depend on now."

Up to a point, hand-holding helps. Almost all investors feel the need from time to time, particularly when market conditions seem to be shifting. But "Make me safe" investors need a great deal of reassurance, like the client I told you about at the beginning of this chapter who spoke with her broker every other day.

That behavior is not unusual, but having one's hand held too much can make a person more risk averse, because risk aversion is strongly linked to lack of confidence, and you can't increase confidence by relying too heavily on others. In fact, this type of dependency is a virtual guarantee of decreased confidence.

The ideal situation, for an extremely risk-averse person, is to work with someone to construct a balanced portfolio, with dollar cost averaging as its method, but to make the basic choices for the portfolio on your own.

That is the situation I established for a client named Ralph Morgan.

A FATHER'S GOAL

Ralph Morgan, a forty-one-year-old public administrator, came to see me shortly after the death of his wife, Ellen.

During the seventeen years of their marriage, Ellen, a substitute teacher, had handled the couple's finances; but Ralph and Ellen always agreed on money matters — both were extremely risk averse.

Ellen had grown up on a hardscrabble farm in the South. Her parents had struggled against poverty and never had enough money to put aside as savings. When the family lost the farm, it was a tremendous emotional blow to Ellen. But she worked her way through college, got a teaching degree, and was determined to be safer financially than her parents had been. Ralph was a city boy, but his childhood financial circumstances were similar to Ellen's. His father had died when Ralph was quite young, and his mother earned only a small amount of money doing factory piecework.

At Ellen's direction, the couple had regularly put 10 percent of their after-tax income into CDs. They made certain to live well within their means and, at Ellen's death, their only debt was a mortgage of $42,000 remaining on their suburban colonial home.

Occasionally, they had talked about investing, but always put that idea on the back burner because they felt that they were doing pretty well without taking any risk.

The Morgans had one child — nine-year-old David — who had been conceived after a long battle with infertility. After David's birth, Ellen left her full-time teaching job and took up substitute teaching. This decision reduced the family income, but Ellen wanted to spend as much time as possible with David, whom the Morgans regarded as "a miracle."

When Ralph came to see me, he, quite naturally, was still grieving deeply for Ellen, and was daunted by having to take on the responsibilities of single parenthood, because, as a child, he had seen how difficult this role was for his mother.

Ralph was determined to fulfill a dream he and Ellen had shared of sending David to Harvard. David was in several "gifted and talented" classes, and his teachers agreed he was extraordinarily intelligent.

Ralph now realized that he and Ellen had not approached their dream realistically. With $44,000 in CDs, then earning interest of 6 percent, he would not be able to fund college in the seven years remaining. But, Ralph told me, he couldn't possibly "risk losing" any of the money because to do so would be to let Ellen down.

Like most highly risk-averse investors, Ralph was asking for the "safety guarantee."

Of course, I couldn't give it to him, but I went over the points I made earlier in this chapter, telling him that the *only* guarantee any investor has is through choosing good-quality companies, holding on to them over time, and selling as infrequently as possible. As I've said a number of times in this book, it is impulsive selling, for emotional reasons, that destroys long-term returns. An excellent "guarantee" of succcess is to avoid panic selling.

I pointed out to Ralph that he was focused on the pain of losing, a pain that he saw as affecting Ellen as well as himself. What he should do was to concentrate on the pleasure he would get from fulfilling his goal, which would have been Ellen's pleasure as well.

I suggested that he close his eyes and visualize David, grown up and walking across a college campus. I asked him to see himself at David's graduation and to experience how proud and pleased he would feel. I was trying to demonstrate to Ralph that the *end* results of his investing program would be highly enjoyable, if he could work through his fear of short-term pain.

THE DRIPs APPROACH

Ralph decided that he wanted to put his entire portfolio in equities, since, we agreed, that would be the best way of meeting his goal. I told him that I would give him support and guidance, but that I wanted him to do as much of the work as possible. This was frightening to him, but I explained how important it was for him to demonstrate to himself that he could make "good enough" decisions out of the many "good enough" possibilities that are available.

Our plan was to build his equities, over time, through DRIPS (dividend reinvestment plans).

As I explained in chapter 3, most companies, if you already own their stock, allow you to reinvest all or some of the dividends, or to buy additional shares, usually with no fees and often at a considerable discount to the market, an important point for Ralph because he was very much concerned about costs. What's not so widely known is that there are fifty or so companies that allow you to make *initial* stock purchases directly from them, including such outstanding companies as AFLAC, Barnett Banks, Exxon, McDonald's, Procter & Gamble, and Texaco. (For a complete list of the companies, with their addresses, see the Resources Section.) Most of these companies require that you buy more than one share, and some charge enrollment fees for opening the accounts.

There is also a little-known back door to the DRIPs programs of the companies that don't allow initial investment, through a plan devised by *The Moneypaper,* a financial newsletter published by Vita Nelson in Mamaroneck, New York. (See the Resources Section.) Subscribers can buy as little as one share and become enrolled in the programs.

You can arrange not only to reinvest dividends but to buy additional shares on a fixed-amount basis, usually monthly (thereby, dollar cost averaging). Generally, the minimums for purchases range from $10 to $25 and the maximums from $1,000 to $10,000. About 270 companies will accept investments of $10. *Using this option, as little as $100 a month is enough to fund a portfolio of ten different high-quality companies.*

To reiterate the advantages of DRIPs for risk-averse investors who want to take care of themselves, while still feeling taken care of:

- You purchase stocks at a discount.
- You demonstrate that you can get yourself enrolled in the program and can select stocks on your own.
- You put yourself on a dollar cost averaging schedule.
- You have subtle protection against impulsive selling because selling shares is not as quick as it would be with a traditional brokerage account — a disadvantage if you have to make a quick sale, but the situations when you have to do that are extremely rare.
- You have to keep records, and that constantly reinforces the message "I can do this myself."

DRIPs also focus on the *emotional power* of dividends.

In chapter 3, on developing a stock portfolio, I advised readers to look for companies that are "shareholder friendly," and I said that one of the things such companies do (instead of, or in addition to, paying dividends) is to buy back shares and reinvest in themselves, so that the value of the shares increases.

For highly risk-averse investors, however, dividends are particularly meaningful. They have an emotional "value added" because they convey a sense of security about the company. *Psychologically, dividends represent the parental power of the company — its ability to take care of its own.*

TAKING THE HELM

In developing his portfolio, Ralph followed several themes to narrow down his choices and ease decision making. The first, I suggested, was to buy companies that had a history of raising dividends regularly. On his own, he developed themes of safety, market leadership, financial strength, and good growth.

After research in *Value Line,* Ralph settled on the portfolio that follows. The emphasis on finance reflects his association of banks with security, and the emphasis on food, with his notion that "people always have to eat." My only contribution was New Plan Realty Trust, a REIT (real estate investment trust), because I thought he needed some real estate exposure, and perhaps because I thought I should do something to earn my fee!

RALPH MORGAN'S DRIPs PORTFOLIO

Air Products & Chemicals — chemical company
AMBAC — reinsurance
Bancorp Hawaii — bank
Bristol-Myers Squibb — drugs and consumer products
Brown-Forman "B" — liquor and china
Exxon — oil company
Hershey — food company
Intel — microprocessors manufacturer
New Plan Realty (listed on New York Stock Exchange) — real estate
Sara Lee — food company
Wendy's — food retailer

If I had selected Ralph's equities for him, I might have made some different choices. I would have added another oil company, Texaco, to the list, because I thought that oil companies were undervalued at the time. My drug company choice would have been Merck, because, as I said in chapter 9, I believe it is the best managed company in the world.

But if I had taken over, I would have defeated the whole purpose of foster-ing Ralph's independence and convincing him that he could make choices that were "good enough."

APPROACHES THAT MINIMIZE DECISION MAKING

While I believe that you should investigate companies before you buy, some highly risk-averse people want to do as little investigation as possible because they find the entire process too frightening. You should work to get over this aversion, but if you're not successful, there are "low energy" ways to get into equities that, while not risk free, have good overall records.

One method of stock selection, called "Beat the Dow," is an old system. The theory is that if your portfolio consists of the ten highest-yielding Dow stocks, it will perform better than the Dow Jones Indus-trial Average itself. These stocks are known as the "Dogs of the Dow," because they are in the "doghouse," the least popular companies of the moment, whose falling prices have caused the yields to climb.

Once a month, the *Wall Street Journal* publishes a list in Section C of the Dow Jones stocks and their records. Pick out the ten stocks with the highest dividend yields, buy them, and hold them for a year. Decem-ber is a good time to buy because that's when investors sell stocks for tax losses and drive prices down further.

After a year, make a new list of the top ten highest yields. Sell any stocks you own that are not among them and replace them with ones that are. Next year, repeat this procedure again, and so forth. From 1954 to the present, this method has averaged an annual return of 18.7 percent, beating the Dow Jones by 4 percent.

An alternative is to play "Flying Five." In this variation, you buy the five of the ten highest-yielding stocks that have the lowest prices, to take advantage of the fact that, in general, low-priced stocks tend to do better than high-priced stocks and just a small bounce in price can mean substantial gains. The "Flying Five" system has averaged a return of 21.7 percent from 1954 to present.

Several brokerage houses sell unit trusts of the ten "Dow Dogs" for as little as $1,000 or $250 for an individual retirement account (IRA). (A unit trust is a pool of securities that all come due at a specific time.) There are fees and at the end of a year, the trusts get broken up, so you have to pay taxes on any capital gains. A newsletter called *Beating the Dow,* published in Old Tappan, New Jersey, edited by John Downes, provides information on this method. (See the Resources Section.)

The psychological advantage of "Beat the Dow" is that it is a contained system, with only a small amount of work to do and not too much decision making. If the system works for you, you simply do the same thing year after year. It is a form of contrarian investing, based on the principle of buying stocks that are out of favor and selling them when they return to favor. One disadvantage of the system is short-term taxes, since you have few successful long-term holds. Another is that you don't learn much about investigating companies, since you never make the "business owner" connection with your stocks.

Another minimalist approach is to put the equity portion of your portfolio into one super index fund. One good choice is the Vanguard Index 500 Trust, which as I said in chapter 2 is on the *Forbes* Honor Roll of top funds. The fund invests in the 500 large- and medium-size companies that compose the S&P Index, and its results mirror the index. (No-load. *Forbes* rating [August 25, 1997]: B for up markets, C for down markets. Five-year annualized total return: 19.62 percent; ten-year: 13.65 percent. *Morningstar* rating, 4 stars.) Every year, the Index 500 Trust average beats 80 percent of equity and balanced funds. Since different funds beat the index each year, very few individual funds can match the 500 Trust's long-term record. Also, the costs of most funds make it extremely difficult for them to outpace indexed funds.

If you want to diversify more broadly, you can put all your money into the Total Stock Market Portfolio of the Vanguard Index Trust. This fund, which mirrors the performance of the entire U.S. equities market, holds over 1,000 individual stocks selected from the Wilshire 5000 Index, including the 500 companies in the S&P Index. (No-load. Not yet rated by *Forbes.* Five-year annualized total return: 19.14 percent. *Morningstar* rating: 4 stars.)

Once you have made the "index fund" decision, you needn't do anything more, because over the long term these funds have been very competitive in terms of net investment performance.

Remember, though, they are not risk free, as many investors, and particularly risk-averse investors, are starting to assume from their good records. Index funds reflect overall market conditions, and they will participate in downturns, just as they participate in upward moves.

"MATTRESS" REGRETS

Sometimes the desire for safety is so overwhelming that a "Make me safe" investor will take his money out of the market and put it all "under the mattress," that is, bank accounts, CDs, or T-bills.

Dropping out is a poor solution because if the person has a healthy level of greed and discovers that he doesn't really love his mattress as much as he thinks, he is bound to have regrets.

At first you get a sense of relief, because you are free of fear of loss, but especially in a strong market, you soon begin to compare your returns from cash instruments with stock returns, and you may start to feel terrible. You may also begin to realize that cash is not risk free, because the value of the money, in terms of buying power, cannot normally keep up with inflation. So as you sleep comfortably (or perhaps you don't), your money is actually losing value.

And, *you* lose the value I mentioned earlier, of being able to deal with some of the issues that cause risk aversion. Not that investing is a form of therapy, but it can be important in terms of building self-esteem, and sometimes you wind up being distressed because you have thought more about protecting your money than protecting your long-range interests.

We all view money as a source of security; that's natural. But extremely risk-averse people have an exaggerated idea of the kind of security that money can provide. They see money as protecting them from pain, loss, emotional distress, and perhaps even from death itself — a reason why they build such a moat around money and try to keep it inviolable.

The image of money as a shrine is destructive because money is a tool, not an all-powerful protector. Money needs to be released, in a sensible way, so that it can do the job of achieving practical goals that bring you pleasure, rather than being enthroned in order to meet emotional goals that it truly cannot fulfill.

CHAPTER 13

The Confident Investor

Several years ago, I conducted a small study designed to discover the personal qualities that make for high investing returns. I surveyed some of my most successful clients and other successful investors and found that they had one trait in common — confidence.

Their confidence didn't stem from experience — it preceded it. These people expected to do well, they acted *as if* they would achieve — and they did.

There are plenty of investors who, like those in my sample, are naturally positive. For them, investing is a welcome challenge and a rewarding adventure. They understand their emotions, accept them, and instinctively know how to manage them.

Of course, their assurance, the product of a strong self-image, isn't really innate. It develops out of having been adequately nurtured and loved as a child, and although we all should have been treated this way, not all of us were.

But no matter what our upbringing, we can learn to be assured investors and that is what the "Mind over Money" program is all about. Time and time again, I have seen confidence develop when clients uncover the emotional pattern that's holding them back, make the necessary alterations, and embrace the rewards.

So being confident isn't only a good idea, *it's the major idea,* and it's where every discussion in this book is intended to lead you.

I keep a list of the characteristics of confident investors tacked to my wall to share with clients — and as a reminder to myself.

Here is a review of what confident investors practice:

- *Being faithful to the style they choose.* Researcher James O'Shaunessey looked at a number of investing "systems" and found that they all worked, *if* you followed them faithfully over time. Value worked the best, but you don't have to be a value investor to be successful. You just have to be consistent.

- *Trusting what they already know.* If they're in medicine, they'll use their knowledge to investigate drug companies. If they're computer programmers, they'll scrutinize computer companies. They start from the inside out, because they think they already have something important to bring to investing — and they're right.
- *Treating investing as normal.* They understand that investing is neither complicated nor intrinsically scary. They make it part of their daily lives.
- *Accepting uncertainty.* They relax, figuring that if things don't work out today, they'll work out tomorrow.
- *Listening to others.* They're always willing to explore other people's ideas, but rely on their own judgment.
- *Competing only with themselves.* They focus on their own skills, not on measuring their returns against those of others.
- *Not being too troubled by mistakes.* They treat mistakes as a learning experience.
- *Welcoming the gratification of growing rich.* No shame or guilt for these investors. They see themselves as deserving, so they feel fulfilled.

Trust is the common element of confident investor practice. Though spirituality is not much talked about in connection with investing, I believe the two are linked, because trust is, after all, a spiritual concept.

By trusting, we give up the need for complete control, we don't fear market fluctuations, and we become comfortable. We learn that the "abiding faith" we seek is in ourselves.

APPENDIX A

Why I Picked My Core Portfolio Stocks

This chart does not constitute stock recommendations, of course, because the selections were made at a certain point in time. The chart is intended to demonstrate the factors that can be relevant to stock selection.

STOCK	INDUSTRY	ENTRY PRICE	WHY I SELECTED THE STOCK
1. Berkshire Hathaway	Multiform, emphasis on insurance	$2,350	1. Phenomenal management — Ben Graham had called Warren Buffett his "most brilliant student." 2. Outstanding "paper trail" of investments. 3. Integrity — the highest. 4. Very shareholders oriented.
2. Capital Southwest Corp.	Venture capital	54½	1. Diversified way for the small investor to be in venture capital. 2. Sound management. 3. Integrity. 4. Exceptionally oriented to shareholder interests.
3. Leucadia National	Insurance and other investments	22	1. Excellent management — Cumming and Steinberg are as smart as they come. 2. Incredible attention to due diligence when making investments. 3. Great eye for value.
4. Markel	Insurance property and casualty	40½	1. Sound management. 2. A business plan patterned after Berkshire Hathaway. 3. Increasing attention to shareholder needs.

STOCK	INDUSTRY	ENTRY PRICE	WHY I SELECTED THE STOCK
5. Merck	Drugs	32	1. Best managed company in the world. 2. Early days of the first Clinton administration created a wonderful psychological opportunity to buy great drug companies.
6. Philip Morris	Tobacco, food, and beer	22	1. Worries around tobacco have created a psychological bargain. 2. Very strong management. 3. Great brand names.
7. PICO Holding	Insurance, financial services, and investments	1½	1. Ronald Langley and John Hart — two super investors at the helm. 2. A potential opportunity to be in on the ground floor of what could be a great company. (NB: PICO is far more speculative than other stocks on this list.)
8. Royal Dutch Petroleum	International oil company	63	1. Second best managed company in the world. 2. A "call" on the next oil "crisis."
9. Thermo Electron	Science and high tech	13¾	1. Unique corporate culture that fosters entrepreneurship while raising capital at bargain rates. 2. High-quality management.
10. United Asset Management	Financial management	19¼	1. A perpetual royalty on a vast pool of capital. 2. Enormous unrecognized cash flow. 3. Practically no capital needs.

APPENDIX B

Net Present Value:
A Calculation for Confident Buying

The concept that stocks have an intrinsic, or private, market value is absolutely critical to my approach to investing, and it is psychologically critical because it takes the guesswork out of buy decisions.

In the long run, the value of the common stock is determined by the company's business value, the price a competitor would pay if the company were for sale today. And what the competitor would pay is based not only on today's figures but also on the company's future cash flow, measured against capital expenditures needed to grow the company and keep it competitive.

If you want to purchase a stock in the same way that a business person would, you need to know several things about the company: its *present value,* which is the discounted value of future cash flows; its *residual value,* the worth of the company ten years hence, and ultimately, its *net present value (NPV),* which is the sum of the present value, plus the residual value, minus capital expenditures in those cases when the company has significant capital expenditures.

When you know the net present value, you have a firm idea of whether the stock is worth the price being asked for it. Of course, the ideal is to buy it for a great deal less. I look to buy when a company is selling for 50 percent or less of its NPV.

You can estimate net present value (I say "estimate" because it's not an exact science) using a method called the "two-stage dividend discount model." In the first stage, you figure the company's present value, and in the second, its residual value. The method takes some figuring but it's basically not too difficult to do. In fact, I teach physicians and other interested investors how to do it, and it makes them far more emotionally secure in their investing.

The word *dividend* is in the title because of an old principle that the investment value of a common stock is equal to the net present worth of all its future dividends. This was first described by John Burr Williams in 1938 in his book *The Theory of Investment Value*.

It's fairly easy to see how present value can be figured in a situation where the dividend yield is predictable, such as U.S. Treasury bonds. The present value of a treasury bond equals its future value divided by one plus the current yearly interest rate, raised to the power of the years of time involved. The mathematical formula is:

PV	=	$FV/(1 + i)^t$
PV	=	present value
FV	=	future value
i	=	interest rate per annum
t	=	time (in years)

So doing the calculations for a bond is fairly simple. (But of course, you don't have to do this work at all because the *Wall Street Journal, New York Times,* and many leading daily newspapers publish tables giving you bond prices and interest rates for a thirty-year period.)

However, for stocks, it's not as simple because the dividend flow from stocks is not as reliable as the interest flow from bonds. A more useful concept is one developed by Warren Buffett called "owner earnings," which he defines as cash flow minus capital expenditures.

To perform the calculations, which are projections over a ten-year period, first make a chart like the one on page 238, which I made in 1996 for United Asset Management, a Boston-based holding company of investment management companies. Fill in the left-hand column as demonstrated. Then proceed as follows:

STAGE ONE: CALCULATING PRESENT VALUE

You are going to figure the discounted value of the cash flow per annum over a ten-year period, add up the discounted values, and arrive at a figure that represents the sum of the present values of the company per share.

1. Average the company's growth rate over the *past* ten years (the figures are available in *Value Line*). This is the figure you are going to project as the company's average growth rate over the *next* ten years.

(If you have special knowledge of a company or its industry, you may adjust this growth rate up or down, according to your best judgment.) In the chart for United Asset Management, I assumed a growth rate for UAM of 22.5 percent. This was based on the fact that its earnings had compounded at 22 percent per annum for the previous decade and my belief that it could sustain this growth for the coming decade.

2. Establish a discount factor, based on the current rate of interest of the long-term U.S. T-bond. The discount factor equals one divided by 1 plus the interest rate, to the power of the year, so for each year out, you are dividing by a larger number, thereby giving you a smaller discount factor each year: $1/(1 + i)^t$

3. Look in *Value Line* and find out the company's actual cash flow per share for the prior year.

For example, for 1995, the year prior to my calculations, UAM's actual cash flow per share was $2.75.

4. Multiply the actual cash flow per share for the prior year by 1 plus the growth rate. This gives you the cash flow per share for Year 1. Then multiply the cash flow per share for Year 1 by the discount factor. This gives you the discounted value per share for Year 1.

In the case of UAM, with a growth rate of 22.5 percent, I multiplied the actual cash flow per share for the prior year, $2.75, by 1 plus the growth rate (1.225), and arrived at a cash flow per share for Year 1 of $3.37. I multiplied $3.37 by a discount factor of .9354 and obtained a discounted value per share for Year 1 of $3.15.

5. To arrive at the cash flow per share for Year 2, repeat the same process: Multiply 1 plus the growth rate by the previous year's cash flow. Then multiply the cash flow per share for Year 2 by the discount factor, thus arriving at the discounted value per share for Year 2.

In the case of UAM, I multiplied 1 plus the growth rate (1.225) by $3.37, the cash flow per share for Year 1, and obtained a cash flow per share for Year 2 of $4.13. I multiplied $4.13 by a discount factor of .8751 (the discount factor decreases each year) and arrived at a discounted present value per share for Year 2 of $3.61.

6. Repeat this process for Years 3 through 10. (If you have a computer, it can be done easily on a spreadsheet program.)

7. Add up the discounted values per share for ten years, obtaining the sum of the present values. This sum is the present value of the company's "owner earnings" per share.

In the UAM example, I arrived at a sum of present values of $62.74 per share.

STAGE TWO: CALCULATING RESIDUAL VALUE

The object is to project what the residual value of the company will be a decade hence. You proceed as follows.

1. Select as the growth rate for Year 11 a rate that is *one-half* of the growth rate you have been using. You assume that, at some point, the company's growth rate will slow down, and since there is no way of figuring exactly when that will be, a standard convention is simply to halve the growth rate figure for Year 11. This covers all bases.

For example, in my UAM calculations, I projected 22.5 percent as the average growth rate over a ten-year period, but I projected 11¼ percent as the growth rate for Year 11.

2. Select for the capitalization rate (the company's costs of borrowing money), the current interest rate of the T-bill. You can find this figure in the *Wall Street Journal.*

3. Multiply the cash flow for Year 10 by 1 plus the new growth rate. This gives you the cash flow per share for Year 11. In the UAM example, I multiplied 1.1125 (1 plus the new growth rate) by $20.92, the cash flow per share for Year 10. I obtained a cash flow per share for Year 11 of $23.27.

4. Divide the cash flow per share for Year 11 by the capitalization rate. This gives you the company's estimated value per share at the end of Year 10.

In the UAM example, I divided the cash flow per share for Year 11, $23.27, by a capitalization rate of 6.39 percent, which was the interest rate at the time of the T-bill. I arrived at an estimated value per share at the end of Year 10 of $364.

5. To revert the company's estimated value per share at the end of Year 10 to its present value per share, multiply it by the discount factor of Year 11.

In the UAM example, I multiplied the company's estimated value per share at the end of Year 10, $364, by .4800, the discount factor of Year 11. The figure I got, $174.72, was the present value of the residual value per share.

6. After you calculate the present value of the residual value per share, add it to the sum of the present values per share, the figure you obtained at the end of Stage One. This gives you the net present value of the company per share.

For example, with UAM, I added $174.72, the present value of the residual value per share, to $62.74, the sum of present values per share, arriving at a net present value for UAM of $237.46 per share.

At the time, the market price for United Asset Management was $27. My calculations showed me that UAM was selling at 11 percent of its net present value, quite a bargain, since I look to buy when companies are selling at 50 percent of their net present value or less.

Note: To demonstrate this exercise simply, I have used as an example a company with no capital expenditures, as is the case with most service industries. If the company you are evaluating has significant capital expenditures, do the following: Before you begin the calculations for Stage One, present value, average the capital expenditures per share over the past ten years (the figures are in *Value Line*). This is the figure you are going to project as the company's capital expenditures per share over the *next* ten years. Then, for each year, after you multiply the cash flow for the prior year by 1 plus the growth rate and get the cash flow per share, subtract the capital expenditures per share. Multiply the remainder by the discount factor to obtain the discounted value per share.

As I noted earlier, these calculations are not an exact science. It is possible to use other assumptions; for example, the T-bond rate plus 3 or 4 percent for the discount factor, to allow for risk and uncertainty. But the point is to have assumptions in place and to do the exercise. By performing it in the case of UAM, I arrived at a reasonable estimate of what the company was really worth, and this, coupled with other good things I knew about the track records of the company's management, increased my sense of inner security about the purchase.

NET PRESENT VALUE CALCULATIONS FOR UNITED ASSET MANAGEMENT

Stage One: Present Value					
Year	Prior year cash flow per share	Growth rate	Current year cash flow per share	Discount factor	Discounted value per share
YEAR 1	$2.75	22.5%	$3.37	.9354	$3.15
YEAR 2	3.37	22.5%	4.13	.8751	3.61
YEAR 3	4.13	22.5%	5.06	.8186	4.14
YEAR 4	5.06	22.5%	6.20	.7657	4.75
YEAR 5	6.20	22.5%	7.59	.7163	5.44
YEAR 6	7.59	22.5%	9.30	.6697	6.23
YEAR 7	9.30	22.5%	11.39	.6268	7.14
YEAR 8	11.39	22.5%	13.95	.5863	8.18
YEAR 9	13.95	22.5%	17.08	.5485	9.37
YEAR 10	17.08	22.5%	20.92	.5131	10.73
Sum of present values per share = $62.74					

Stage Two: Residual Value

Cash flow Year 10	$20.92	Estimated value per share at end of Year 10	$364
Growth rate	11.25 percent	Discount factor Year 11	.4800
Capitalization rate	6.39 percent	Present value (residual) per share	$174.72
Cash flow Year 11	$23.27		

Net present value = Sum of present values and present value residual
Net present value = $62.74 + $174.72
Net present value = $237.46

Current market price per share $27.00

Current market price, $27.00, is 11 percent of net present value, $237.46

UAM is currently selling for 11 percent of its net present value.

Resources Section

BOOKS:

Carlson, Charles B. (1996) *No Load Stocks.* New York: McGraw-Hill. The best single discussion of DRIPs (Dividend Reinvestment Plans).

Chilton, David. (1991) *The Wealthy Barber: Everyone's Common Sense Guide to Becoming Financially Independent.* Rocklin, CA: Prima Pub. A wonderful first investment book, simply written in anecdotal style, yet covering all the bases. A great gift for college graduation.

DeBenedictis, Daniel J. (1989) *The Complete Real Estate Adviser.* New York: Pocket Books. Makes the complexities of real estate investing understandable for the average reader. A solid introduction to the field.

Dines, James. (1996) *How Investors Can Make Money Using Mass Psychology.* Belvedere, CA: James Dines & Co. An overview of market psychology from the famous "gold bug."

Engel, Louis. (1994) *How to Buy Stocks.* 8th ed. Boston: Little, Brown. A classic. The basics of equity investing, in simple language, that have helped generations of beginning investors get off on the right foot.

Fisher, Philip A. (1996) *Common Stocks and Uncommon Profits.* New York: John Wiley. The second best investment book ever written. A must for anyone who plans to invest.

Graham, Benjamin. (1986) *The Intelligent Investor.* New York: Harper & Row. The best book on investing ever written. I reread it every year and never fail to learn more.

Graham, Benjamin, David L. Dodd, and Sidney Cottle. (1988) *Security Analysis: Principles and Technique.* 5th ed. New York: McGraw-Hill. This "bible" of professional investing is complex, with many math-

ematical formulas and tables, so it's too intimidating for most beginners, but important for the advanced investor.

Gurney, Kathleen. (1988) *Your Money Personality.* New York: Double-
day. A psychologist's research on investment personalities and the
stocks they favor. Useful for financial planners and general readers
as well.

Hagstrom, Robert G., Jr. (1994) *The Warren Buffett Way.* New York:
John Wiley. A comprehensive biography of the investor with emphasis on his investment philosophy.

Hallowell, Edward M., M.D., and William J. Grace. (1989) *What Are
You Worth?* New York: Weidenfeld & Nicolson. A popular psychology treatment of the relationship between emotions and spending
patterns.

Kilpatrick, Andrew. (1994) *Of Permanent Value.* Birmingham, AL:
AKPE. The author, an experienced financial adviser, became so impressed with Warren Buffett that he mortgaged his house and put
the money into Berkshire Hathaway. His excellent volume chroni-
cles that experience and other aspects of Buffett-oriented investing.
The most reliable of all the books on Buffett.

Lefevre, Edwin. (1923) *Reminiscences of a Stock Operator.* New York:
George H. Doran. Reprint, 1995, New York: John Wiley. Written
under a pseudonym, perhaps by Jesse Livermore, the Wall Street
stock manipulator of the 1920s. Valuable for insights into the psychology and economics of speculation.

Lynch, Peter. (1989) *One Up on Wall Street: How to Use What You
Already Know to Make Money in the Market.* New York: Simon &
Schuster. A highly readable account of Peter Lynch's style; helpful
in demystifying the investing process. Reassuring for beginners and
all investors.

Pring, Martin J. (1993) *Investment Psychology Explained.* New York:
John Wiley. One of the most comprehensive explanations of market
behavior (as opposed to individual behavior in the market), by a
seasoned professional trader.

Quinn, Jane Bryant. (1991) *Making the Most of Your Money: A Compre-*

hensive Guide to Financial Planning. New York: Simon & Schuster. Written for the average reader, this book covers all aspects of finance and investing in a down-to-earth style; a splendid guide that belongs in every home library.

Smith, Adam. (1967) *The Money Game.* New York: Random House. The first, and the wittiest, of a series of marvelous books about Wall Street. Anyone who is interested in investing and reads Smith (aka Jerry Goodman) is in for a treat.

————. (1972) *Supermoney.* New York: Random House. See above.

Soros, George. (1994) *The Alchemy of Finance: Reading the Mind of the Market.* New York: John Wiley. Legendary investor Soros shares his insights on market psychology and offers useful advice as well.

Train, John. (1994) *The Craft of Investing.* New York: Harper Business. An explanation of winning in the market from a practitioner who writes as well as he invests. I recommend all of Train's books, but this, the most recent, is the best place to begin.

————. (1980) *The Money Masters.* New York: Harper & Row. A study of the common attributes of nine famous investors: Warren Buffett, Paul Cabot, Philip Fisher, Ben Graham, Stanley Kroll, T. Rowe Price, John Templeton, Larry Tisch, and Robert Wilson.

Williams, John Burr. (1938) *The Theory of Investment Value.* Cambridge, Mass.: Harvard University Press. A classic scholarly work, reputed to be the source of Warren Buffett's dividend discount model of assessing net present value.

Whitman, Martin J., and Martin Shubik. (1979) *The Aggressive Conservative Investor.* New York: Random House. Not an easy read, but worth the effort, because it explores ways of making big profits at low risk — by a major practitioner of the bankruptcy school of value investing.

Zweig, Martin. (1986) *Martin Zweig's Winning on Wall Street.* New York: Warner Books. An excellent book on equity investing, written by one of the most diligent market scholars. Few pundits love the market as intensely as Zweig, and even fewer share his brilliance.

NEWSLETTERS:

Beating the Dow, 184 Central Ave, Old Tappan, NJ 07675. John Downes, editor. Published monthly. $125. 201-767-4100. Chronicles a simple method that has historically topped Dow returns.

BI Research, 130 Fieldcrest Drive, Ridgewood, CT 06877. Thomas Bishop, editor. Published ten times yearly. $90. 203-438-9924. One of the five best market newsletters over the long haul. Editor Bishop has a good nose for underfollowed and undiscovered stocks.

Dick Davis Digest, Dick Davis Publishing, P.O. Box 350630, Ft. Lauderdale, FL 33335-0630. Steven Halpern, editor. Published biweekly. $165. 954-467-8500. Researches 400 financial services. If you like market letters, you'll love this well-written digest that excerpts highlights from hundreds of letters.

Growth Stock Outlook, Box 15381, Chevy Chase, MD 20825. Charles Allmon, editor. Published twice monthly. $195. 301-654-5205. Allmon's letter is controversial because he has been almost 100 percent in cash since 1987, but he is one of the best stock pickers in the country, with a knack for finding good companies at low prices.

Hulbert Financial Digest, 316 Commerce St., Alexandria, VA 22314-2802. Mark Hulbert, editor. Published monthly. $135. 703-683-5905. Rates other financial services. Hulbert applies a well-trained philosophical mind to measuring the results of market newsletters, performing a valuable service with a high level of integrity.

IQ (Investment Quality) Trends, 7440 Girard Ave., La Jolla, CA 92037. Geraldine Weiss, editor. Published twice monthly, $275. 619-459-3818. Weiss pioneered the theory that one should buy when a stock's dividends are in the top 20 percent of their historic yield and sell when in the lowest 20 percent. Over the years, this method has produced excellent results with less-than-average volatility. A caution: Currently, many companies are buying in shares rather than increasing dividends, making the Weiss method less reliable.

The Moneypaper, Temper of the Times Communications, 1010 Mamaroneck Ave., Mamaroneck, NY 10543. Vita Nelson, editor. Published monthly. $81. 800-388-9993. Does a nice job of covering

DRIPs (Dividend Reinvestment Plans). Subscribers can participate in a special arrangement with many companies to start a DRIPs account with just a single share purchase.

Morningstar Mutual Funds, 225 W. Wacker Dr., Chicago, IL 60606. Published biweekly. $425. 800-735-0700. The "bible" of mutual fund reporting. Analyzes and rates funds, providing investors with invaluable data for decision making. Any fund manager would die for a five-star rating, the highest *Morningstar* has to give.

Systems & Forecasts, Signalert Corp., 150 Great Neck Rd. #204, Great Neck, NY 11021-3309. Gerald Appel, editor. Published biweekly. $225. 516-829-6444. One-time therapist Appel is a proponent of charting and market timing. I'm not a believer, but this interesting letter has an excellent record.

The Schott Letter (TSL), Schott Investment Corporation, 120 Centre Street, Dover, MA. John Schott, editor. Published monthly. $110. 800-797-9678. If you like this book, you'll like *TSL,* in which I also write about market psychology and the psychology of individual investors. One company is investigated in detail each month and there is a mutual funds section and reports on past recommendations.

Value Line Investment Survey, 220 E. 42nd St., New York, NY 10017. Published weekly. $570. 800-833-0046. With a database that's probably the best in the industry, *VL* covers and rates over 1,700 individual companies. The rating system was controversial in the past, but since *VL* switched to a more complicated system that takes momentum into account, its record has improved substantially. The *Hulbert Financial Digest* ranks *VL* highly. *VL* publishes three other letters with similar formats, the *Expanded Value Line,* covering over 1,800 medium- and smaller-size companies; *Value Line No-load Fund Advisor* (see below); and *Value Line Convertible Bonds and Preferred Stocks.*

Value Line No-load Fund Advisor. Same address and phone number as above. Published monthly. $107. To compete with *Morningstar,* *Value Line* decided to put out its own mutual fund newsletter. Low-load funds are also covered.

ONLINE RETRIEVAL SERVICE:

Dow Jones News/Retrieval Service and Stock Quote Reports, Dow
Jones & Company, Inc. Provides texts of articles appearing in newspapers and magazines. Different packages available. Order by
phone, 800-522-3567, 800-369-7466.

DIVIDEND REINVESTMENT PLANS (DRIPs) THAT WILL ACCEPT
INITIAL INVESTMENTS:

(Phone number given is sometimes that of trustee.)

AFLAC, Inc. (insurance)
1932 Wynnton Rd.
Columbus, GA 31999
800-227-4756

AirTouch Communications, Inc.
(wireless telecommunications)
One California St.
San Francisco, CA 94111
800-233-5601

Arrow Financial Corp.
(banking)
250 Glen St.
Glens Falls, NY 12801
718-921-8200

Atlantic Energy, Inc.
(utility–electric)
6801 Black Horse Pike
P.O. Box 1334
Pleasantville, NJ 08232
609-645-4506

ATMOS Energy Corp.
(utility–gas)
P.O. Box 650205
Dallas, TX 75265-0205
800-543-3038

Barnett Banks
(banking)
P.O. Box 40789
Jacksonville, FL 32203-0789
800-328-5822

Capstead Mortgage Corp.
(financial services)
2711 North Haskell Ave., Ste. 900
Dallas, TX 75204
800-527-7844

CMS Energy
(utility–electric, gas)
212 West Michigan Ave.
Jackson, MI 49201-2236
517-788-1868

COMSAT Corp.
(global telecommunications)
6560 Rock Spring Dr.
Bethesda, MD 20817
800-524-4458

Crown American Realty Trust (REIT)
Pasquerilla Plaza
Johnstown, PA 15907
718-921-8247

Dean Witter, Discover & Co.
(financial services)
2 World Trade Center
New York, NY 10048
800-622-2393

DeBartolo Realty (REIT)
7655 Market St.
Youngstown, OH 44513
800-446-2617

The Dial Corp.
(consumer products)
Dial Tower
Phoenix, AZ 85077-1424
800-453-2235

DQE
(utility–electric)
Box 68
Pittsburgh, PA 15230-0068
800-247-0400

DTE Energy Company
(utility–electric)
2000 Second Ave.
Detroit, MI 48226
800-551-5009

Eastern Co.
(manufacturer of locks and metal
products)
112 Bridge St.
Naugatuck, CT 06770
800-736-3001

Enron Corp.
(gas distributor)
1400 Smith St.
Houston, TX 77002
800-519-3111

Exxon Corp.
(oil refining)
5959 Las Colinas Blvd.
Irving, TX 75039-2298
800-252-1800

Hawaiian Electric Industries
(utility–electric)
P.O. Box 730
Honolulu, HI 96808
808-532-5841

Home Properties of NY (REIT)
850 Clinton Square
Rochester, NY 14604
212-936-5100

Houston Industries, Inc.
(utility–electric)
P.O. Box 4505
Houston, TX 77210-4505
800-231-6406

Integon Corp.
(insurance holding company)
500 W. Fifth St.
Winston-Salem, NC 27152
800-446-2617

Interchange Financial Services
(commercial banking)
Park 80 West, Plaza Two
Saddle Brook, NJ 07663
212-509-4000

Johnson Controls
(electrical equipment)
5757 North Green Bay
P.O. Box 591
Milwaukee, WI 53201
414-276-3737

Kellwood Co.
(apparel)
600 Kellwood Pkwy.
St. Louis, MO 63017
800-321-1355

Kerr-McGee
(oil and gas)
Kerr-McGee Center
P.O. Box 25861
Oklahoma City, OK 73125
405-231-6711

Madison G&E Co.
(utility–electric, gas)
P.O. Box 1231
Madison, WI 53701-1231
800-356-6423

McDonald's Corp.
(restaurants)
McDonald's Plaza
One Kroc Dr.
Oak Brook, IL 60512
800-621-7825

MidAmerican Energy Co.
(utility–electric)
666 Grand Ave.
P.O. Box 9244
Des Moines, IA 50306-9244
800-247-5211

Mobil Corp. (oil)
3225 Gallows Rd.
Fairfax, VA 22037-0001
800-648-9291

Morton International, Inc.
(air bags, salt, chemicals)
100 North Riverside Plaza
Chicago, IL 60606-1596
800-990-1010

NorAm Energy Corp.
(utility–gas)
P.O. Box 21734, Rm. 401
Shreveport, LA 71151-0001
800-316-6726

O.G.&E Electric Services
(utility–electric)
P.O. Box 321
Oklahoma City, OK 73101-0321
800-395-2662

ONEOK Inc.
(utility–oil, gas)
P.O. Box 871
Tulsa, OK 74102-0871
800-395-2662

Philadelphia Suburban Corp.
(utility–water)
762 Lancaster Ave.
Bryn Mawr, PA 19010
800-756-3353

Piedmont Natural Gas
(utility–gas)
P.O. Box 33068
Charlotte, NC 28233
800-633-4236

Pinnacle West Capital Corp.
(utility–electric)
P.O. Box 52132
Phoenix, AZ 85072-2132
800-457-2983

Portland General Corp.
(utility–electric)
121 SW Salmon St.
Portland, OR 97204
201-324-1644

Procter & Gamble
(household goods, food)
P.O. Box 5572
Cincinnati, OH 45201-5572
800-742-6253

Regions Financial Corp.
(banking)
P.O. Box 1448
Montgomery, AL 36102-1448
800-446-2617

SCANA Corp.
(utility–electric)
1426 Main St.
Columbia, SC 29218
800-763-5891

Tenneco, Inc.
(energy, auto parts, packaging)
P.O. Box 2511
Houston, TX 77252-2511
800-446-2617

Texaco Inc.
(oil company)
2000 Westchester Ave.
White Plains, NY 10650
800-283-9785

Tyson Foods "A"
(poultry)
2210 West Oaklawn
Springdale, AR 72764
800-822-7096

U S West Communications Group
(telecommunications)
7800 East Orchard Rd.
Englewood, CO 80111
800-537-0222

U S West Media Group
(multimedia)
7800 East Orchard Rd.
Englewood, CO 80111
800-537-0222

UtiliCorp United
(utility–electric, gas)
P.O. Box 13287
Kansas City, MO 64199-3287
800-884-5426

Western Resources, Inc.
(utility–electric, gas)
P.O. Box 750320
Topeka, KS 66675-0320
800-527-2495

Wisconsin Energy Corp.
(utility–electric)
231 W. Michigan St.
P.O. Box 2949
Milwaukee, WI 53201
800-558-9663

WPS Resources Corp.
(utility–electric, gas)
700 N. Adams St.
P.O. Box 19001
Green Bay, WI 54307-9001
800-236-1551

Source: "Guide to Dividend Reinvestment Plans." *The Moneypaper*. (See newsletter listings above for address.)
A compehensive list is also available in Charles B. Carlson's *No Load Stocks*. (See book listings above.)

Index

accounting firms, change in, 55–56
advance-decline line, 83–84
aerospace industry, 142
Aetna Life & Casualty, 60, 169
AFLAC, 221
Aggressive Conservative Investor, The (Whitman), 124
Agouron, 132
AIM Balanced Fund, 166
AirTouch Communications, 158
American Software, 66–67
American Stock Exchange, 117
America Online, 131–132, 138
Amgen, 73–74, 125, 139, 146, 169
Ann Taylor, 181, 183
annual reports, 54–55, 140, 186–187
annuity contracts, 202–203
Aquinas-Equity Growth Fund, 162
asset allocation, 31–32, 85
asset allocation mutual funds, 215
assets, company, 50
Autoimmune, 132

balanced funds, 166
Bank of Granite, 204
banks, 41–42, 204

Barnett Banks, 169, 221
Barron's Weekly, 49, 83, 84, 142
Baruch, Bernard, 26
bear market depressive syndrome (BMDS), 14, 97, 99–100, 103
bear markets, 82, 90
buying during, 102–105
defensive stocks and, 88
and dollar cost averaging, 218
emotions in, 97–102
fear in, 14, 77, 95–97, 99, 105
and mutual funds, 28
selling during, 94–96, 101
stop/loss orders and, 122
warning signals, 84
"Beat the Dow," 224, 225
Beating the Dow, 225
Ben & Jerry's Ice Cream, 162
Berkshire Hathaway, 146, 162, 169, 231
annual reports, 34
price per share, 130
shareholder identification with, 130, 141–142
subsidiaries, 192
BHC Communications, 157
"bid-ask" spread, 159, 197
biotech companies, 44, 139

blue chip stocks, 145, 163
Bombay Company, 181
bonds, 192
  corporate, 37, 88, 125, 159
  interest rates and, 88, 125–126
  "junk," 159
  "laddering," 158
  mutual funds, 64, 119, 217
  portfolio share, 125–126
  safety of, 88, 125, 158–159
  zero coupon, 90–91, 190
books on investing, 33
Boston Chicken, 80, 198
Bradley Realty, 159
Bristol-Myers, 95
brokers, 61, 127, 148–149, 209
Browne, Christopher and Will,
  158
Buffett, Warren, 30, 91–92
  and Berkshire Hathaway, 34, 192,
    231
  and Coca-Cola, 124–125, 191
  and Graham, 8, 231
  on junk bonds, 159
  on owner earnings, 234
  on successful investing, 27, 34,
    59, 89
  on unique companies, 41
  and value investing, 28
bull markets
  buying during, 90
  crowd behavior in, 77–78
  and dollar cost averaging, 218
  emotions in, 79–82, 94
  and gambling investing, 199–200
  greed in, 14, 77–79, 82–83, 91–
    93, 98

and impulsive investing, 179
market cycles and, 82, 96, 102
of 1990s, 96, 114, 179
portfolio protection in, 85–90
selling during, 86–88, 89
warning signals, 83–85
"business partner" psychology, 48,
  101, 103
Business Week, 51
buying
  in bear markets, 102–105
  blocks of shares, 42
  in bull markets, 90
  delaying decision on, 43, 57,
    143–144
  directly from companies, 42,
    221
  investigation of companies and,
    43, 48, 54–57, 140, 185–186,
    202, 224
  momentum investing and, 132–
    133
  and performance expectations,
    62
  and selling decision, 74–75

Cabot Market Letter, 143
California Energy, 169
call options, 196–197
capital expenditures, 55
capital gains, 22, 29
capital reinvestment, 41
Capital Southwest Corporation, 231
Caterpillar, 169
Centocor, 132
CGM Realty, 161

Charles Schwab, 192
charting, 46
Chilton, David
  The Wealthy Barber, 42
Chiron, 139
Chris-Craft Industries, 49, 157
Circuit City, 146
Cisco Systems, 53, 146
Citgo, 207
Citizens-Emerging Growth Fund,
    162
Clinton administration, health insur-
    ance plan, 142, 158
Coca-Cola, 55, 102, 110, 144, 145,
    191, 192
  bull market and, 114
  fall of communism and, 142
  undervaluation of, 125
Coca-Cola Enterprises, 55
Cohen & Steers Realty Shares, 159,
    161
Colonial Penn Insurance Company,
    101
Columbia Real Estate Equity, 161
commission costs, 42
commodities trading, 79–80
Common Stocks and Uncommon
    Profits (Fisher), 33
communism, fall of, 142
companies
  annual reports, 54–55, 140, 186–
    187
  dividend payments, 222, 223
  earnings, 41, 55
  identification with, 188
  initial stock purchase direct from,
    42, 221

investigation before buying stock
    in, 43, 48, 54–57, 140, 185–
    186, 202, 224
  management, 50–51, 54, 56
  market capitalization, 52
  net present value, 53, 233–237
  profitability, 40, 55
  shareholder friendliness, 41, 188–
    189, 222
  10K forms, 54, 55, 140
  trustworthiness, 41, 54
  unique, 41–42
Complete Real Estate Adviser, The
    (DeBenedictis), 203
computer industry, 66
computerized trading, 84
"concept" stocks, 136, 138–139, 201
confident investors, 16, 228–229
Congress on the Psychology of In-
    vesting, 4–5, 148
conservative investing, 201
Cornell University, 151–152
corporate bonds, 37, 88, 125, 159
Corus Bankshares, 169, 204
covered options, 206
crowd psychology, 8, 35–36, 77–78
CSX Corporation, 188–189
Cumming, Ian, 122

Davis New York Venture Fund, 204
Dean Witter, Discover, 123
Death of a Salesman (Miller), 148
DeBenedictis, Daniel J.
  The Complete Real Estate Adviser,
    203
defensive stocks, 88

DHA Communications, 49
Disney Corporation, 188, 191, 192
diversification, 26, 81–82
dividend reinvestment plans
    (DRIPs), 42, 221–222
dividends
    automatic reinvestment of, 42
    company history, and buying deci-
        sion, 223
    company history, and selling deci-
        sion, 71
    and net present value, 233–234
    psychological value of, 222
    and taxes, 22, 29, 41
    yields, 83
Dodd, David
    Security Analysis, 8
"Dogs of the Dow," 224, 225
dollar cost averaging, 121, 218
Domini Social Equity Fund, 162
Dow, Charles, 163
Dow Jones Industrial Average
    bear markets and, 103, 104
    bull markets and, 84, 96
    change in composition of, 163
    measuring performance against,
        63, 64
    P/E ratio, 52, 103, 104
    stock selection methods and, 224
Dow Jones News Retrieval Service,
    49–50, 67, 140
Downes, John, 225
Dreman, David, 36, 45, 77
DRIPs (dividend reinvestment
    plans), 42, 221–222
Duke Power, 169
duPont, Alfred, 123

earnings, 55
    compound, growth rates, 45
    forecasting, 141
    predictability of, 41
EBIDTA (earnings-before-interest-
        depreciation-taxes-and-
        amortization), 55
emotions, 179
    in bear markets, 97–102
    in bull markets, 79–82, 94
    and investing, 3–4, 8–9, 12, 16–
        17, 18, 22
    money and, 3, 22
    and selling decisions, 14, 61
    and stock market, 5, 47, 77
employment insecurity, 5
Energy Conversion Devices, 162
Engel, Louis
    How to Buy Stocks, 33
Enrico, Roger, 124
estate planning, 176–177
Extreme News, Law of, 37
Exxon, 72, 157, 169, 221

fair market value, 47–48, 53
Fidelity Blue Chip Growth Fund,
    125
Fidelity Contrafund, 175
Fidelity Equity-Income II Fund, 166
Fidelity Puritan Fund, 133, 166
Fidelity Real Estate Investment, 161
First Call, 50
Fisher, Philip A.
    *Common Stocks and Uncommon
        Profits*, 33
fixed annuities, 203

Florida East Coast Railroad, 123, 157

"Flying Five," 224

Forbes
  mutual fund ratings, 28, 161, 216
  small company ratings, 51
  on socially conscious funds, 162

401(k) plans, 82

Franklin-Templeton Group, 124

Freud, Sigmund, 78, 154

"friction" costs, 159, 197, 200

Gamblers Anonymous, 212

gambling investors, 196
  brokers and, 209
  bull markets and, 199–200
  portfolio strategies for, 202–204, 210
  psychology of, 16, 198–199, 200–202, 207–211
  and trading, 197, 199, 200, 205–207, 210–211

Gates, Bill, 146, 191

Gayner, Tom, 146

Geist, Dick, 4–5

General Electric Corporation, 163

General Motors, 145, 146

Genzyme, 139, 182

Gillette, 142

Graham, Benjamin, 8, 30, 231
  The Intelligent Investor, 8, 33
  Security Analysis, 8
  and value investing, 27–28, 47

Greater Fool Theory, 46

growth investing, 45, 51–52
  mutual funds, 64

growth stocks, 124–125, 145–146, 158, 190–192

Guardian Park Avenue Fund, 31, 168, 203

Hart, John, 57, 232

Hatsopoulos, John, 41

hedging, 89, 90, 207–208

Heine, Max, 124

Hershey, 88, 188

Hewlett-Packard, 158

Honda, 169

How to Buy Stocks (Engel), 33

Hughes Electronics, 146–147

Hulbert, Mark, 65

Hulbert Financial Digest, 65, 186

IAI Growth & Income Fund, 166

IBES, 50

IBM, 53, 103, 142, 145, 169

Impact Project, 163

impulsive investors
  bull markets and, 179
  identification with companies, 183–184, 188–189, 196
  and investigation of stocks, 185–187
  and media information, 179–180
  and money managers, 193–194
  portfolio strategies for, 189–192
  psychology of, 15–16, 179–188, 194–195

independent thinking, 8

index funds, 30, 65, 225–226

inflation, 226

information explosion, 40, 127, 179
inheriting investors, 151–152
  attitudes toward money, 154–
    155, 177
  estate planning and, 176–177
  and money managers, 171–174
  portfolio strategies for, 157–159,
    165–171
  psychology of, 15, 151, 152–156,
    163–165
  and real estate investments, 159–
    161
  and socially conscious investing,
    155, 161–162
  "windfall" inheritors, 174–175
initial public offerings (IPOs), 83,
  134
"inner investor," 10
"insider" knowledge, 81
Insull, Samuel, 9
insurance companies, 41–42, 204
Intel, 144, 145, 158
  P/E ratio and earnings, 45
  price fluctuations, 60, 75, 102
Intelligent Investor, The (Graham),
  8, 33
interest rates, 82, 125–126, 217
International Flavors & Fragrances,
  190–191
international funds, 158
internet, information from, 149,
  210
internet stocks, 132, 140
investing
  asset allocation, 31–32
  emotions and, 3–4, 8–9, 12, 16–
    17, 18, 22

getting started, 13, 21–27, 34–
  35
learning about, 22, 33–34
personal styles, 12, 14–17
psychology of, 3, 4–5, 77
systems for, 228–229
investment advisers, 171–174, 193–
  194
Investor's Business Daily, 33, 45, 49,
  67
Iomega Corporation, 138
IPOs (initial public offerings), 83,
  134

J. P. Morgan bank, 157, 169
Japanese stocks, 82
Johnson, Samuel, 83
Johnson & Johnson, 53–54, 142,
  147, 162, 191–192
"junk" bonds, 159

Kellogg, 88, 90, 102, 192
Kemp, Jack, 60
Kennedy administration, 142
Kohut, Heinz, 148

"laddering," 158, 216
Lakonishok, Josef, 77, 84
Langley, Ronald, 56–57, 232
Lapham, Lewis, 177
large capitalization funds, 119
learning about investment, 22, 33–
  34
LeBon, Gustave, 78

legislation, 142
Lehman Brothers Bond Index, 65,
    119
Leucadia National, 122–123, 204,
    231
leverage, 160, 197
Lexington Corporate Leaders Trust
    Fund, 31, 167
Life, 84
Lifson, Larry, 4–5
Lipper Company, 142
load funds, 29, 203–204
losses
    psychological valuation of, 27, 69,
        214
    selling and, 14, 60, 73, 220
lottery winners, 178
Lutts, Carlton, 143
Lynch, Peter, 48, 180
    One Up on Wall Street, 33, 185

McDonald's, 145, 192, 221
Magellan Fund, 185
Making the Most of Your Money
    (Quinn), 33
Mamis, Justin, 147–148
Markel Corporation, 146, 169, 204,
    231
market capitalization, 52
market cycles, 23, 96, 120
Merck, 92, 110, 125, 144, 232
    management of, 158, 223
    undervaluation of, 53–54, 142,
        158
Mercury Finance, 60
Merrill Lynch, 123

Microsoft, 81–82, 92, 102
    overvaluation of, 53
    power investors and, 129, 144,
        145–146, 189, 191
Miller, Arthur, 148
momentum investing, 45–46, 68,
    132–133, 143
money
    impulsive investors and, 194
    inheriting investors and, 154–
        155, 177
    power investors and, 147, 149,
        150
    risk-averse investors and, 226–
        227
Money Game, The (Smith), 163
money managers, 171–174, 193–
    194
Moneypaper, 222
Morgan, J. P., 92
Morgan, Stanley, 123
Morningstar Mutual Funds, 28
Motorola, 102
Munger, Charley, 28
mutual funds
    asset allocation, 215
    balanced, 166
    bear markets and, 28
    bond funds, 64, 119, 217
    and celebrities, 180
    gambling investors and, 203–204
    getting started with, 24–26, 29–
        31, 32
    growth, 64
    index funds, 30, 65, 225–226
    inheriting investors and, 157–
        158, 166

mutual funds—*Continued*
  international, 158
  load and no-load, 29, 203–204
  performance expectations, 64–65,
    119–120
  power investors and, 147
  psychological benefits of, 24
  ratings, 28
  real estate, 161
  risk-averse investors and, 215,
    216, 217
  selection criteria, 27–29
  socially responsible, 161–162
  transaction trends, 142
  value, 27
  worrying investors and, 119–120,
    123–124, 125
Mutual Funds, 162
Mutual Series Qualified Fund, 124,
  167
myopic loss aversion, 214

naked options, 206
National Opinion Research Center,
  177
N&B Socially Responsible Fund,
  162
Nelson, Vita, 222
net present value (NPV)
  and buying decision, 53–54
  calculation of, 233–238
  and selling decision, 72
Netscape, 129, 132
"new paradigm," 17, 82, 86
New Plan Realty Trust, 159, 223

news articles, 66–67, 84
  online retrieval services, 49–50,
    67
newsletters, 127
newspapers, 33–34, 127, 234
New York Stock Exchange, 37, 117
New York Times, 234
Niederhoffer, Victor, 37
Nordstrom, Inc., 191

oil companies, 223
One Up on Wall Street (Lynch), 33,
  185
online retrieval services, 49–50, 67
options trading, 196–197, 206–207
O'Shaunessey, James, 228–229
over-the-counter stocks, 117
overvalued stocks, 70–72, 80, 139
owner earnings, 234

Pacific Telesis, 158
Parnassus Income-Balanced Fund,
  162
partnership, limited, 160
Pax World Fund, 162
Pennzoil, 207
PepsiCo, 124–125, 142
pharmaceutical companies, 53–54,
  142
Philip Morris, 61, 64, 92, 110, 169,
  232
physicians, survey of investing by,
  25, 60, 92–93
Physicians Insurance Company of
  Ohio (PICO), 56–57
PICO Holding, 232

PNC Bank, 192
Polaroid, 53, 169
power investors, 196
  brokers and, 148–149
  and "concept" stocks, 136, 138–139, 201
  and investigation of companies, 140–141
  and momentum investing, 132–133, 143
  overidentification with stocks, 15, 130–131, 137
  portfolio strategies for, 137–147, 201
  psychology of, 15, 129–137, 147–150
  and speculative stocks, 137, 139, 144, 146–147
preferred stock, 88
present value, 233, 234–236
Presstek, 143
Price, Michael, 124
price-to-earnings ratio (P/E)
  and buying decision, 36–37, 45, 52, 80, 103
  and selling decision, 71
price-to-sales ratio (PSR), 52
Princeton University, 57
Pring, Martin J., 101
Procter & Gamble, 88, 221
professional investors, 35–36, 142
  traders, 205–207
profitability, 40, 55
Progressive Insurance, 204
"psychological value," 58
psychology
  crowd behavior, 8, 35–36, 77–78
  of investing, 3, 4–5, 77
  stock market and, 6, 17–18, 46–47
put options, 90, 196

Quinn, Jane Bryant
  Making the Most of Your Money, 33

real estate, 159–160, 203
real estate investment trusts (REITs), 159, 160–161
rebalancing, 86, 88–89, 94
residual value, 233, 236–237
retirement security, 5, 6, 32
return on equity (ROE), 40, 55, 63
returns, 21–22
  risk-averse portfolio, 217
  Rule of 72, 22
  Standard & Poor's 500 index, 37, 182
risk-averse investors
  and dividend reinvestment plans, 221–222
  portfolio strategies for, 223–226
  psychology of, 16–17, 213–221, 226–227
  and safety, 213, 218, 226
  and stocks, 216–217
risk-free investments, 90–91
Robertson Stephens Emerging Growth Fund, 147
Rogers, Will, 160
Rorer, Ted, 40, 95
Royal Dutch Petroleum, 169, 232

Rubel, Fred, 9
Rule of 72, 22
Russell 2000 Index, 52, 64, 103

St. Joe Companies, 123, 157
Sara Lee, 185
satellite portfolio, 44–45, 63, 87
savings, 42–43
Schloss, Walter, 28
Schott Letter, 10
Sears, 169
Securities and Exchange Commission, 54, 140, 171
Security Analysis (Graham and Dodd), 8
self-employment plans (SEPs), 5
selling
  in bear markets, 94–96, 101
  brokers and, 61
  in bull markets, 86–88, 89
  buying decision and, 74–75
  emotions and, 14, 61
  forced, 75–76
  importance of resisting, 59, 74–75, 95, 220
  and losses in investing, 14, 60, 73, 220
  net present value and, 71–72
  performance expectations and, 62, 68, 70–71
  psychology of, 14, 59–62
  standards for, 61, 68, 71–74, 87, 134
  stop/loss orders and, 64, 119
  worrying investors and, 111, 114–115, 118, 119

Sepracor, 44, 63
ServiceMaster, 145, 162
shareholder friendliness, 41, 188–189, 222
short selling, 89
"short squeeze," 89
Siegel, Herbert, 49, 51, 157
small capitalization funds, 64
Smith, Adam
  The Money Game, 163
socially conscious investing, 155, 161–162
societal change, 66
Spears, John, 158
speculative investments, 79–80
  portfolio rebalancing and, 86–87
  power investors and, 137, 139, 144, 146–147
Spyglass, 132
Standard & Poor's 500 index
  average returns, 37, 182
  measuring performance against, 28, 63, 64–65, 119
  P/E ratios, 52, 103
Standard & Poor's Reports, 49, 52, 161
Steinberg, Joseph, 122
stock market
  crash of 1929, 101
  crash of 1987, 95, 102
  crowd psychology in, 8, 35–36
  cycles in, 23, 96, 120
  impossibility of timing, 35
  Law of Extreme News, 37
  Law of Unexpected Results, 36–37
  mood swings and, 8, 47

predictability in, 36
psychology and, 6, 17–18, 46–47
trouble signals, 83–85
stock portfolio
"Beat the Dow" system, 224
core, 40–42
psychology of, 13–14, 39–40
rebalancing, 86, 88–89, 94
rules for building, 42–44, 202
satellite, 44–45, 63, 87
stocks
direct initial purchase, 42, 221
investigation of companies, 43,
    48, 54–57, 140, 185–186, 202,
    224
net present value, 53–54, 71–72,
    233
performance expectations, 62–63,
    67, 70
psychological benefits of, 24, 39,
    216–217
psychological identification and
    attachment, 4, 39, 57, 130–131,
    137, 183–184
"psychological value," 58
ranking, 49
tracking and evaluating, 66–67
Stone & Webster, 169
stop/loss orders, 63–64, 116, 117,
    118–119, 207
"straddle," 207
supermarket chains, 52
support groups, 162–163

taxes, 22, 72, 160, 200
technical analysis, 46

technological shifts, 66
Telefonos de Mexico, 60
Templeton, Jack, 7
Templeton, Sir John, 7–8, 28, 82,
    102, 167
10K form, 54, 55, 140
Texaco, 169, 207, 221, 223
Thaler, Richard, 77
Theory of Investment Value, The
    (Williams), 234
Thermo Electron, 41, 232
Third Avenue Value Fund, 30, 123–
    124, 168
3M Company, 188
Time, 84
"Time-Life Indicator," 84
"tips," 80–81
tobacco industry, 64, 66
Total Stock Market Portfolio, 225
trading, 199, 200, 205–207, 210–
    211
"trailing" stop/losses, 116, 118–119
Train, John, 46
trend surfing, 142
Trump, Donald, 154
TWA, 136–137
Twain, Mark, 26
Tweedy-Browne Global Value Fund,
    157–158
two-stage dividend discount model,
    53, 233–234

U.S. Surgical, 147
U.S. Treasury bonds, 26, 88, 125,
    158–159, 190, 215, 216
    average returns, 37

undervalued stocks, 103
Unexpected Results, Law of, 36–37
United Asset Management, 123,
    169, 232, 234, 235–238
United Paramount Network (UPN),
    157
unit trusts, 225
University of Michigan, 87

value investing, 46
    Law of Unexpected Results and,
        37
    mutual funds, 27
    and stock selection, 52
    successfulness of, 27–28, 45, 47,
        229
Value Line Investment Survey, 48–
    49, 51, 52, 83, 161, 186
value stocks, 45, 120, 122–123, 157
Vanguard Group, 30, 65, 203
Vanguard Index 500 Trust Fund,
    30, 225
Vanguard Wellington Fund, 166
variable annuities, 202–203
venture companies, 50, 63–64
Virginia Carolina Chemical, 7
volume, trading, 83

Wall Street Journal, 49, 60, 67, 127,
    234
    advance-decline graph, 84
    Dow Jones stock records, 224
    "Heard on the Street" column,
        33–34

Washington Post, 192
Washington Real Estate Investment,
    159
wealth accumulation, 151
Wealthy Barber, The (Chilton), 42
Wells Fargo Bank, 192, 204
Whitman, Martin J., 30, 124
    The Aggressive Conservative Inves-
        tor, 124
Williams, John Burr
    The Theory of Investment Value,
        234
Wilshire 5000 Index, 225
"windfall" inheritors, 174–175
Winnicott, D. W., 215
Winning on Wall Street (Zweig), 33
"wish list," 102, 105
worrying investors
    brokers and, 127
    and buying decision, 116–117
    and perfectionism, 114, 215
    and performance evaluations,
        119–120, 126–127
    portfolio strategies for, 120–126
    psychology of, 14–15, 109–116,
        128
    and selling decision, 111, 114–
        115, 118, 119
    and stop/loss orders, 116, 117,
        118–119, 126
Wrigley, 102

zero coupon bonds, 90–91, 190
Zweig, Martin, 84
    Winning on Wall Street, 33